ONE
TRUTH

LIBERATING – NOURISHING – UNIFYING

HENRY HON

Foreword by Doug Krieger
Northern California – USA

TABLE OF CONTENTS

DEDICATION

The first time my wife and I visited Africa we went to Nigeria--September 2016. We were astounded by the amount of Christian activities there. At least 50% of the population of Nigeria is Christian. We met scores of believers there; even at random in the hotels or airport; they came across fervent, knowing their Bible, well-read and kept up to date with various great Bible teachers throughout history.

Prior to our visit we met brother Dayo from Nigeria while he was traveling through the USA in 2015. Dayo was excited with the fellowship we had and his participation of an ekklesia gathering over a weekend with diverse believers. Therefore, he invited us to visit Nigeria. When we visited about a year later, he brought us to fellowship with various groups of believers in 4 cities. We ended our 10-day trip there with a conference. Around 75 saints gathered--I shared from my first book, *ONE*, which had just been published. For three days we had fellowship regarding the matter of the ONEness of believers based on the Lord's prayer in John 17. The fellowship was sweet and genuine. We found the saints to be seeking and open to the Lord; we were humbled.

During that small conference, I met a brother who had been serving the Lord full-time as a minister/evangelist for over 25 years. He had been seeking the Lord for a way to go on concerning God's eternal purpose which is the building up of His people into ONE according to the Lord's prayer in John 17. After enjoying the fellowship at this small conference, brother Femi took my book, *ONE,* and read it carefully over the next number of months. After reading the book, he felt lead by the Lord to redirect his focus of ministry to build up the One Body of Christ in Nigeria--and in other places in Africa. He felt the Lord opened a way for him to serve according to what the Lord first called him to do.

In early 2018, my wife and I went the second time to Nigeria. Brothers there set up a 3-week schedule for us to visit 7 cities. I spoke the message of *ONE* to hundreds of believers in about every city, including a pastors/ministers' conference. Again, the Lord had gone before us to prepare the saints for the message of oneness. In these conferences, I met believers from different backgrounds, churches, and perspectives. They were hungry for knowing and experiencing the One Body of Christ.

The Lord has mightily moved in Nigeria over the last eighty years. There were a couple of revivals that powerfully swept through the nation. However, at this juncture in time believers are highly divided into various denominations and sects. They love the Lord, yet, they also recognize their divided state of affairs. On the one hand, they thank the Lord for the Western missionaries who brought them the gospel; on the other hand, the sectarian system of Christianity came with the gospel; whereby, it caused much division among the Nigerians. Today, they recognize the destructiveness of what division has caused. The Lord has truly prepared them to hear the message of a vision and way to practice oneness among believers.

During my second visit, brother Femi introduced me to brother Tobih, a medical doctor who also teaches at a medical university, and a minister of the gospel. Brother Tobih has a ministry reaching across Nigeria and into Europe. The Lord also put on his heart concerning the oneness of the Body of Christ. After fellowship with brother Tobih, it was clear we were in one accord for the Lord's purpose for the Oneness of His Body in answer to His prayer in John 17.

Brother Tobih holds an annual conference of a few thousand ministers, pastors, and spiritual leaders from across various churches and denominations. This 4-day "Christian Workers Congress" has been taking place at a campground for almost 15 years. In February 2019, for the first time, he made the subject of the entire conference on the oneness of the Body of Christ. **My associate**, Doug Krieger, along with my wife, Sylvia, and I went and spoke on the *One Ekklesia* for three days, morning and evening to about 3000 saints. The Lord energized us and encouraged us due to the tremendous reception of this message of oneness. We saw the Lord moving mightily within the conference. There was an awe-inspiring, resonating acceptance among the saints for the Lord's desire for His people to be one--the «Gospel of Peace» was proclaimed!

I am dedicating this book, *ONE TRUTH*, to God's people in Nigeria. I am praying the Lord will have His way to set up an inspiring pattern of oneness in Nigeria for His Body on earth. The saints there have suffered much for the Faith; now, the blessing of oneness is coming upon them. We are witnessing a coming together into one fellowship, loving one another for the building up of the Lord's one ekklesia. The Lord said, the last shall be first. Yes, God has chosen the despised. Africa was one of the last places the gospel reached. The African people generally have been seen as underdeveloped, even less civilized--yet, the Kingdom of God has begun to prevail in Africa! Now, our prayer is that the Lord will do something marvelous on the earth starting from Nigeria. A wonderful move of God to shame the wise. This coming together of divided believers in Nigeria, spreading throughout Africa and beyond, will generate a revival all over the earth. This is for the Kingdom of God in preparation for the Second Coming of Christ at the end of the age!

Henry Hon

FOREWORD
by
Doug Krieger

Pontius Pilate starred Truth right in the face and sarcastically inquired of Jesus: WHAT IS TRUTH? Seems to me Pontius didn't hear a word Jesus said. Oh, yes, he heard with his ear Jesus saying something like this: "*I have come into the world, that I should bear witness to the truth . . . Everyone who is of the truth hears My voice*" (John 18:37-38).

Another religious cabal beat Pilate to the punch when Jesus told them:

> "You [those who wished to kill Jesus] have sent to John, and he has borne witness to the TRUTH . . . But you do not have His word abiding in you, because whom He sent, Him you do not believe. You search the Scriptures, for in them you think you have eternal life; and these are they which testify of Me. But you are not willing to come to Me that you may have life."
>
> ~ John 5:33, 38-40

There's "truth" and then there's Truth. Indeed, John's Gospel starts off by this astounding statement: "*For the law was given through Moses, but grace and truth came through Jesus Christ*" (John 1:17). What? Here all along I thought Moses and the law given through him was the pure, unadulterated truth — but Jesus sounds like He's inflating His importance above and beyond the "truth found in Scripture." Such a juxtaposition — comparing the Law of Moses vs. Jesus as "Grace and Truth" seems what got Jesus into all sorts of conflict with these religious leaders of His day who espoused the Law, but especially their "traditions" or interpretations of the Law, well, it seems that at every opportunity Jesus broke those traditions

Especially disconcerting to the religious leaders of Jesus' day were those interpretations having to do with the Sabbath. We ought to rest on the Sabbath, right? Well, how much, as in if we took a walk how far should we walk on the Sabbath? The "oral traditions" developed by Jewish authorities figured it out: We should walk no more than 2,000 cubits because that was the distance the Israelites had to keep between themselves (the tribes) and those bearing the Ark of the Covenant . . . this distance became known as a "Sabbath's Day journey."

Scores of examples like this can be cited; however, cutting to the chase, the same Law which Paul, the Apostle, says is *"holy and just and good"* (Rom. 7:12) is the same Law whereof Paul says: *"The letter kills, but the Spirit gives life"* – said in this context: *"Who also made us sufficient as ministers of the New Covenant, not of the letter but of the Spirit"* (2 Cor. 3:6).

Thus, and apparently, there's life and then there's Life! Instead of coming to Him for truth and life, we just make things up like this Sabbath's Day's journey and then rigidly go about setting up our "oral traditions" as if they somehow are comparable to the Lord Himself? That's what it sounds like.

These oral traditions of the "fathers" became known as *"the law of commandments contained in ordinances"* (Eph. 2:15). Alas! These ordinances with their "touch not, taste not" rigidities had little to do with the truth embedded in the Law of Moses revealing God's righteous character – no, but they had a whole lot to do with man's supercilious efforts to look "holier-than-thou" religious, but hardly righteous!

Ever wonder why Jesus said: *"For I assure you that unless your righteousness greatly surpasses that of the Scribes and the Pharisees, you will certainly not find entrance into the Kingdom of the Heavens"* (Matt. 5:20 – World English Bible)?

The bad news is man continues to invent more and more "oral traditions" – more *"law of commandments contained in ordinances"* . . . oblivious to the fact the lot of them have been NAILED TO THE TREE – that's the good news/gospel – along with the animosities, hatred, jealousies, envy, strife and ENMITY these extraneous ordinances and their *"middle wall of separation"* erected between folks like Jews and Gentiles.

Now, bless God Almighty – through the CROSS – *"He Himself is our peace"* – yes, peace between these polar opposites . . . you know, between folks who can't stand each other, although we're all claiming we're all God's people – forbid we ever act like we are!

Anyway, all this to say, you're going to discover encapsulated in Henry Hon's book, ONE TRUTH, are these amazing breakthroughs which really *"proclaim liberty to the captives . . . recovery of sight to the blind"* . . . and . . . *"set at liberty those who are oppressed"* (Lu. 4:18).

Jesus, the God-man, is starring at us all, right in the face . . . Hon, in ONE TRUTH, brings these contrasts into stark focus — be it Pontius or Caiaphas the high priest, Elijah or Peter . . . the secularist, religious, the prophet or the apostle . . . eventually, all of us come face to face with the Truth . . . but will we recognize Him; will we come to Him or will we rigidly hold to our philosophies and ordinances, content in our trite secular state or blinded by our traditions?

This is tough . . . breaking through these facades which keep us separated from the Way, the Truth and the Life, let alone from one another while we're at it! It's time to lose control, brethren — give it up for Jesus; humble ourselves under the Mighty hand of God for He wants us to be exalted in due season above the fray of our trivialities which keep us from the Savior Who is Truth and from our brethren who are afar off when God wants us not only to preach the Gospel of His Grace but the Gospel of His Peace . . . grace to save us and peace to unite us.

Finally, imagine, not a word about Satan until you get completely through the book of Romans when you hear the "*God of peace*" will CRUSH SATAN under our feet shortly! That's the TRUTH of the Gospel which Paul, now Henry Hon — and, hopefully, the Holy Spirit — will enlighten us while plowing through this text. There's a whole lot in here . . . take it slowly, prayerfully but press on . . . when finished, it is my prayer and hope that "*seeing through a glass darkly*" — ever so dimly — will break forth in Light and Life, right here and now, until face to face with Him Who is TRUTH!

Doug Krieger
Editor, Tribnet Publications
Co-Chair, One Body Life — Northern California

PREFACE

I left Hong Kong with my mom and brothers when I was 8 years of age. I arrived in the United States after turning 9. It took us a month to get here because we traveled by boat — well, by ship. Back then we were stigmatized by a derogatory nick name: F.O.B. (fresh off the boat).

When I arrived in the USA, I did not know a word of English. That was back in the '60s when there were no ESL (English (as a) Second Language) classes. Basically, I was tossed into all those regular classes where everybody spoke English. I was the only one who did not understand a word of English. It was learning English by osmosis — a little at a time. I still struggle with English — even up through my university years. Therefore, I got an engineering degree. I was much more comfortable with numbers than with words. My kids, sometimes my wife, still make fun of my grammar when I speak — I'm getting a little better at it!

It was when I started studying the Bible after graduation from UC Berkeley when my English language structure started to become critical to me. I became aware prepositions are keenly important. Sentence structure and punctuation, if misplaced, can easily alter the meaning of a sentence or even a word. Studying the Bible helped me in business with legal contracts both in reading, negotiating, and writing agreements. Nevertheless, I always had an uneasiness and felt unqualified to write anything; therefore, I disliked writing . . . anything. I would only write if it were part of my job. Writing for me has always been a chore — I do so, reluctantly.

So, for me to finish my first book in 2016 was a huge accomplishment. Frankly, I never would have undertaken it if not for receiving both inspiration and what I felt to be an assignment from God. Once the heart of Jesus in His prayer for oneness was unlocked and revealed in me, it became the central focus of my ministry.

Although I have studied the Bible for more than 40 years, yet when I started to focus on the subject of the Lord's prayer in John 17 for His people to be one, I received more illumination of Scriptures through the enlightening of the Spirit. I started to understand portions of Scriptures as never before. I saw them through the light of God's eternal purpose for the oneness of His people. Puzzling Scriptures became crystal clear.

One Ekklesia, my second book was published in 2018. It was the first book in a trilogy. The trilogy breaks up my first book, ONE, into these three separate writings. As the title of the book says, *One Ekklesia* is all about the Lord's ekklesia (most English versions mistranslated this word to "church"). It covers the vision and the practice of the Lord's ekklesia — from a universal, mysterious view of God's ekklesia to the very practical expression of the same on a day-to-day basis. *One Ekklesia* has about 70% new material in it which was not covered in the initial book, *ONE*. Much of the new unveiling of Scriptures I received was incorporated into this text.

Light continued to pour forth; therefore, this book on truth has about 25% new material not covered in the first book, ONE; plus, revisions which should improve the clarity on points of truth. The new material is centered on the **Completion Gospel of Jesus Christ** with a focus on the gospel of peace.

The third book in the series will be *One Life & Glory*. As with the book *ONE*, the trilogy is a continuing exposition on John 17 which is a record of Jesus' prayer at the last supper the night before His death on the cross. His prayer from the depth of His heart unveils God's eternal purpose and desire, which includes the gifts He provided to all His disciples in order to fulfill God's eternal purpose.

I hope you will benefit by reading and studying the truth with the help of this book.

Henry Hon

ONE
TRUTH

LIBERATING, NOURISHING
AND UNIFYING

HENRY HON

1

LIBERATING, NOURISHING, AND UNIFYING

Jesus Prayed for His followers to be ONE

Before Jesus Christ's agony at the Garden of Gethsemane and the subsequent crucifixion, there were only four recordings of His prayers. The first three were very short, only one to two sentences (Luke 10:21; John 11:41-42; John 12:28). The fourth prayer was lengthy and detailed, which was recorded in the entire chapter of John 17. He spoke this mysterious and momentous prayer to the Father at the end of the last supper, immediately prior to His betrayal and judgment that night. He was crucified early the following morning.

In this most significant prayer, Jesus prayed three times for His followers to be one. Oneness or unity was the focus of His petition. This oneness is not natural or human, for they may be one as the Father and the Son are one . . . that's supernatural Oneness. The oneness He prayed for flowed from His very nature and life within the Triune God. How mysterious is the Trinity: He is simultaneously expressed as *three and one*. He is both corporate and singular.

In the same breath, God is addressed as both "He" and "they" (Gen. 1:26-27), and "I" and "us" (Isa. 6:8). God is ONE: Eternally existing – distinctively the Father, the Son, and the Spirit. It is only in Jesus Christ this mysterious and extraordinary unity can be realized among once divided and hostile people. It is in Him alone people so diverse, even hostile one to another, having conflicting backgrounds, can literally become one. Prior to each petition to the Father in John 17 for His people to be one, He gave a gift to His believers. It is through these three wonderful gifts His followers were to be made one.

In the beginning of the last supper, after Jesus Christ washed His disciples' feet, He gave them a commandment — known as His New Commandment. He waited until the very end of His ministry to release His new commandment: "You are to love one another as I have loved you" (John 13:34). There was only one commandment Jesus claimed to be His own. This was it! Believers were to love one another just as Jesus Christ loved them. How did Jesus love us as His people? He loved us by dying for us. His love was not just in words, but in action. His action of love included kindness, forgiveness, caring, receiving, accepting, supporting, supplying, respecting, appreciating and much more. His love is all-inclusive; therefore, throughout the New Testament, out from "love one another" gave birth to at least 30 more "one anothers." All these "one anothers" positively describe all aspects and experiences of LOVE. To love one another is not simply saying "I love you." It took Paul an entire chapter in 1 Corinthians 13 to described in detail what love means and how love acts.

In the beginning of the last supper, Jesus gave this unique commandment. At the end of the last supper He prayed for His people to become ONE. Being one as the Triune God is one is the ultimate manifestation of love. The Trinity has the same expression: The Father loves the Son (Matt. 3:17), and the Son loves the Father (John 14:31). They are two; yet, absolutely and singularly one. Therefore, the Lord's commandment and His prayer for His people to be one as the Father and Son are one declares the reality in which believers are in God and God in them. This oneness shared by believers within the Trinity declares the manifestation of His heart's eternal desire and purpose.

Jesus declared in Matthew 16:18: I will build my *ekklesia* (Greek). This is His ekklesia: The oneness of God's people within the Triune God. (For an in-depth study of God's ekklesia, read *One Ekklesia* by the same author.)

If there is a desire to know and experience the oneness of the Lord's people, which is God's eternal purpose and desire, it is essential to understand and experience the three gifts given by Jesus Christ. Oneness among God's people is the very character of the Lord's ekklesia (unfortunately, in most English versions of the Scriptures it is mistranslated to "church"). The Lord's ekklesia has many descriptions, such as the Household of Faith, the Temple of God, the Body of Christ, the Bride of Christ, the One New Man, the New Jerusalem, the Pillar and Ground of Reality, and much more. God's people becoming one or unified as one cannot be organized or systematized by human manipulation. It is not through compromise or negotiation. Neither are God's people unified via the Trinity as a matter of conformity or uniformity. Just as the Trinity is mysteriously three yet one, the inexplicable and transcendent oneness of people distinctly diverse and separate can only take place within the realm of the Triune God – outside is but human manipulation . . . whereas, the Triune God never had to be organized for He always was, is and shall ever be: I AM.

The three gifts Jesus gave to His followers for them to be one are: (1) *Eternal life*, which bears the Father's name (John 17:2, 11); **the truth**, which is God's word manifested in the Living Word, Jesus Christ (John 17:14, 17); and the **Lord's glory** (John 17:22), which we find is the Spirit transforming the ministers from glory to glory (2Cor. 3:18). Thus, these three gifts mirror the very essence of the Triune God: The Father, the Son and the Holy Spirit. The more believers have a heart to fulfill God's eternal purpose by utilizing and enjoying these three gifts, the greater will be the manifestation of God's eternal purpose – the oneness of His people.

The first gift of eternal life is what believers have received through their second birth, which is called regeneration (born again). It is through this birth God became our common Father. Believers have the Father's name because they are born of Him, His offspring. This eternal life received through faith needs to grow, bear fruit and mature. There are four ingredients needed for every life form to flourish: nourishment, air, exercise and sleep. If these four elements are present then life will spontaneously and automatically grow, reproduce and mature. Every believer needs to be nourished with Christ as food and drink. Experiencing Christ as our very environment by incessantly breathing in the Spirit of God – He is the very breath we breathe! Thus, we are enabled to minister the riches of Christ to others, while we rest in Christ as we serve in ministry. The ultimate manifestation of maturity in this divine life, incorporated in the Father's name, is the ability to be one – to unite with all kinds of different believers (Eph. 4:13).

The third gift is the glory of Jesus Christ, which He received after His death, resurrection and ascension. It was His humanity which was crowned with glory and honor matching what He already possessed in His divinity. This glory He gave to His people through the out pouring of His Spirit empowers His disciples to serve and minister as He did with lowliness and humility. Pride is one of the biggest and deadliest dividers among God's people. But now we can serve one another with love, kindness and humility allowing us to become one with those totally contrary to our own disposition. Jesus laid aside His divine glory — rightfully His — in order to serve all humanity as a slave, no matter the opposition. Now, it is His glory clothed upon all His believers enabling and empowering them to minister as He did as servants for the building up of His ekklesia. Having His glory as the source of our Unity, believers can keep and extend unity in meekness and gentleness (Eph. 4:2-3).

These three gifts are expounded in more detail in the book *ONE* by the same author.

The Gift of Truth

> "I have given them Your word . . . Sanctify them by Your truth. Your word is truth . . . That they all may be one, as You, Father, are in Me, and I in You; that they also may be one in Us, that the world may believe that You sent Me."
>
> — John 17:14, 17, 21

The second gift is God's Word, which is truth. God's Word here must refer to the Son of God since according to John 1:1 and 14, the Son is the Word who became flesh. The Word is the truth. No doubt Jesus Christ, the Son of God — as the Word of God — is the truth. Therefore, Jesus said: "*I am the truth*" (John 14:6).

The truth is the topic and focus of this book. The Word of God is the truth which sanctifies. This sanctifying truth liberates, nourishes, and results in the unity of all believers. At the end of this second part of the Lord's prayer beginning with giving His followers God's Word, which is truth, He prayed again for their oneness within the Father and the Son. How astounding and wonderful is this oneness shared by all believers in the Trinity: in the Father, the Son and the Holy Spirit! How powerful is this manifestation whereby the world will believe!

> . . . who [God] desires all men to be saved and to come to the knowledge of the truth.
>
> — 1 Timothy 2:4

God's basic desire for all people is expressed herein: salvation and the knowledge of the truth. He is truly a loving God. He has no ill-will toward humankind. Although all men have sinned and have become "enemies" against God (Rom. 5:10-11); yet, God's desire is for all men to be saved. He has done everything to accomplish so great a salvation by sending His Only Begotten Son to die in order for all men to be saved through obtaining this salvation through the gift of faith — not of our own works (Eph. 2:8-9). His mercy and loving kindness are wonderful.

However, this is only half of God's desire for humanity. His second desire is for mankind to come to the knowledge of the truth. This shows why having faith in Jesus Christ for salvation is not altogether sufficient — it's incomplete. Just as salvation is essential, we must recognize that coming to the knowledge of the truth is the rest of the "divine mandate." If one only has salvation, but not the knowledge of the truth, then a vital half is missing.

Some may consider, "Well, I am saved; so, that is good enough for me." It may be good enough from a selfish point of view, but it is not good enough for God. His eternal purpose depends on people coming, AS WELL, to the knowledge of the truth. Without this knowledge of the truth, there may be millions upon millions of "saved" people, but they may still be in bondage, malnourished, spiritual infants, scattered and divided — leaving the building up of His ekklesia incomplete. Therefore, God's second desire for all men is just as essential as the first. Coming to the knowledge of the truth is co-equal with salvation!

Truth is a matter of knowledge. The word knowledge in the Greek is *epignōsis* which connotes "*exact or full knowledge--a greater participation by the 'knower' in the object 'known,' thus more powerfully influencing him*" (Vine's). This knowledge is from learning, understanding, logically considering, and retaining. Without inception and progress in learning and understanding, full knowledge cannot be attained. Without using the mind given by God to study and learn rationally, we cannot come to the knowledge of the truth.

In the first gift given by the Jesus in His prayer for His people to become one was the gift of eternal life. Life is mysterious. Where is life located in a person? What is life? It is simply impossible to accurately explain and define. All a person really knows is he/she is alive. Even physically, we may know all about pumping and circulating of blood, the electrical pulses in the brain, and DNA affecting physical traits, but where is life? It is truly mysterious and incomprehensible.

However, relating to the second gift of truth, it is completely understandable and logical. In fact, without the use of our minds to think, to remember, to consider, and to retain, it is not possible to progress in the knowledge of the truth. Yes, the Spirit's enlightening is needed, but without applying efforts to reason and recall, then knowledge of the truth is absent.

Some believers have depreciated knowledge and uplifted the experiences wrought by the Spirit. They need to recognize both are equally important and essential. The Spirit is not more important than truth nor truth more important than the Holy Spirit. Actually, truth and Spirit are eternally joined, they are one.

In emphasizing the need for the knowledge of the truth, a case can be made whereupon it is through truth that men receive God's Spirit. Consider the Lord's words in John 6:63, "the words (truth) that I speak unto you, they are spirit, and they are life." It is when there is the understanding of truth that the Spirit is received (Eph. 1:13). The Spirit is even called the *Spirit of truth*. In other words, it is the truth which possesses the Spirit. Without truth, the Spirit is also absent. Therefore, let's come and progress into the full knowledge of the truth. Let's consider the many items of truth, logically and prayerfully, so the knower will participate fully in the object known.

Sanctifying Truth

> I have given them Your word . . . Sanctify them by Your truth.
> Your word is truth.
>
> — John 17:14, 17

Let's consider the word "sanctify" since it is the truth that sanctifies. Sanctify means "being made holy" because it is the verb form of "holy." Holy (Gk. *Hagios)* means to revere, especially relating to God, to be held in awe (Thayer's). According to *Vine's Expository*, holy also means to be "separated" i.e. separated from the common and profane; thus, consecrated to God.

Often when Christians speak of holiness or sanctification, their consideration is one of sinlessness, perfection, methods of overcoming sins, worldliness, lifestyles, or what holiness among God's people should look like. All these considerations, many of which are Scripturally based, have caused more debate and spiritual fratricide among Christians than just about any other topic. Arguments and divisions have been formed over whether Christians can sin, levels of sin, or how often can a person fall into the same sin before they should be ostracized.

Is there a "second blessing" which will cause a Christian not to sin? If there is, how can we secure such a blessing? What are the methods

Christians should practice in order to overcome sin? Christians shouldn't be worldly even if it is not sinful. Then what constitutes worldliness? What kind of music can, or cannot, Christians listen to? How should we dress? What kind of movie, house or car to avoid if you are to be saved from worldliness? Included in this debate is whether a person who receives the gift of tongues and obeys God's voice will be delivered from sin — viz., how the "gifts of the Spirit" might possibly affect our "sinful habits?" There are thousands of ways to arrange the various shades of sins and worldliness with a combination of methods employed to be holy. Therefore, it is easy to recognize how the topic of sanctification or holiness and its practice has and still does divide multitudes of believers into different groups.

However, according to the Lord's prayer, it is the truth which sanctifies. Instead of focusing on sanctification, why not focus on the truth? Since it is the truth which makes one holy, diving into the truth for understanding and nourishment results in sanctification. Christians should trust in this sanctifying truth working within each believer doing a work based on the timing and circumstances of each individual rather than expecting a one-size-fits-all outcome-based solution where each believer is rigidly placed within a framework whereby the expression of holiness is according to a schedule. Far too often this "sanctimonious effort" is shrouded in some form of "discipleship steps" that, if followed, commend the believer is on the right pathway to holiness.

Furthermore, genuine sanctification by the truth produces oneness among believers. Holiness should unite believers rather than divide. However, it seems among Christians today, those who focus on holiness, who may have achieved some amount of *sinless perfection*, or have been delivered from an appearance of worldliness, are more prone to be judgmental, while rejecting those who have not met up to the standard of holiness estimated by whatever "group think" is out there. It seems Christians have made holiness as their goal in and of itself. When holiness is the goal and the measurement of spirituality or alleged maturity, it can become divisive. It will be used to measure one another. Therefore, many groups, and churches have been organized around various doctrines and practices relating to holiness. Holiness has become a quick yardstick to receive or reject another believer — so-and-so either "measures up" or does not.

Those who reject others due to holiness can feel justified based on their understanding of sanctification. Doesn't the Bible say don't be unequally yoked (2 Cor. 6:14). Didn't Paul say not to eat with a Christian who sins (1 Cor 5:11); didn't the Bible say, "bad company corrupts good morals"? Thus, Christians under the influence of external "holiness" are often much harsher in mercilessly condemning fellow believers since they should know better. Of course, unbelievers are sinners, but this person calls himself a Christian so he shouldn't have fallen into temptation.

However, **according to the Lord's prayer, sanctification or holiness should ultimately produce oneness or unity with other believers.** That means a believer who is holy is one who can receive and minister life to other people around him/her regardless of whether they are deemed holy or not. One sanctified can love, care and be kind to those who are in various levels of holiness or lack thereof. It is through this kind of sanctifying truth believers are made one — NOT "holier than thou!"

Only God is Holy

According to the revelation of the Scriptures, only God is holy (Psalms 99:9; Lev. 11:44). Throughout the Old Testament, Jehovah God was called the "Holy One" 45 times. When Jesus Christ as the Son of God was born, since He was truly God, He was also called the "Holy One" (Luke 1:35; 4:34). Similarly, the third "person" of the Trinity is called the Holy Spirit (Matt. 1:18; 2 Cor. 13:14). Only God in His Trinity is holy and no one else is (1 Sam. 2:2). Therefore, no matter how hard men try to be sinless and consecrated to God in order to be holy, it is not possible without the essence of the Spirit of God doing His work within men. At the same time, while God is uniquely the Holy One, He has become the most approachable. He can unite and join Himself with diverse humanity. He can be one with anyone who would receive Him.

In other words, God being the Holy One has now become the most approachable, the easiest with Whom we humans can develop a relationship. He is the One who can unite with any person no matter their background, preference, and personality. This has everything to do with the Son's death and resurrection which brought redemption and justification for all humanity. Therefore, in the case of Jesus Christ, holiness does not separate Him from people; rather, as the Holy One he is seeking to receive and unite with all people.

Intrinsically, without God: His life, nature, essence, or Spirit, nothing in this entire universe is holy. Therefore, the temple in the Old Testament can be the holy temple because God was in it. When God left, it is just another building left in ruins. Believers are literally called saints, which means holy, because they have received Jesus Christ, the Holy One, into them. Eventually the New Jerusalem, the bride of Christ, is called the Holy City because she is completely identified, joined, perfected as one entity with Him, since God is in His people and they are in Him.

Without a direct and intimate relationship with the Trinity: The Father, Son and Holy Spirit, there is no holiness with humanity. Therefore, truth is needed. The Word was given to men in order for them to possess the truth. Truth is the only method prescribed for holiness by Jesus Christ in His prayer for unity. Therefore, it is critical to know and enjoy truth, and what it produces: The oneness of His people within the Triune God!

Religion is defined by fear

Among various religions of the world, such as Islam, Hinduism, and Buddhism, all have their views and methods of holiness. This quest for holiness, of course, extends to Judaism and Christianity. Each of these religions pursues holiness which pursuits include aspects of overcoming evil, detachment from the secular world, and a form of ceremonial worship. Nevertheless, the quest for holiness in religion is driven by fear – their methods may have nothing to do with God Himself.

The word religion in the Greek is *thrēskeia*. The primary meaning is the fear of the gods and the religious practice of ceremonial worship (Thayer's). The root word is derived from "crying aloud with fear" or being frightened. Therefore, in the New Testament, the word "religion" was used negatively by Paul when he spoke about the strict religious sect he was in which persecuted Christians (Acts 26:5). It was translated as the "worship" of angels for those with fleshly minds (Col. 2:18). Even when James used the word religion more positively by saying pure religion is "*to visit orphans and widows in their trouble, and to keep oneself unspotted from the world*" (James 1:27) – here, the word is related to actions or a to a lifestyle to which most religions would approve; yet, Jesus Christ was not mentioned. In other words, Jesus Christ is not needed in order to be religious or be a religion. Therefore, in contrast to Jesus Christ Himself being life, truth, love, forgiveness, supply, and everything positive intended to be for humankind's enjoyment – this is juxtaposed to religion with all its legalism, lifestyles, and ceremonial worship practiced by men in order to please "god" due to their fear of "god."

No matter the amount of perfection, sinlessness, or consecration and sacrifices religion offers to their gods, the religious abide unholy according to the revelation of Scripture. Even in Christianity, there are various efforts and methods to achieve perfection and deliverance. However, Christians can easily take their focus off the Holy One while being distracted by their pursuit of holiness. Once Jesus Christ is not the center and focus of a believer's quest in their daily living, they too will fall into a mere outward religious form. Christianity can be just another religion with a set of rules and methods to achieve an appearance of holiness in order to please God due to a fear of God's judgment.

However, true holiness is simply God Himself. Whenever and wherever a person has a relationship or fellowship with God, that person is being sanctified. It is at the moment of direct and personal relationship with God when a person is holy or being sanctified.

This is not to say when believers are sanctified by the truth, they will not be freed from sins and experience deliverance. Neither should Christians continue to sin without repentance and confession of sins. The point to be made here is to refocus the attention on Jesus Christ instead of on holiness, while measuring holiness by one's ability to fellowship and become one with diverse believers instead of one's own sinless perfection. A truly holy person is one with the ability to be one with others, which includes a life of loving, caring, forgiving, kindness, and bearing those who may be dissimilar and contrary.

Truth Liberates

> And you shall know the truth, and the truth shall make you free... therefore if the Son makes you free, you shall be free indeed.
> – John 8:32, 36

The sanctifying truth liberates, sets people free. The ignorance of truth is bondage. Knowing truth is freedom. Truth is the Son, Jesus Christ. Accordingly, true sanctification or holiness is freedom, it's liberation.

In the beginning of John 8, the scribes and pharisees brought a woman caught in adultery to Jesus for Him to condemn her to death by stoning in accordance with Mosaic Law. This woman was caught in the very act of adultery. She should have been condemned to death. Jesus was tested: If He were not in agreement with the Pharisees in condemning her to death, then He would be contradicting God's law and be considered unrighteous. On the other hand, if He were to follow God's law as the Pharisees wanted, He would not be the Savior. In His wisdom, the Lord said those without sin cast the first stone at her. Eventually, the religious accusers started leaving from the oldest to the youngest. When all had left the scene, only Jesus was left with the woman. Jesus said *"neither do I condemn you"* (John 8:11). She was free to leave. She was liberated. Jesus saved her!

After this episode, religious Jews wanted to kill Jesus (John 8:37, 40, 59). First, they wanted to kill the woman for breaking their religious laws. Then they wanted to kill Jesus because in their estimation He was not holy (John 8:48) — He sorely offended their religious traditions. Throughout history, religion has been a major cause of killings and wars. In fact, the first murder according to the Bible occurred when Cain killed Abel over religious envy: God accepted Abel's sacrifice and rejected Cain's. Today, major conflicts on earth are perpetrated by religious people aiming to please their god.

Certainly, people willing to kill for their religion are in bondage. They are enslaved to their understanding of holiness, their religious laws, and their ways of worship. Those under such bondages are driven by their religiosity to kill others. If not literally killing, then at least they will condemn, trouble, ostracize, or shun those not abiding by their religion and its strictures.

It is in John 8 where Jesus declared *"the truth* (the Son) *shall make you free."* Certainly, the woman who was condemned by religion was set free. Instead of death by stoning according to the Mosaic law, she was liberated to live. The religious Jews would not receive the truth, the words of Jesus (John 8:37); so, they stayed in bondage. The woman who sinned and was condemned to die gladly received the words of Jesus — she was liberated. The religious Jews, thinking they were holy because they subjected themselves to the law and worshipped the God of Abraham, rejected the Truth before their very eyes.

In John 8 the contrast between the truth being Jesus the Word of God, and a religion having a desire to worship and please God according to law and man's tradition is in view. Truth sets people free from bondage and condemnation endemic in religion. Religious people would find it their duty to kill those transgressing their religion. Without truth, any attempt to be holy and perform worship to please God becomes religious and results in bondage. Whereas truth liberates people from religion and those condemned by it. In religion, there are two groups of people: those condemning and those being condemned. The truth sets both groups free: liberation from casting judgment on others and freedom from being condemned.

It is this ignorance of the truth which fosters religion. All humanity has an innate interest in God, but due to sin and the presence of evil they also have a natural fear of a higher power. That is the reason religion is by definition fear based. Religious men do all they can to limit sin and perform ceremonial worship in order to appease either their idea of god or appease the religious requirements of their system. Without truth, humankind lets their imagination wander into all sorts of religious practice; ironically, it also generates anger, hatred, and killings on those transgressing their religious systems.

Truth is needed. Truth shall liberate men from the darkness and blindness of religion.

Truth Nourishes

> That He might sanctify and cleanse her with the washing of water by the word, For no one ever hated his own flesh, but nourishes and cherishes it, just as the Lord [does] the church [ekklesia].
>
> – Eph., 5:26, 29

> Like newborn infants, desire the pure milk of the word, so that you may grow up into your salvation, 3 if you have tasted that the Lord is good.
>
> – 1 Peter 2:2-3, CSB

> If you instruct the brethren in these things, you will be a good minister of Jesus Christ, nourished in the words of faith and of the good doctrine which you have carefully followed.
>
> – 1 Tim. 4:6

Ephesians 5:26 supports the Lord's prayer by repeating sanctification is by the word of God. Ephesians 5:29 unveils the sanctifying word nourishes. Most Christians consider holiness is merely the elimination of sins and worldliness in order to be consecrated to God. Holiness then becomes the absence of a negative. However, Scriptures unveil holiness needs an addition of a positive. This is nourishment. Nourishment is an addition of an element outside a person which feeds, strengthens, and builds up when food is ingested.

This **addition** is God Himself. God came to humanity as the Word--Truth. He became food for humanity in order for Him to be ingested by man. The Word is nourishing. Eating physical food and understanding the science of metabolism is a wonderful analogy when comparing it to the reality of the Word--Truth. Truth is food to man. Metabolism is the process activated within a body when food is consumed. Here is the simplified meaning of metabolism according to www.merriam-webster.com: *the processes by which a living organism uses food to obtain energy and build tissue and disposes of waste material.*

Therefore, by enjoying food, the body is built-up, and negative things are expelled. In the process of metabolism, the old and dead cells with any impurities in the body are disposed. Simultaneously, nourishing ingredients are assimilated to supply energy, reproduce cells, and cause the body to grow. Physically, the way to expel negative elements in the body is through the positive enjoyment of food.

Based on this understanding of God's Word being man's food for nourishment, it is futile for people to struggle with their self-efforts to become "holy" by eliminating these negative elements of sin and worldliness. Spiritual nourishment in the Word is needed not only for adding God's divine nature, but to expel the negative effect of sin in humanity.

In 1 Peter 2:2 nourishing milk is in the Word. It is by this nourishment babes can grow up into salvation. Certainly, salvation includes sanctification as clearly defined through the book of Romans. The way to grow spiritually is like physical growth; it is through the nourishing milk of the Word. Spiritual food is in the Word, the truth. How do people know whether they are receiving nourishment? It is because they are tasting the Lord — He is good. When you see Jesus in the Scriptures, you begin to appreciate how wonderful and good He is, then you are tasting and getting nourished. Later, we shall see it is essential to differentiate between mere understanding of Scriptures and partaking of the Word as food.

"But He answered and said, "It is written, 'Man shall not live by bread alone, but by every word that proceeds from the mouth of God.'"

– Matthew 4:4

"As the living Father sent Me, and I live because of the Father,
so he who feeds on Me will live because of Me. This is the bread
which came down from heaven--not as your fathers ate the
manna, and are dead. He who eats this bread will live forever . . .
It is the Spirit who gives life; the flesh profits nothing. The words
that I speak to you are spirit, and [they] are life."

– John 6:57-58, 63

Religion, overall, is a system designed to help humanity behave in
a way of avoiding sin while becoming well-pleasing to god(s) through
a set of laws, normally, incorporating some form of ceremonial worship;
whereas God's desire is to become food for man to enjoy Him and partake
of Him and thereby become man's life – manifesting His character. This is
sanctification or holiness according to scriptural revelation. How different is
religion from God's desire! How contrasting it is between a religious person
and one who is truly holy by partaking of God's divine nature (2 Peter 1: 4)
through being nourished by His Word.

This is how His Word as the truth sanctifies human beings: by being our
spiritual food and nourishment by which God's life and nature permeates
humanity and, simultaneously, through this process of spiritual metabolism
expels sin and death.

The Word as Truth Is Contained in the Scriptures

"You search the Scriptures, for in them you think you have
eternal life; and these are they which testify of Me. But you are
not willing to come to Me that you may have life."

– John 5:39-40

Then He said to them, These [are] the words which I spoke to you
while I was still with you, that all things must be fulfilled which
were written in the Law of Moses and [the] Prophets and [the]
Psalms concerning Me." And He opened their understanding,
that they might comprehend the Scriptures.

– Luke 24:44-45

John 17:14 states: *"I have given them Your word . . . ."* John 17:17
continues: *"Your word is truth."* The "word" in this verse does not refer to

the actual text in Scripture (the Bible). The Bible contains and conveys the Word; however, people can read and study the Scriptures, yet *miss* the Word. John 1:1 says, "*In the beginning was the Word and the Word was with God and the Word was God.*" This verse alone shows us the "word" in John 17:17 is not simply referring to the Bible, since the Bible was not written in the beginning of eternity! Then, in John 1:14 we read: "*The Word became flesh….*" This "Word" is God Himself, incarnate. The Son of God became man, in the form of Jesus Christ, the Son of Man. *The* Word is Jesus.

In John 5:39–40, Jesus as the Word was separated from plain Scriptures. The religious Jews studied the Scriptures. They knew the Scriptures thoroughly and what they received in their understanding was law, ceremonial worship and ordinances with traditions. What they missed was the Person to Whom the Scriptures testified. Jesus Christ whom the entire Scripture was speaking about was right in front of them; yet, they missed Him. They would not come to Him to have life. Since they missed Jesus the Word, all they obtained from Scripture was a religion ready to kill the One of Whom the Scriptures spoke.

The entire Hebrew Scriptures are composed of Moses, the prophets and the psalms; therefore, all Scripture is concerning Jesus Christ. Paul in 2 Timothy 3:16 said all Scripture is God's inspiration or breath. Why? Because God speaks of His Only Begotten Son Who is embedded throughout the Scriptures. If you do not see Jesus Christ in the Scriptures, then you have not understood the Scriptures. People can obtain ethics, law, history, stories, ceremonies, rituals and more from the Bible, but if they do not see Jesus and *come to* Jesus, they have not received understanding to comprehend the Scriptures. Although the contents of the Bible are factual and without error, still one can read and study the Scriptures without coming to Jesus. Life is in Jesus, not in mere Scripture absent of Jesus.

The Greek word for "*word*" is *logos*. It means "a speech, something said, and reasoning." It is the root word for "logical" (Gr. *logikos*). Jesus being the "Word" is the expression or effulgence of God as speech. This Word comes in a way which is reasonable — it can be logically understood. We find in John 1:18 our God is hidden — no one can see or perceive Him but the Son, Who is the Word . . . the Word manifests or "declares" God. It is through the Word — Jesus Christ — man can see and know God. The New American Standard Version captures the essence of the verse: "*No one has seen God at any time; the only begotten God who is in the bosom of the Father, He has explained Him."* Although logical, it does not mean there are no mysteries or that everything can be known through the Word. Mathematics clearly is composed of logic, but in an equation, there can be an unknown value called "x." In the case of spiritual logic, although the Word explains God; yet, how God is both three and one simultaneously can be an unknown. Therefore, the Word is for man to understand the things of God; yet, there can still be unknowable mysteries which can only be resolved in eternity.

Words can be written down, passed on, and reproduced in an accurate manner; this is how the Word has been recorded in the Scriptures. God will be manifested to those who seek Jesus as the Word in the Scriptures through understanding and reasoning — the Word explains Who God really is. Believers need to do more than simply read and study the Bible because it contains the Word; they should simultaneously come to Jesus, seek Him, see Him, speak to Him, know Him, handle Him, and have fellowship with Him; otherwise, they will miss the words of eternal life (1 John 1:1–2).

In John 1:14 it says, *"The Word became flesh and dwelt among us . . . full of grace and truth."* A few verses later in verse 18 John writes, *"For the law was given through Moses, but grace and truth came through Jesus Christ."* These two verses reveal *"grace and truth"* were introduced through the Word, Jesus Christ, when God was manifested in the flesh.

According to Vine's Expository Dictionary, **truth** *(Gk: alethia)*, as used in the New Testament, is "the reality lying at the basis of appearance and manifestation." According to this definition, truth is much more than not telling a lie or saying something factual; *it is the reality of the universe.* Truth is eternal. When a person realizes what is hidden behind what appears or what is manifested, *that is truth.* No wonder "truth" has such prominence! It is one of two profundities which came through Jesus Christ. It is important to elevate the understanding of the word "truth" to a high and spiritual level, and not relegate it to a simple secular concept such as, "Tell me the truth! Did you take a cookie?"

John says Jesus Christ is full of grace and truth. He continues to say grace and truth came through Jesus Christ. Based on the above definition, when a person receives Jesus Christ as the Word, they possess *the* truth, *the* reality. They will know and discern what is real, what is behind the entire "shadow" of the universe (Col. 2:16–17). Without Jesus Christ, men are stuck knowing only what they see and what is physically manifested. Men's lives and all they strive for — money, fame, pleasure and material gain — all are vanity. Even the physical universe is not reality; the real frame holding together the observable universe is the Word (Heb 11:3)! Receiving and believing in Jesus Christ brings people out of the pit of vanity, emptiness, falsehood – into truth, veracity, and something solid which is eternal.

The more a believer stands in truth alone, the more open and receptive in fellowship this person will be with all other believers. When a child of God is established in the truth, that person is not blown about by various doctrines (*Didaskalia*) and practices. Neither will there be objections to or insistence on any peripheral doctrines, nor the wide array of Christian practices. A person grounded in the truth of Jesus Christ is a person who is peaceful, comfortable, confident and bold.

Truth Unifies

There is only one truth in the entire universe: Jesus Christ, the embodiment of the Trinity (Col. 2:9), who He is, what He has done in relation to His people in time and for eternity. It is the truth of Jesus Christ in His person and work which makes His people one.

In the New Testament the word *truth* in Greek is *aletheia* and is used 110 times. Every time it is translated in the singular, never in the plural, which confirms there is only one unique truth. There are not many truths. Even among Christians, many speak of *truths* in the plural. Due to this misunderstanding, there is division because you can have your truth and I can have my own truth. No, there is only one truth for all followers of Jesus Christ. Believers are made one by this one truth.

Just about every division and faction among Christians use the Bible as the basis to support their division. There are literally tens of thousands of denominations[1], each quoting Scriptures to justify their position. For example, major doctrinal differences among churches divide from each other whether or not salvation is predestined versus salvation as free-will or a choice. Others include the manifestation of the Spirit (such as speaking in tongues) is needed versus those teaching miraculous gifts have waned (aka, cessationism). Even those divided over such similarly trivial practices such as methods of baptism or music suitable for worship use the Bible to support their stance.

Just about all these various doctrinal and Christian practices, which have divided Christians for centuries, are not based on truth as has already been discussed. Most of these arguments on Christian practice or peripheral beliefs are outside the realm of truth. Believers who have been divided could readily become one if they refocused their attention on *the* truth. What is the faith that saves and makes a person a believer in Jesus Christ? It is this: Jesus Christ being the Son of God who became man. He was the sinless God-Man who died for the sins of the world. He resurrected on the third day and ascended to be the Lord of lords. He has poured out His Spirit and He is indwelling all those who believe and receive Him; thus, making them the children of God.

Every genuine Christian church should preach such a gospel, and every believer should have this same faith. This is *the* truth which makes His believers one. The more a person understands the truth, appreciates the truth, and is firmly established in this truth, the more the person can love and be one with all other believers. A person who is established in truth will not be drawn into divisive arguments over so many contentious Christian doctrines and practices; rather, this person will seek for ways to bring others into truth and minister life through speaking truth.

2

WHAT IS & IS NOT TRUTH

Truth: God and His Eternal Work

In the New Testament, the word *truth* is always used in the singular. It is never *truths*, plural. Secularly, the expression "truths" is used and preferred. Due to this influence, even Christians would use the plural rather than the singular truth. To people of the world, there are many truths, such as many ways to enlightenment. In other words, truth in the secular world is relative — not absolute (i.e., "truth" is in the eye of the beholder).

Therefore, one person's truth can be different from another. This kind of thinking has also impacted Christians so they can have conflicting truths. Conflicting and contrary truths have led to divisions and sectarianism. Therefore, it is critical to recognize in the divine revelation within Scriptures: There is only one truth. Since there is a unique truth in this universe, all believers are one in the truth. This may sound to some ears rather simplistic; however, as we examine the profound nature of truth or reality it will become more than clear to us.

Just as God is one and three (Father, Son, and Spirit) simultaneously, truth is one with multiple facets. The more Christians understand and appreciate these facets, the more grounded and established they will become in walking in truth (3 John 1:4).

Let's briefly consider the major items of the truth.

First and foremost, God is truth. "*In the beginning was the Word and the Word was with God, and the Word was God . . . and the Word became flesh . . . full of grace and truth*" (John 1:1, 14).

Second, Jesus Christ who is God in the flesh is truth. Truth was revealed in Jesus Christ. Jesus said, "*I am the truth*" (John 14:6), and Paul declared "*the truth is in Jesus*" (Eph. 4:21).

Third, the Spirit is Truth. The Scriptures declare the *Spirit of truth* (John 14:17, 15:26, 16:13; 1 John 4:6); this *Spirit is truth* (1 John 5:6). The Spirit of

Truth guides believers into all truth by declaring and infusing the reality of all Who the Father and the Son are into believers (John 16:13–15).

Fourth, all that the Father, the Son, and the Spirit have accomplished in the New Covenant for His eternal purpose is truth. This includes the death of Jesus Christ on the cross, His resurrection, His ascension and enthronement, and His work of redemption for the forgiveness of sins, justification, sanctification, the believers' regeneration (new birth) and glorification. Therefore, the person of the Triune God dwelling bodily in Jesus Christ (Col. 2:9) and His work of redemption and regeneration is the Word of truth — that is, the gospel of salvation. It is through believing the truth people are saved and sealed by the indwelling Spirit (Eph. 1:13). It is in truth God and humanity are joined and unified together to be the Lord's ekklesia, His body — the new man spoken of in Ephesians 2:15. This is God's eternal purpose: A corporate entity, ultimately the New Jerusalem, created and built up into maturity in truth (Eph. 4:24).

Finally, the Word as recorded in the Bible is truth. The Bible conveys the truth; therefore, in Daniel 10:21 the term "Scripture of Truth" is used. Truth is the possessor of Scriptures. This means if one reads the Scriptures and only understood law, history, ceremonies, ethics or morality, and missed truth, then they missed the entire point of Scriptures. Therefore, when reading or studying Scriptures, it is critical to come to the embedded Word. Truth is experienced when the Word is made real to a person. The Word, the *logos*, speaks to people and communicates to their reasoning. When the Word is received, understood, and becomes real in a person, then it is truth. That is why people need to know and come to the full knowledge of the truth (2 Tim. 2:25, 3:7; 1 Tim. 2:4).

For example, the Bible says Jesus Christ is God who became man, died for mankind's sin and was resurrected on the third day. Many unbelievers have heard this, but it is not truth or real to them. One day as they consider this word, they will hopefully open their heart and connect with Jesus through faith. At that very moment, the Spirit of Truth will enter them and make the word of God they heard real; they will understand with a living knowledge, and then, that will be real to them because they have encountered *the* truth!

The sum of New Testament revelation of the *truth* is rich and deep. It is God in Jesus Christ as the Spirit with all that they have accomplished for man and in man, which includes the eternal purpose of God's ekklesia (assembly) fulfilled in Jesus Christ. Therefore, truth is God Himself, with His life, nature, and essence, intrinsically joined with humanity. The truth is eternal (2 John 1:2). Anything which is temporal and has no effect in eternity is not truth.

This book, *ONE TRUTH*, and another book, *ONE EKKLESIA* are dedicated to exploring the various facets and items of the truth as outlined above.

What Is __Not__ Truth?

Jesus prayed in John 17 for believers to be made one through the truth. Thus, anything which divides believers — things over which Christians argue becoming sectarian — is not truth. Most Christian groups agree truth is what was outlined above. Any doctrines not defined as truth are non-essential. What has divided Christians include doctrines (Grk: *Didaskalia* which will be defined later), various Christian practices, or human causes. Christians have been divided, have fought over, and have rejected each other over some of the most ridiculous items such as musical style in worship, whether women should have their head covered, whether the rapture is pre, mid, or post-tribulation, methods of baptism, and even methods of leadership. Some of these items are tantamount to the rise and fall of denominations — if you're not pre-trib you're deceived, maybe not even saved!

There are literally thousands of such things which have divided Christians; yet, the truth remains the same. A believer who has a growing understanding of the truth stays anchored in the truth and will not be distracted by positioning themselves in non-essentials; they will remain one with all believers.

The tactic of the enemy (Satan) is to use men and women — specifically Christian men and women — to elevate non-essential doctrines and practices thereby forming groups and churches around those doctrines. For example, a major dividing doctrinal point among Christians is centered on the debate over predestination or free will. Churches have been grouped together on one side or the other. Both sides can show supporting Bible verses and speak of how their doctrine is better for Christians, but the fact is, neither of those doctrines died for humankind or was resurrected!

Nowhere in the Scriptures does it say in order to receive eternal life a person needs to believe in one of these doctrines. Ultimately, it does not matter in eternity which doctrine is correct. Therefore, neither doctrine is truth, and certainly not worth dividing over. Whether a person espouses one side or the other, or even both, is not a problem unless it becomes a condition for fellowship — and a rejection of those with contrary views.

Another major point of division is whether the Holy Spirit is still doing works of power as in the days of the early apostles, or if these works of power have ceased. Again, using the definition of truth above, this belief is not truth either way. A person who is established in the truth will be able to have fellowship and receive believers no matter what their doctrinal position or preference is. Those who are not standing in truth may be so biased with their personal doctrinal stance they end up taking an extreme position. For example, some may not acknowledge a genuine miraculous healing today can be from God; others may belittle believers for not receiving any manifestation of the Holy Spirit.

Practices are much more common than doctrinal differences in dividing believers. For example, the moment a person believes in Christ and receives salvation, this person is regenerated in Christ; this is biblical truth. It is faith which brings a person into Christ. Baptism is a physical symbol declaring the truth of being in Christ. Every believer agrees with the truth that faith uniquely brings a person into Jesus Christ; however, many sectarian groups have formed over the physical symbol of baptism. Some insist on water baptism, while others insist baptism must be by immersion and not by sprinkling. Still others within the same immersion camp insist the following phrase has to be recited at baptism: "In the name of the Father and of the Son, and of the Holy Spirit." Others insist the wording should be: "In the name of Jesus Christ."

All the above are various *ways* to practice baptism, but not the truth of being immersed into Jesus Christ, the Triune God. Different teachings on baptism use different scriptural verses as their foundation, and many believers are helped by their way of baptism. However, it is against the truth to use any of these practices to build up an entire sectarian group hindering believers in that group from accepting and fellowshipping with other believers if they do not hold to the same practice.

It's Easy to Be Distracted Away from the Truth

At this juncture, let's consider the story in Matthew 17 because it shows how easily and quickly the Lord's disciples forgot the revelation they received just eight days earlier. Here, Jesus brought a few of His disciples up to a high mountain. Peter was included — one who recently received the revelation concerning Jesus being the Christ, the Son of God (Matthew 16). On this mountain, Jesus was transfigured before them; He became shining as the sun. Together with this glorious Jesus were Moses and Elijah, also standing there conversing with Jesus. Peter grew excited and immediately said they should make three tabernacles, one for each of them. Moses represented the Law given by God, since Moses gave the Law (John 1:17); therefore, many times the Law was associated with Moses throughout the Bible. After Moses, the major prophet who performed many miraculous works was Elijah. He was the only prophet prominently named in the New Testament, twenty-nine times; therefore, Elijah represents the prophets with God's supernatural power.

When encountering all three, Peter viewed them the same, giving them "equal honors": Jesus, Moses, and Elijah. Since he wanted to build three tabernacles, one for each, this demonstrated Peter considered them with equal standing, requiring equal reverence. Suddenly, the Father spoke from a cloud and said, "*This is my beloved Son, hear Him.*" The disciples fell in fear of such a voice. When Jesus came to lift them up, and when they looked up, they saw "*no one, but Jesus alone.*" Both Moses and Elijah were gone; only Jesus was left for them to behold.

This is the experience of most Christians. They are saved by a wonderful revelation concerning Jesus being the Christ, the Son of the Living God. Then they immediately view the law and so many other items on an equal level as Jesus. "Now that Jesus saved me," they think, "I have to learn these doctrines, keep these laws, pursue these spiritual gifts, do these works, and on and on." Even though Jesus is the shining One, from their perspective, Jesus is now just another item among a long list of things. No, no, no! Another revelation is needed after believing — there is no one else other than Jesus. It is not Jesus plus this and that. It is Jesus Himself alone!

It is unfortunate when most believers study the Bible, they consider it elementary to stay focused on Jesus Christ. There is a thought "deeper truth" is how to behave as a Christian, understand the end times, learn self-denial, obtain a special gift from God, or many other topics. Some think, "I already know Jesus Christ died and resurrected; let's learn about all the other Biblical matters." One can study, know, and discuss many topics in the Bible; yes, it is advisable to read the Bible from cover to cover thoroughly, but a mature believer is one who can only be satisfied with the excellence of the knowledge of Jesus Christ (Phil. 3:8–15). Those items which expand upon Him are focused on the "knowledge of the Son of God."

A mature believer is one who has lost the taste for all peripheral topics other than Jesus Christ, and His pursuit of the truth is to see and know how Jesus Christ's person and work is revealed upon the pages of the Bible. There is a recognition and appreciation Jesus is unsearchable and unlimited in His riches; therefore, it is an eternal pursuit to come to the full knowledge of the Son of God. In fact, Jesus is INCOMPARABLE!

Confusion: Doctrine Unites, Doctrine Divides

The matter of Biblical "doctrine" or "teaching" has also been a great source of division in the Body of Christ . . . let me explain. These two words "doctrine" and "teaching" can be used interchangeably. It simply means "that which is taught" (Vine's). There is a doctrine which is essential and unites and there are many doctrines causing division. Which is which?

The Bible is full of doctrines, unless you do not read the Bible, but if you do, it is unavoidable to pick up all sorts of doctrines. Believers are encouraged to study the Bible in order to be taught by various doctrines. Some have such a strong emphasis in learning doctrines with a desire to resolve all seemingly contradicting ideas in the Bible; consequently, they formulate and organize these various doctrines into a more uniformed and cohesive arrangement for easier understanding. That body of doctrine is what can be defined as "systematic theology."

The difficulty is this: There are literally thousands of teachings in the Bible ranging from the mysterious and heavenly concerning the person and nature of God . . . to the mundane and earthly such as what one should wear and eat. The more students of the Bible desire to teach and live according to the doctrines in Scripture, the more conflict they discover — interpretations widely vary.

Therefore, Christians are inclined to simplify doctrine by asking: "Just tell me the right doctrine to believe and live by." Depending on personality and influence, some will emphasize one side of conflicting teachings while others will highlight the other side. For example, the Bible does not actually have a doctrine of the Trinity. Sometimes it refers to God in the singular and at other times it speaks of God in the plural, specifically: Father, Son and Holy Spirit. Some can then emphasize their teaching on the side of God being one, while others on the side of three persons within the "Godhead." This has caused great divisions in the past.

Salvation by faith or works can also have conflicting verses. Some will cite why believers are saved by grace, not by works (Eph. 2:8-9), while others will cite "*faith without works is dead*" (James 2:20). This is the same for whether salvation is eternally secure or whether a believer can lose their salvation. This has been a major divider among Christians for hundreds of years — right up to the present. Beyond these major theological doctrines, there are hundreds or thousands more concerning church practices, methods of prayer, end times, Christian blessings and even life-style doctrines such as marriage, diet, clothing, music, etc.

Due to the many doctrines throughout the Bible, many divisions and factions have been formed among Christians. Additionally, the misuse of Biblical doctrines has placed many people into bondage. They feel if they do not follow and abide by the teachings in the Bible then they are breaking God's laws and are thereby susceptible to God's judgment.

Reacting to how Christians have used doctrines to divide and oppress God's people, numerous believers begin to devalue and even belittle doctrine. They may say something like: "We don't need doctrines; we just need the Spirit." Or, "Doctrines kill and divide." Or, "Studying the Bible is not necessary, it's the Spirit that gives life." They have pitted the experiences of the Spirit against the understanding of the Bible; yet, that is in and of itself their doctrine. Ironically, Christians pushing-back on this "no-doctrine" teaching respond by doubling-down, emphasizing all controversies can be explained with intensive study and "cutting-straight" (e.g., "rightly dividing") Scriptures. It seems constant arguments over doctrines in the Scripture are unavoidable and unending. Those who clamor for "sound doctrine" warn us to beware of those who deprecate the same.

The English word for "doctrine" or "teaching" comes from two different Greek words. The two Greek words are used differently and have two distinct meanings, but since they are both translated as "*doctrine*" in English, the exact meaning of each is lost. It is a source of confusion for English readers when these two Greek words are not clearly delineated. It would be a great help for believers to understand "doctrine" which they need to embrace as truth, and those doctrines which are flexible in application so as not to divide nor be oppressed by them.

The two Greek words translated to "doctrine" or "teaching" are: *Didachē* (Strong's #1322) and *Didaskalia* (Strong's #1319). According to Biblehub. com, *Didachē* means: Established teaching, especially a "summarized" body of respected teaching (viewed as reliable, time-honored). However, *Didaskalia* means: Applied teaching; systematic theology; Christian doctrine (teaching) as it especially extends to its necessary *lifestyle* (applications).

Didachē is used 30 times in the New Testament and 25 out of the 30 times refers to the doctrine spoken by Jesus (Matt 7:28, Luke 4:32); the doctrine of Jesus Christ (2 John 1:9-10); and, the doctrine of the apostles (Acts 2:42, 5:28). The other five times are used negatively (Heb. 13:9) — specifically, doctrines of: the Pharisees (Matt. 16:12), Balaam (Rev. 2:14), Nicolaitans (Rev. 2:15), and Jezebel (Rev. 2:24). Both the positive doctrines relating to Jesus Christ or the damaging ones are consistently time-honored and reliable for acceptance or rejection. There are no situations where the doctrine of Jesus Christ should be rejected, or the doctrine of Jezebel should be accepted.

The constant and eternally profitable ***doctrine*** (*Didachē*) represents the teaching concerning the person and work of Jesus Christ. It is this fundamental doctrine wherein the truth of the New Testament is found. It teaches people to know God, Jesus Christ, the Holy Spirit, the entire work of Christ from incarnation, human living, death, resurrection, ascension, the outpouring of the Spirit, regeneration of His people unto the building up of His ekklesia, the assembly, His Body until His bodily return in glory. This is the doctrine all believers should speak (1 Cor. 14:6); and from which Christian teachers should not deviate (Rom. 16:17). The above usages fit the definition of a "summarized body of respected teaching (viewed as reliable, time-honored)."

Didaskalia, on the other hand, is used 21 times. It refers to applied-teaching, application to Christian lifestyle with a view to systematizing theology. Therefore, this kind of doctrine instead of being "time-honored" is more contemporaneous. It seeks influence on the hearer's lifestyle. The effect on the hearer can be positive: leading them toward seeking and living a well-pleasing life before the Lord Jesus. However, it could also be negative: leading them away from the Lord toward self-efforts and bondages. Whether positive or negative, those influenced believe the source of this doctrine is divine or Scriptural — sound Biblical teaching.

On the positive side, we are told this teaching (*didaskalia*) of Scripture is for learning, providing us patience, comfort, and giving hope through difficulties in conflicting situations (Rom. 15:4). The Scriptures also provide doctrine (*didaskalia*), corrections, and instruction in righteousness. When one comes to the Scripture for Spiritual breath (life-sustaining), he/she receives the proper "doctrine" to be instructed to live and work in an evil generation (2 Tim. 3:16). How we apply Scriptures becomes the doctrine which governs how we live and act as Christians from day to day (2 Tim. 3:10).

Therefore, ministers of the Word should do their best to apply Scriptures in a way that is healthy or sound. When it comes to applying Scripture to a lifestyle, one can imagine all these various approaches. Thus, Paul stressed it needs to be healthy (1 Tim. 1:10; 2 Tim. 4:3; Titus 1:9; 2:1). "Healthy" points to life and growth, not merely behavior. When applying Scriptures, it needs to be in a way leading people to grow in their spiritual life.

It is by this strengthening and growing through the indwelling life of Christ believers are transformed. It is through life-transformation the daily life of believers is truly affected. The Christian life should not be governed by a set of rules; rather, it should be by God's eternal life within each believer. Healthy doctrine (*didaskalia*) is applying Scripture in a way leading the hearer to turn to Jesus Christ, so His life will cause the believer to grow and be transformed from within. Nevertheless, applying Scriptures improperly can also have a very harmful effect — the opposite of applying them in a healthy manner:

> And in vain they worship Me, Teaching [as] doctrines [didaskalia] the commandments of men.
> — Matthew 15:9

> In order that we may be no longer babes, tossed and carried about by every wind of that teaching [didaskalia] in the sleight of men, in unprincipled cunning with a view to systematized error . . ..
> — Ephesians 4:14 DBY

In Matthew 15, when Jesus condemned the Pharisees, their teaching was about tithing. They were not teaching something sinful, such as lying or stealing. They were teaching something according to God's command: tithing — giving something to God. However, in their application of God's law concerning tithing, they negated another one which is to honor one's father and mother. This doctrine of "If anyone tells his father or his mother, 'what you would have gained from me is given to God'" became a commandment of men. It sounded so spiritual and Scriptural, but it was also in direct disobedience to another one of God's commands: *honor your father and mother.*

The Scriptures are full of seemingly competing and contrary ideas. When a person applies only one set of verses and negates conflicting verses, the doctrine derived by a one-sided application, no matter how Scriptural, is of man and not of God.

In Ephesians 4:14, the doctrines which were like a wind blowing young believers about can be assumed to be doctrines from the Bible. These differing emphases in applying Scripture became a wind to toss and carry immature believers from one side to another. Bible teachers can use their cunning ways of interpretation to come up with doctrines in support of their sectarian systems. Babes are blown about, captured into such a system by doctrines (*didaskalia*) or "systematized error."

Even doctrine (*didaskalia*) of demons as described in 1 Tim. 4:1-3 were not related to idolatry or some other sinful act; rather, they can be traced to applying scriptural and spiritual references. Didn't Paul say it is better for a man not to marry, so he can be pleasing to the Lord (1 Cor. 7:1, 8, 32)? A doctrine to forbid marriage is just a codifying of a portion of Scripture to help believers to love the Lord without entanglement. As far as abstaining from foods, isn't this also Scriptural and spiritual? Jesus Himself spoke of fasting (Matt. 6:16) — believers in Acts also fasted (Acts 13:2-3; 14:23). Demons merely formulated a doctrine by applying Scripture to regulate a Christian lifestyle.

Today, doctrines (*didaskalia*) which are causing arguments and divisions are mostly focused on how Scriptures are applied. It is not over the doctrine (*didaskalia*) of Jesus Christ. Understanding and appreciating the doctrine of Jesus Christ as the truth brings believers into oneness. Attempting to systematize the Bible correctly among certain Christian lifestyles continues to segregate and divide believers. One desiring to serve the Lord needs to be grounded on and enriched by the doctrine of Jesus Christ with all His unsearchable riches, and simultaneously, be able to apply the appropriate Scriptures to a person in need with a particular condition.

For example, if a person's doctrine (*didaskalia*) is "once saved, always saved" or "saved by grace" alone, then that person cannot apply verses such as

Philippians 2:12 "*work out your own salvation with fear and trembling*" in order to help a believer who is lackadaisical in his pursuit of the Lord. Likewise, if a person's doctrine is "you can lose your salvation," there will be another list of verses concerning the security of the believer's salvation which will not be used for comforting one who is under condemnation due to willfully sinning. Rather, a person who is fortified with the doctrine (*didache*) of Jesus Christ will be able to apply all verses without negating any. A healthy word can be spoken based on the need of the person at any specific time. This healthy word will turn the hearer to Jesus, strengthen his or her faith to pursue and serve the Lord. We're not talking about "situational ethics" — we're sharing the riches of Jesus Christ!

There are many more examples of doctrinal (*didaskalia*) applications: head covering for women, the exercise of miraculous gifts, name and claim, modesty, choice or life, social equality, prosperity and health by faith, repentance and many more teachings in the Bible that can be applied to Christian living and practice. Some of these teachings have no doubt helped many believers; therefore, it is precious to them. However, according to the definition given to *didaskalia*, all these doctrinal applications are not truth at their core. Although these kinds of applications have helped many, they have also stumbled many. They have become a source of division and confusion if applied "religiously" in order to compel a certain lifestyle or Christian practice.

Therefore, it is crucial for those desiring to answer the Lord's Prayer for the oneness of His people to understand these two different kinds of doctrine. On the one hand, we need to be those who keep mining the unsearchable riches of Jesus Christ so the doctrine (*didache*) of Jesus Christ becomes fuller and deeper for our enjoyment and our ministry to people. Satan's strategy is designed to distract believers from focusing on and knowing Jesus Christ.

On the other hand, we need to be wary of Satan's other tactic: motivating ministers to emphasize Biblical doctrines (*didaskalia*) to the point of divisiveness whereby these "healthy teachings" turn into unhealthy food. Instead of teachers divisively tossing believers around by every wind of doctrine, what is needed are teachers who can apply Scriptures to a person in need at the right moment to bring individuals back into fellowship with Jesus for the building up of His One Body. Jesus alone is precious.

"*Sound doctrine builds up the Body of Christ.*" Know this: the doctrine (*didache*) of Jesus Christ is always beneficial for building up; whereas spiritual discernment is needed when applying doctrine (*didaskalia*) to a person's lifestyle. Ministers are needed to equip the saints, so all believers can speak the doctrine of Jesus Christ, which is the knowledge of the Son of God, producing the Perfect Man (Eph. 4:13). This will build up the Body of Christ into one ekklesia.

What will be covered in the following chapters are major points affecting the general understanding of *the truth*. This is what would be considered as the doctrine (*didache*) of Jesus Christ or the apostles' teachings (*didache*). These chapters will not focus on the various doctrines (*didaskalia*) in their sundry applications: the how, when, and to whom teachings of the Scriptures are applied. The application of teachings is where divisions and factions have been generated. Even disagreements concerning so-called deeper and richer points of truth, such as the Triune nature of God, should never break fellowship. Only the essential faith which brings salvation determines whether one is in fellowship with Jesus Christ. This saving faith is the only item for which believers should contend.

An Overview of the Points of the Truth

> endeavoring to keep the unity of the Spirit in the bond of peace. [There is] one body and one Spirit, just as you were called in one hope of your calling; one Lord, one faith, one baptism; one God and Father of all, who [is] above all, and through all, and in you all.
> – Ephesians 4:3-6

This portion of Scriptures made clear unity among believers is based on the one truth common among all believers. Believers are to keep the unity already possessed by each because of the indwelling Spirit. Now, they are to recognize the truth which is the foundation of their oneness. This list of seven items of one may constitute the various aspects comprising the truth.

The first item is *one Body*. This being the first is the most important understanding needed by all Christians to guard their unity. There is only one Body of Christ consisting of all genuine believers of the Lord Jesus Christ. The author of this book wrote *One Ekklesia* to have a focused consideration on this critical topic of one Body; because the vision and practice concerning the Lord's ekklesia as His one Body is still sorely lacking. It is against *the truth* for Christians to refer to their church as one body and another church as another body. No matter which church a believer may or may not attend, they are all in the same Body.

There is one Body because there is only *one Spirit*. Scriptures have assigned various titles to the one Spirit: Spirit of God, Holy Spirit, Spirit of Christ, Spirit of Jesus Christ, and seven Spirits. They all refer to the same one Spirit. This one Spirit is both the indwelling Spirit within all believers and also the empowering Spirit clothing believers. Divisions have been caused over different manifestations of the Spirit or various methods of obtaining the Spirit; yet, it is clear believers receive the Spirit through faith alone (Gal. 3:2, 5). The truth is the Spirit is one; therefore, the Body immersed into and drinking of the Spirit is also one (1 Cor 12:13).

One hope – Christ in His believers is the hope of glory (Col. 1:27). All believers have the same hope: the hope of full salvation resulting in ultimate glorification. All those who have the faith of Jesus Christ (Gal. 2:20) will arrive at the same destination of glory. Christians divide over various experiences and methods of sanctification, but we should be united in the reality that we will all arrive in glory. We have no other eternal hope in the present world, but this one hope. Additionally, the followers of Jesus are all called in one Body (Col. 2:15). The Spirit is not merely seeking fragmented individuals to indwell; rather, the Spirit needs one Body to manifest His glory. He needs one Body coordinated with every member functioning as they should under His moving and influence. Therefore, all individual believers are called in one Body. They were not called as mere individuals, but within the realm of the one Body. In God's plan He is not bringing each individual believer into glory – it is the corporate Body of the Spirit arriving in glory.

The *one Lord* is Jesus Christ. He is the Lord of lords. Jesus Christ was made Lord (i.e., the Lordship of Christ) at His resurrection and ascension. When a person proclaims Jesus is the Lord, in essence he declares Jesus is God who became man to die on behalf of humankind; He was resurrected on the third day; and ascended to be made both Lord and Christ (Acts 2:36). This is the one Lord whom all believers must confess to be saved. There is no other name given among men whereby one can be saved (Acts 4:12). When Christians put their trust in and exalt any other person, no matter how great a minister, teacher, or pastor, division is generated. When believers lift up in admiration and give praise to their one Lord, they are made one.

One faith is the faith in the one Lord — Jesus Christ. All believers are saved by the same faith of Jesus Christ. He is the sole object of our trust. He authored and perfected the faith we have received from Him. If anyone preaches there is additional requirements other than faith in Jesus Christ for salvation, it will certainly cause divisions. Therefore, all Christians must unify in the one faith of the one Lord.

One baptism — through this one faith, believers are baptized or immersed into Christ. According to Romans 6, the baptism of believers declares the fact their old man, the fallen man, has been buried and they have been raised to walk in newness of life. The termination and burial of the former life which was without Christ is a reality. It is a fact which has already been accomplished through the death of Christ. Through faith, believers are immersed into Jesus Christ and cannot exit without being in Him. They are no longer in their fallen flesh, for they are living in the resurrected Christ. This is the truth of One baptism. Christians have divided over various methods and formulas of baptism, but the truth is no matter what methods, when, where, or by whom, it is this one faith which makes this one baptism real for all God's children.

Finally, there is *one God and Father of all*. Every believer of Jesus Christ has the same God who is now their Father. Those of the one faith in the one Lord have been regenerated with a new birth — they are born of God. That means the regenerated people of God partake of the Father's life and nature. God is literally their Father. All believers have the same Father; therefore, they are brothers and sisters in truth. God's family cannot be divided with His children fighting and not having fellowship with one another.

In these seven items of the truth, the Triune God is integrated throughout. The one Spirit is within the one Body and all the members have this one hope of glory. The Son is their one Lord in Whom believers have their one faith, and through faith, one baptism immerses them into Christ with a new birth as God's children. Their one God is now the believers' one Father, Who is residing in all of them.

When believers have the knowledge of this truth how can they be divided? How can they not unite together as one? How can they not love one another in fellowship?

... until we all attain to the unity of the faith and of the knowledge
of the Son of God, to mature manhood, to the measure of the
stature of the fullness of Christ,

– Eph 4:13 ESV

As Ephesians chapter 4 progresses, it shows that within this sphere of
truth is the essential faith concerning Jesus Christ and the knowledge of the
Son of God (Eph 4:13-15). It is this faith which is essential for salvation;
simply put: Jesus is God who became man to die on the cross for man's sins;
He was resurrected on the third day with a mysterious physical/spiritual
body enabling Him to indwell all believers (i.e., the "Comforter") as the
Lord of all. The knowledge of the Son of God is the entire truth abounding
in unsearchable riches. His riches cannot be exhausted. Therefore, what is
presented in the following chapters can only be a framework of the riches
of Christ providing believers a clear direction in appreciating their pursuit
of the truth. However, not every point in the following chapters is truth
according to the definition given in previous pages. Some of the points
can be classified as healthy teachings providing support for the truth. The
following chapters will present:

1. Jesus Christ, His person: He is both God and man. This point is
   essential to a believer's faith. This is what a person must believe to
   have salvation and be born of God.
2. Jesus Christ, His work: Jesus died on the cross for man's sin,
   resurrected on the third day, and ascended to be Lord of all. As the
   Spirit, He is now indwelling His believers, His One Body. These
   matters are also essential: One cannot claim to be a follower of
   Christ, a believer in Him, without clearly accepting this sequence of
   events as the work of Jesus Christ.
3. Satan and man, his creation and fall: This chapter would not be
   considered as truth. There can be disagreement concerning Satan's
   nature, his position, whether human beings possess original
   sin, what the makeup of man is, or whether his spirit is the same
   as his soul. However, this chapter offers Scripture opening the
   reader's understanding (or consideration) concerning Satan and
   humankind; each person can then *be convinced in his own mind*
   (Rom. 14:5).

4. God's redemption and salvation: This chapter unveils the effect of the work of the Lord Jesus when applied to humankind. How this chapter slices and dices various words may result in differing opinions among believers, but the overall effect on a man's sins is forgiveness resulting from Christ's redemption and man's salvation through the work of Jesus Christ. This is truth.

5. God's economy: Although this point is infrequently mentioned among Christians, it is God's purpose and method of accomplishing His eternal goal through Jesus Christ. Therefore, it is truth. The more believers understand and enjoy God's economy (aka, dispensing or administration), the more they can and will be one with other believers. God's economy is a description of how Jesus Christ is working out God's plan.

6. The New Covenant: This is also truth. To implement the New Covenant, Jesus Christ shed His blood (died) and resurrected. Additionally, the essence and power of the New Covenant is the indestructible Life of the Lord Jesus Christ. It is through the New Covenant believers are made one.

7. The final two chapters of this book concern the completion gospel. The gospel is not only an aspect of the truth, but truth itself that needs to be preached as the gospel. The gospel of grace has been preached to almost every corner of the earth, but the gospel of peace, which is the second part needed, has been mostly hidden and kept silent. Both parts are needed to complete the gospel of Jesus Christ.

3

JESUS CHRIST – HIS PERSON

Jesus Christ: The Topic of the Entire Bible

First, let us consider the Person of Jesus Christ. *Who is He?* When people read the Bible, they can read for various reasons and often come away with different impressions. A person can read the Bible for its intriguing stories. Another might read it to learn morality and ethics, while still others read it to learn law and history. However, what is the real goal of the Bible?

God's intention is to reveal His purpose – hidden and fulfilled in the Person and Work of Jesus Christ. If a person reads the Bible and misses Jesus Christ, it is like they never read the Bible. It would be like reading a book on American History, and, at the end, knowing nothing about the United States. Let's look at the Bible itself, to see what it reveals as the main topic in its pages.

The New Testament Starts and Ends with Jesus Christ

> Book of the generation of Jesus Christ, Son of David, Son of Abraham.
>
> – Matthew 1:1 DBY

The very first verse of the gospel of Matthew, the first book of the New Testament, says it is the book of *the generation of Jesus Christ*. Some translations use the term "historical records" of Jesus Christ. Some believe the word "book" in this verse only refers to Jesus' genealogy, those who came before Him; but the point of any person's genealogy is to bring focus on that person based on history. God in His sovereignty designed this to be the first verse for the entire book of the New Testament. This verse can then be applied to the entire New Testament, *the* book that is about Jesus Christ.

It is a book about where He came from, what He did, what He is doing, and who He is in the future unto eternity.

The New Testament begins with Jesus' ancestry spanning from Abraham to King David, from King David to the Babylonian Captivity, and from the Babylonian Captivity to birth of Jesus. Then His youth, work, teachings, life, death, resurrection, with His relationship and continuation, through His Spirit, with His disciples is presented. In another section of the New Testament written by the apostle John it says Jesus Christ is God without a beginning or "*in the beginning with God*" (John 1:1-2). Jesus created all things, and He put on flesh to become a man (John 1:3, 10, 14). In yet another section of John's gospel he describes Jesus living in His disciples (John 14:19-20). Because of their preaching Jesus Christ, those disciples were multiplied. Believers in Him became His expansion, His body — His assembly or *ekklesia* (Greek — Matthew 16:18).

Also, recorded in the New Testament are various letters written by apostles to woo believers back to Jesus Christ, since many were becoming distracted and turning away to other things such as the ordinances of the law (including Jewish fables — Titus 1:14; Col. 2:14; Eph. 2:15) and meaningless philosophies (Greeks — Col. 2:8). Satan, the enemy, has done his best to confuse believers, distract them, and pull them away from the simplicity that is in Jesus Christ (2 Cor. 11:3-4). The apostles, on the other hand, made it their life's work to keep believers focused on *Christ*, the Messiah.

Revelation: The Unveiling of Jesus Christ

Revelation, the last book of the Bible, concludes the New Testament concerning Jesus Christ:

> The Revelation of Jesus Christ, which God gave Him to show His servants — things which must shortly take place. And He sent and signified [it] by His angel to His servant John.
> — Revelation 1:1

> He who testifies to these things says, "Surely I am coming quickly." Amen. Even so, come, Lord Jesus! The grace of our Lord Jesus Christ be with you all. Amen.
> — Revelation 22:20, 21

Revelation is the end of the *entire* Bible, both Testaments. In this last record written by John, the apostle begins by saying it is "*the revelation of Jesus Christ*" (Rev. 1:1). Revelation includes graphic descriptions of the end times in the form of signs and wonders, but if the reader misses the unveiling of Jesus Christ, then they miss the actual revelation. The purpose of the New Testament from Matthew to Revelation is to unveil Jesus Christ — His person and work.

Finally, the last two verses of the Revelation conclude with Jesus Christ coming again, and the joy and rejoicing of Jesus Christ dwelling physically and visibly with all His saints. Explicitly, Jesus Christ is the subject and focus of the entire New Testament.

The Old Testament Speaks of Jesus Christ in Prophecies, Types and Allegories

> You search the Scriptures, for in them you think you have eternal life; and these are they which testify of Me. But you are not willing to come to Me that you may have life.
>
> – John 5:39–40

> Then He said to them, "These are the words which I spoke to you while I was still with you, that all things must be fulfilled which were written in the Law of Moses and the Prophets and the Psalms concerning Me." And He opened their understanding, that they might comprehend the Scriptures.
>
> – Luke 24:44–45

> Paul talked to them all day, from morning to evening, explaining everything involved in the kingdom of God, and trying to persuade them all about Jesus by pointing out what Moses and the prophets had written about him.
>
> – Acts 28:23 (The Message)

During Jesus' time on earth many of the Pharisees (considered to be the religious people of the day) were persecuting Jesus seeking to kill Him (John 11:46-48, 53). These religious leaders were very familiar with the Scriptures, which, at the time, included only the Hebrew Bible or its Septuagint version in the Greek language. As religious people, they diligently searched and studied the Scriptures, but focused intently on the Law. They used God's command to keep the Sabbath as a reason to persecute Jesus; in their minds, they believed He had broken this religious law by healing on the Sabbath (Luke 13:14).

However, Jesus directly addressed the Pharisees: they got it completely wrong. Instead of drawing laws from the Scriptures which cannot give life, they should have realized the purpose of the Scriptures was to testify, even prophesy, concerning Jesus Christ (1 Peter 1:10-12). If they would have known this, they would have come to Jesus for eternal life. Everything in the Hebrew Scriptures, which were written over a period of a thousand years, and hundreds of years before the birth of Jesus Christ, pointed to the person and the purpose of Jesus. When a person reads the Scriptures in this way, as originally intended, they will come to Jesus Christ for eternal life. The prophets riveted their attention upon the Savior (1 Peter 1:10-11)

The gospel of Luke reveals how a person's mind may be opened to understand the Scriptures: by looking for and seeing Jesus in the Law, in the prophets and in the psalms.

These three sections comprise the entire Old Testament and each makes Jesus Christ known through types, allegories and prophecies. When someone looks for anything other than Jesus when reading the Scriptures — and His purpose — their mind will remain closed . . . they will not truly understand the Scriptures. May the readers of *this* book be directed to Jesus Christ with an open mind to really understand the Bible!

Let's consider a few examples of how the Old Testament speaks of Jesus Christ.

Adam, the First Man Created by God

Genesis begins with creation. Adam, the first man, completed God's creation. Paul wrote in Romans 5:14 about Adam as a type of Jesus Christ. Jesus was referred to as the *last* Adam in 1 Corinthians 15:45. That means the ultimate *real* man was not Adam, but Jesus; He is the man who fulfills God's purpose which the first Adam failed to do. As the real man, Jesus Christ both expresses God and completely subdues God's enemies.

The Tree of Life in Genesis

In Genesis man was given to eat of the Tree of Life. Eating of the Tree of Life would have given man eternal life (Gen. 3:22). The Tree of Life in Genesis is a picture of Jesus Christ, the *real* Tree of Life for man to eat, to have eternal life. Since Jesus is life (John 14:6), He is the true vine (John 15:1; Rev. 22:2), He also said to eat Him (John 6:54); therefore, He is the Tree of Life for man to eat in order to have eternal life.

The Passover Lamb in Exodus

In Exodus, before the tenth plague was to come on Egypt to kill the first born of the land, God told Moses to instruct each family to kill a lamb. They were then to paint its blood on the outside of the house on the doorposts and lintels and eat the lamb. This lamb was called the "Passover" lamb (or "Pascal lamb") because God's judgment "passed over" the houses when He saw the lamb's blood during the plague of the death of the first-born.

Jesus is the *real* Passover Lamb of God (John 1:29; 1 Cor. 5:7) Who was slain to take away the sins of the world. His blood satisfied God's wrath on mankind (Romans 5:8-10), and His flesh is for man to eat (John 6:53).

Manna in Exodus

During Israel's journey through the wilderness for forty years, the Israelites received bread from heaven six days each week to sustain them. This bread was called "manna." This manna in the Hebrew Scriptures, however, was not the real bread from heaven. When Jesus came, He declared *He* is the real bread from heaven; those who ate manna died in the wilderness, but anyone who eats Him as the bread of life shall have eternal life (John 6:32–35).

The Tabernacle and the Temple Built by Israel

A major portion of the story of Israel surrounds the tabernacle in the wilderness and temple (Solomon's). Jesus is the real tabernacle where God dwells among men (John 1:14), and the true temple that was destroyed and raised up in three days (John 2:19). In resurrection, Jesus as the real temple was enlarged to include all believers in Jesus (Eph. 2:21–22; 1 Peter 2:9). He is the real temple God wanted in the Hebrew Scriptures.

These are just a few examples which show how Jesus Christ is the focus of the entire Hebrew Scriptures. There are volumes of books available today that discuss the various types, figures, and prophecies of Jesus Christ. The hidden riches of Christ will continue to be discovered by those who seek Him while reading the Torah (Law), Prophets and Psalms.

Witness to See Jesus in the "Things"

> But rise and stand upon your feet, for I have appeared to you
> for this purpose, to appoint you as a servant and **witness to the
> things in which you have seen me** and to those in which I will
> appear to you.
>
> Act 26:16, ESV
> (emphasis added)

The Lord appeared to Paul and called Him to be a servant and a witness of Jesus Christ. The Lord showed him many things, and in each he was to see Jesus. A few of these "things" included:

- Adam is Jesus Christ, the real man (Rom. 5:14)
- Husband and wife are Jesus Christ and His body, the wife, the assembly (Eph. 5:23–32)
- The good land is the expansive and all-inclusive Jesus Christ (Col. 1:12)
- Melchizedek is Jesus Christ who is ministering bread and wine (Heb. 5)
- Sarah and Hagar are the grace of Jesus Christ versus the enslaving law (Gal. 4:24)

Paul saw many things when caught up into the "third heaven" (paradise) in 2 Corinthians 12:2–4. Imagine how many books might have been written about this experience had it happened to someone else! However, Scripture says Paul did not have the heart to talk about it; he was called to be a witness to Jesus alone, and no other thing. When something was not about Jesus, Paul doubted if it was necessary to talk about it at all (see the example of marriage in 1 Cor. 7:25–40)

Today, Christians have seen and heard many things on various topics or read books about such things as the end times, Christian marriage, raising children, Christian finance, leadership, miraculous gifts, predestination and so on. However, how much is Jesus unveiled in these topics? If Jesus is not unveiled and witnessed, then those topics do not bear much spiritual value. In fact, these things themselves can divert people away from Jesus Christ.

Many things can distract believers. It is time to come back to see and witness Jesus Christ — as John the Beloved said: *"Who bore witness to the word of God, and to the testimony of Jesus Christ, to all things that he saw"* (Rev. 1:2).

Who, or What, Is God?

God Is the Self-Existing One

> 'The God of your fathers has sent me to you,' and they say to me, 'What is His name?' what shall I say to them?' And God said to Moses, 'I AM WHO I AM.' And He said, 'Thus you shall say to the children of Israel, 'I AM has sent me to you.'
>
> – Exodus 3:13–14

> Therefore I [Jesus] said to you that you will die in your sins; for if you do not believe that I am *He*, you will die in your sins.
>
> – John 8:24

When Moses asked God to reveal His name, God answered, "I AM." The word "I AM" in Hebrew means, "be" or "existing."[2] God simply *is*. He is self-existing, but He also *existed*.

The Hebrew word Jehovah (or Yahweh/YHWH) is derived from "the existing one"; therefore, "Jehovah" or "Yahweh" means the same as "I AM," or "the existing one."[3] The self-existing one without a beginning or ending is the very name of God. That is who God is. He is the "I AM."

Jesus said in John 8:24 that men must believe that He is the "I AM" in order to be saved. In the translation above, the "He" was added; it was not there in the original Greek text. Jesus said that *He is the I AM*. He is the same I AM as the I AM in the Hebrew Scriptures.

There is only one I AM. In the Hebrew Scriptures the I AM is called *Jehovah*. In the Christian Scriptures, He is called *Jesus*. Jesus is the very self-existing God. Unless men believe that Jesus is the I AM, they will die in their sins.

"Jesus" is the transliteration of the name *"Joshua"* in Hebrew. The etymology of the word *Joshua* comes from two words: *"Jehovah"* and *"save."*

Thus, *Jesus* literally means, *"Jehovah saves."*[4] Jesus is the very Jehovah, the name of God in the Hebrew Scriptures, the I AM, who came to save. Jesus is *not* another person sent by God to save, but *He is God Himself* who came to save.

God Is the Creator and Source of All Things

> In the beginning God created the heavens and the earth.
>
> — Genesis 1:1

> Thus says God the LORD, Who created the heavens and
> stretched them out, Who spread forth the earth and that which
> comes from it, Who gives breath to the people on it, and spirit to
> those who walk on it.
>
> — Isaiah 42:5

God, as the always existing One with no beginning or ending, created. God is the Creator. He created the heavens and the earth and gave breath (life) to all those living on the earth. This is the second characteristic of God: He is the Creator. Without Him, nothing would exist. God existed on His own and through Him all things came into existence and all things are "held together." This is a definition of God.

> In the beginning was the Word, and the Word was with God,
> and the Word was God. He was in the beginning with God. All
> things were made through Him, and without Him nothing was
> made that was made.
>
> — John 1:1–3

The Word — Jesus — was God. Since God is both singular (one) and plural (three), the Word was both *with* God and *is* God — the Son is the pre-existing One. The Word as God was the Creator. All things were made through Jesus as the Word, and without Him, nothing exists. These and other verses (see Col. 1:15–16) make it clear that Jesus Christ is the Creator, since He is God.

If you would, Jesus Christ is the "creating agency" of the Godhead. To suggest that "the only begotten of the Father full of grace and truth" (John 1:14) did not exist in eternity past and was always in fellowship with the Father, is an absolute denial of the deity of Christ. Those who deny the pre-existence of the Word made flesh, are denying that Christ (the Messiah) was incarnated as a man and are of the "*spirit of antichrist*" (who deny the Father and the Son — 1 John 2:22). "*For you loved Me before the foundation of the world*" (John 17:24b). This was not a "foreseen" love but an eternal love which always existed between the Father and the Son.

God Is the Source of all Life

> Nor is He [God] worshiped with men's hands, as though He needed anything, since He gives to all life, breath, and all things.
> – Act 17:25

> (as it is written, "I have made you [Abraham] a father of many nations") in the presence of Him whom he believed – God, who gives life to the dead and calls those things which do not exist as though they did.
> – Romans 4:17

God is the one who refers to things that do not exist "as though they did" (creation), but also gives life to all things – even life to the dead. God is the author and giver of life. He initiated life, and He sustains it. Satan, God's enemy, is death. His mission is to kill – to end life.

> For as the Father raises the dead and gives life to them, even so the Son gives life to whom He will.
> – John 5:21

Jesus, the Son of God, does the same. As God, Jesus has the same life-giving ability, and grants life to whomever He desires. The Son and the Father are one God. Jesus is the self-existing and ever existing I AM. He is the Creator and gives life. Jesus is nothing less than God Himself.

God Is Omnipotent, Omnipresent and Omniscient

> "I am the Alpha and the Omega," says the Lord God, "who is and who was and who is to come, the Almighty."
> –Revelation 1:8

> I am [Jesus Christ] the Alpha and the Omega, the Beginning and the End, the First and the Last.
> –Revelation 22:13

"Omnipotent" means "all-powerful" or "all-dominion." That God is omnipotent means He has power, authority and dominion over all things. The word "*almighty*" in the original Greek literally means all-powerful or omnipotent.[5] God is omnipotent, and so is Jesus Christ. It is not clear from Revelation 1:8 who John was referring to, but Revelation 22:13 answers that question: *Jesus* is the Alpha and Omega declared in Revelation 1:8. Jesus as God is the almighty, omnipotent one.

> "Can anyone hide himself in secret places, So I shall not see him?" says the LORD; "Do I not fill heaven and earth?" says the LORD.
> — Jeremiah 23:24

> For where two or three are gathered together in My name, I am there in the midst of them.
> — Matthew 18:20

God's omnipresence means He is everywhere, even throughout time and space. There is not one place in the entire universe, or time period, that God's presence does not occupy. There is nowhere to hide from God. In space, on earth, or even under the earth, God is there.

Jesus is also omnipresent. Two-thousand years after His birth, death and resurrection, Jesus is still everywhere. There is not a place in the universe where He is not. Anyone who calls on the Lord Jesus will find Him, wherever the caller's location.

> Declaring the end from the beginning, and from ancient times [things] that are not [yet] done; saying, 'My counsel shall stand, And I will do all My pleasure.'
> — Isaiah 46:10

> But Jesus, knowing their thoughts, said, "Why do you think evil in your hearts?"
> — Matthew 9:4

God is also omniscient. This means He knows all things, before things even take place or exist. He knows what is in the hearts of man, and He knows their thoughts. There is no place for mankind to hide physically, and even the thoughts of men cannot be hidden from Jesus Christ.

God Is One–Three: The Trinity, or Triune God

God Is One (Singular)

> . . . and that there is no other God but one.
>
> ~ 1 Corinthians 8:4

> I am the LORD, and there is no other; There is no God besides Me. I will gird you, though you have not known Me.
>
> ~ Isaiah 45:5

The Bible teaches there is only one unique God in the universe. The word "one" in 1 Corinthians 8:4 in the original Greek is *heis*, the word for the numeral "one."[6] It is a singular word, indicating there is no other God besides the one God. This is what "monotheist" means: one God.

God Is Three, Existing at the Same Time

> Then God said, "Let Us make man in Our image, according to Our likeness . . ." So God created man in His own image; in the image of God He created him; male and female He created them.
>
> ~ Genesis 1:26a–27

> Also, I heard the voice of the Lord, saying: "Whom shall I send, and who will go for Us?" Then I said, "Here am I! Send me."
>
> ~ Isaiah 6:8

Although today's Judaism does not believe that God is both one and three[7], the Jewish Bible or the Tenach/Tenakh (aka, the complete Hebrew Scriptures) gave clear indications that God is indeed one and yet three.[8] The very first chapter of Genesis says, "*Then God* (singular) *said, 'let Us make man in Our image according to Our likeness'*" (Gen. 1:26a). The words "Us" and "Our" are both plural in number. These are not "royal entitlements" when referring, in this case, to the "King of the Universe" as in "Our Highness" vs. "His Highness." Then in Genesis 1:27 it reverts to using the singular pronoun "His": "*So God created man in **His own** image.*" The mystery of God as both singular and plural was revealed in the very first words of the Bible! This conflict of pronouns used for deity also occurs in Isaiah 6:8: "*Whom shall I send, and who will go for Us?*" Did Isaiah mean "I," or "Us"?

The revelation of the Bible shows Isaiah meant *BOTH*. If God is purely one, there is no ground for plural pronouns, but the Hebrew Scriptures do not clarify how many are included.

This, however, is revealed and affirmed in the Christian Scriptures. The number THREE is clearly defined within the singular God:

> Go therefore and make disciples of all the nations, baptizing them in the name of the Father and of the Son and of the Holy Spirit.
>
> – Matthew 28:19

The one God who is also three is clearly referenced in Matthew 28. In fact, this is a foundational concept that runs throughout the Christian Scriptures from the beginning of Matthew to the last words of Revelation: the three-one God is clearly defined and interwoven throughout. The three are: The Father, Son, and Holy Spirit. The words "Trinity" or "Triune God" have been designed to describe the God Who is both one and three. God being Triune is a mystery Who cannot be fully explained, but can be enjoyed, appreciated, and experienced by all believers.

Matthew refers to a singular name for three in Matthew 28:19: The Father, Son, and the Holy Spirit . . . all three are distinct but only *one* name. When a person calls on His name, they receive all three. When baptized into His name, people are immersed into all three. Believers are in the Father, in the Son, and in the Holy Spirit. This is truly a wondrous mystery!

Sadly, there are some who affirm that the Triune God is only Jesus (aka, "Jesus Only" teaching). Such a teaching, even by Christians, is a direct departure that each "Person" of the Godhead is distinct, but inseparably one. The Son has before the foundation of the world had FELLOWSHIP with the Father — this fellowship within the Triune God is now made, through the Spirit of Promise, the Holy Spirit — available to all who would believe (John 14:16-18; 15:26-27; 16:7, 13-15; Acts 2:33). "Jesus only" does not express the "fellowship" within the Triune God — if you would, Jesus does not "fellowship with Himself" but shares in fellowship with the Father . . . it is into this fellowship within the Triune God we have been called! The very "nature of God" is "sharing" — therefore, the Triune God created man to share in His eternal fellowship.

The name of God, the "I AM," always existed with no beginning or ending, and it applies to all three. The Father, the Son, and the Holy Spirit existed from eternity to eternity and each existed simultaneously, concurrently. They pre-existed in inseparable union – never in conflict but in perfect harmony – because they are in fact, one God. Believers cannot fully explain how this works, but they can accept their one God is also three. This unfathomable truth is at the very nexus of the Christian faith!

Though distinct, the three are not separate. If a person focuses on "three" too much, they, in reality, worship three gods or are "tri-theist." If a person emphasizes "one" too much, they may lose God's distinction of being three. The Bible does not teach that the one God is sometimes the Father, switching at times to the Son, and becoming another mode of the Spirit at other times. This is called *modalism,*[9] and it is not the description of the Trinity in the Bible. Both errors are because of the limits of the human mind. People try to logically define the mystery of the one–three God or the "three-in-one" God, Who is not able to be logically defined! Believers need to accept by faith that God is one and three, existing simultaneously from eternity to eternity, but never the three are separate; they exist within one another. In a real sense, our God is "multi-dimensional."

> The grace of the Lord Jesus Christ, and the love of God, and the communion of the Holy Spirit be with you all. Amen.
> – 2 Corinthians 13:14

In the Hebrew Scriptures, where there is a clear separation between God in heaven and man on earth, God in the singular is fully unveiled. In the Christian Scriptures, where God's intention of being joined with man is realized, the three are unveiled and emphasized. Paul unveiled the three in 2 Corinthians 13:14; man can now apply and experience the Triune God, Who was not seen as clearly nor was available as three in the Hebrew Scriptures. However, even there in Isaiah 63 the ONE-THREE God is distinctly presented as the Savior/Son (vss. 1-9); Holy Spirit (vss. 10-14); the Father (vss. 15-19).

The love of God the Father, the grace or enjoyment of the Son, and the fellowship of the Holy Spirit are practical and experiential for all situations today.

In the Hebrew Scriptures the focus of the relationship between God and man was evidenced through the Law; God was seen primarily as either a judge or a giver of physical and material blessings. While man was either keeping or breaking God's Law on earth, God in heaven was judging or blessing man based on one or the other. This relationship is codified by what is known as the Mosaic Covenant (or "*He takes away the first* [the "old/Mosaic covenant"] *that He may establish the second* [the "New Covenant"] – Hebrews 10:9; also, Hebrews 9:10 and Hebrews 8:6: "*He has obtained a more excellent ministry, inasmuch as He is also Mediator of a BETTER COVENANT, which was established on BETTER PROMISES . . .AND . . . In that He says, 'A New Covenant,' He has made the FIRST OBSOLETE . . . Now what is becoming obsolete and growing OLD is ready to vanish away*" – Hebrews 8:13).

In the New Testament, however, God's purpose is revealed: to have a life relationship directly with humanity. God desires to participate in human life, and He longs for man to participate in His divine life. God wants to be in man and wants man to dwell in Him in perfect, inseparable unity.

For this purpose, the one God is unveiled as three: Father, Son, and Holy Spirit. God's desire to be one with man originated out of His love – the love of the Father for many sons. God as the Father was rarely mentioned in the Hebrew Scriptures; whereas the Father God is prominently revealed throughout the Christian Scriptures. The Son as the Lord was sent to solve man's problem of sin through His redemption and to give His eternal divine life to humanity. This is grace!

Finally, the Holy Spirit brings man into this same fellowship within the Trinity. Believers participate in all that the Father's love entails and the Lord's grace provides. This fellowship is available for believers 24/7 wherever they are, and in whatever circumstances they find themselves. Through this fellowship, God as the Father fulfills His joy of having many sons within the sphere of the Triune God (Eph. 1:5).

"Love," "grace" and "fellowship" are wonderful words describing the experiential relationship between God and man. For man to be included within the fellowship of the Trinity, all three – love, grace and fellowship – work together to fulfill God's awesome purpose. Without the **love of the Father God**, there would be no such fulfilled purpose. Without the coming **grace of the Son**, the Father's plan would not be realized. And without the **fellowship of the Spirit**, there would be no way for humanity to be included and brought into participation of all these divine riches contained in God's divine life and nature. God, one and yet three, cannot be fully comprehended, understood, or explained. But because He is **one–three**, God can be enjoyed and experienced through the deepest union that exists: the oneness between

God and man – wrought in the spirit of man by the regenerating power of the Holy Spirit (John 3:3, 5). Recall again the focus of John 17 – *Jesus' prayer that believers would be one*. The foundational concept of John 17 is the Trinity, the source of oneness among all believers.

The *first gift* discussed in John 17 was eternal life, the **Father**'s name (John 17:2-3); the *second gift* was the **Son** who exists as the Word, the truth (John 17:8, 17); and the *third gift* was His glory through the Lord's **Spirit** (John 17:22-23; 2 Cor. 3:18).

The first gift does not need any explanation: The name to be kept in view is clearly the Father. The second gift is the Word. John 1:1 clearly reveals the Son, Jesus, is the Word. The third gift is the Lord Jesus' glory manifested through service, or ministry via the Spirit. Paul discussed that the apostles were ministers of the New Covenant, or ministers of the Spirit, in 2 Corinthians 3. The chapter ends with the apostles being transformed into the same image as the Lord Jesus, from glory to glory. It is through ministering to people that believers behold the Lord and receive His glory through the Spirit.

Therefore, the source and the structure of oneness among believers occurs through knowing the Triune God in a real and experiential way.

Jesus Christ Is the Embodiment of God

> For in Him [Jesus Christ] dwells all the fullness of the Godhead bodily.
>
> – Colossians 2:9

> To them belong the patriarchs, and from their race, according to the flesh, is the Christ, who is God over all, blessed forever. Amen.
>
> – Romans 9:5, ESV

Jesus, who is I AM, came in a bodily form. Colossians 2:9 reveals the entire Godhead – the fullness of deity (Father, Son and Spirit), dwells inside the body of Jesus. It is too wonderful to even attempt to explain this awesome reality. Jesus Christ contains the entire Triune God because He *is* God. He is not just a part of God, or even a third of God. He is the entire fullness of God. There is no other God outside of Jesus Christ. As shown earlier, Jesus Christ is the subject, center, and focus of the whole Bible but especially the

New Testament. He is unveiled in plain words. As the focus, Jesus Christ is God in fullness and in His completeness (John 1:16: *For of His fullness we have all received, and grace upon grace.*). Also, the Amplified Version of the Scripture demonstrates Jesus Christ, the Son, in all His fullness as God:

> No one has seen God [His essence, His divine nature] at any time; the [One and] only begotten God [that is, the unique Son] who is in the intimate presence of the Father, He has explained Him [and interpreted and revealed the awesome wonder of the Father].
>
> – John 1:18

Jesus Is the Son, He Is the True God, and He Is Equal to God

> And we know that the Son of God has come and has given us an understanding, that we may know Him who is true; and we are in Him who is true, in His Son Jesus Christ. **This is the true God** and eternal life.
>
> – 1 John 5:20

The Son of God, who is Jesus Christ, came so believers might not only know Him but also be in Him . . . to know and experience His relationship with the Father. The apostle John affirms in 1 John 5:20 Jesus Christ is the Son of God, and the Son of God is the true God. The true God means there is no other God besides Him.

> Therefore, the Jews sought all the more to kill Him, because He not only broke the Sabbath, but also said that God was His Father, making Himself equal with God.
>
> – John 5:18

When hearing that Jesus is the Son of God, most people, including some Christians, think Jesus as the Son of God is somehow less than the Father. They misunderstand the true expression of the Trinity and think the Father must be higher in rank and have more authority than the Son since the Father should have existed before the Son. However, John 5:18 says Jesus made himself completely equal with God by calling God His Father. The "essence" of the true Trinity is the "fellowship" – the "relationship" within the Godhead – the eternal fellowship the Son has always had "...*for You loved Me before the foundation of the world*" (John 17:24). He is not less than God, or inferior; He is equal, the same as God, for He is God! What the Jewish leadership missed, and what many Christians miss, is the profound truth Jesus revealed concerning the eternal "relationship" or "fellowship" enjoyed by the Father and the Son; and the astounding disclosure believers were, through the Son, by the power of the Spirit of God, being brought into that eternal fellowship which always existed within the Triune God!

In the Bible, the relationship between God the Father and God the Son is *not* one of birth; this would mean the Father existed first and gave birth to the Son. Rather, the Father may be considered as the invisible source, and the Son is the expression, or the image of that which is invisible (John 1:18). In the NASV we read: "*No one has seen God at any time; **the only begotten God** who is in the bosom of the Father, He has explained Him.*"[10]

Jesus, the Expression of the Father

Jesus is the expression of the Father, and is *called* the Father, because He and the Father are one (Col. 1:15; Heb. 1:3):

> Jesus said to him, "Have I been with you so long, and you still do not know me, Philip? Whoever has seen me has seen the Father. How can you say, 'Show us the Father'?"
> – John 14:9, ESV

It is impossible to see the Father. However, because Jesus is the manifestation of the Father (Heb. 1:3: "*Who* [Jesus, the Son] *being the brightness of his* [the Father's] *glory, and the express image of his* [the Father's] *person...*"), seeing Jesus is the same as seeing the Father. Searching for the Father outside of Jesus is a complete waste of time and energy, but when the believer sees Jesus, he sees the Father fully expressed.

> For to us a child is born, to us a son is given; and the government shall be upon his shoulder, and his name shall be called Wonderful Counselor, Mighty God, **Everlasting Father**, Prince of Peace.
> – Isaiah 9:6, ESV

Tucked away in Isaiah 9:6 is a wonderful prophecy concerning Jesus. A child, born of a human virgin, is the unique, mighty God of the universe. This is the faith of Jesus Christ: He was born of a virgin, yet He is the *mighty God.* Jesus is also, "Immanuel," which is translated, "God with us'" (Matt. 1:23).

Believing this gives man life, but one should also believe the rest of the verse: The Son is called the *everlasting Father.* Just as the child (Jesus) is God, the Son (Jesus) is the Father. He is truly wonderful! He came as a child, but He is called the mighty God. He came as the Son, but He is called the Everlasting Father. Therefore, He is a child; yet, He is God, the Son and the Father.

> I [Jesus] and the Father are one.
>
> – John 10:30, ESV

> Believe me that I am in the Father and the Father is in me, or else believe on account of the works themselves.
>
> – John 14:11, ESV

The Son and the Father not only "agree in one" – they are inseparably ONE! The Son and the Father, though two, they are only one. The word "one" in John 10:30 is, again, the *number* one. Jesus and the Father are literally only one person (Please note: Not "three persons" but "three in One Person" when the Holy Spirit is expressed within the Godhead — See Doug Krieger's Footnote#11 at the end of this chapter.). Within this one person dwells the Father, and the Son (and the Spirit); and this one person is Jesus Christ. Jesus Christ is the Son with the Father. Jesus, the "I AM" and "Jehovah saves," is the complete God, the Son and the Father. Yes, there is DISTINCTION but absolutely, utterly, NO SEPARATION within the Godhead. Within this ONE PERSON there is the Father, the Son, and the Holy Spirit – they are the "I AM" – in this most mysterious sense, the "Father sent the Son" . . . and the Son said, "*I will not leave you orphans; 'I will come to you*" (lit. the "*I am* coming to you" the entire Triune God is coming to you — the great *I AM* is coming to you) speaking of the Comforter, the Helper, given by the Father (John 14:16-18).

Men Are Saved by Believing that Jesus Christ Is God

> But these are written so that you may believe that Jesus is the Christ, the Son of God, and that by believing you may have life in his name.
>
> – John 20:31, ESV

Believing that Jesus Christ is the Son of God is the very essence of the Christian faith. To believe that Jesus is the Son of God means that He is God – not a third of God, but the complete God. This is an essential part of the faith in order to have eternal life.

Jesus Christ Is a Genuine but Sinless Man

His Incarnation – God Put on Flesh to Become Man

> Now the birth of Jesus Christ took place in this way. When his mother Mary had been betrothed to Joseph, before they came together she was found to be with child from the Holy Spirit. . . .behold, an angel of the Lord appeared to him in a dream, saying, "Joseph, son of David, do not fear to take Mary as your wife, for that which is conceived in her is from the Holy Spirit. She will bear a son, and you shall call his name Jesus, for he will save his people from their sins."
>
> . . . Behold, the virgin shall conceive and bear a son, and they shall call his name Immanuel (which means, God with us).
>
> – Matthew 1:18, 20b–21, 23, ESV

Here, Matthew records the birth of Jesus Christ. Mary was found to be with child from (or out of) the Holy Spirit. The source of this child is the Holy Spirit. Jesus was produced from a combination of the divine source and a human vessel. His divinity is from the Holy Spirit, and His humanity was from Mary. Since He was born of Mary, He is a man; but, since He is also born of God, then He is God. Thus, He is both human and divine.

Matthew focuses on the fact that Jesus is a genuine man, born of a real human virgin – He is presented as the "King of Israel" (upon the earth – as man). This is also essential to the Christian faith: Jesus Christ is a man, but He is God *in* man. He is the God–Man who came to save. He is "Jehovah saves."

His name is Jesus.

The fact that God can be joined to a human virgin to produce Jesus corroborates Genesis 1, where God said that He made man in His own image and likeness. Everything else God created was after its own kind, after a certain species of creatures. But when it came to man, the "kind"

ONE Truth

or "species" He created man after Himself! Man was fashioned after God's kind. Biologically, cross species cannot mate and give birth; this is a well-understood fact. However, mankind is so closely aligned to God, with His same image and likeness, that God could impregnate a human virgin by the Holy Spirit. Jesus is the product of the joining of God and man. How wonderful!

> In the beginning was the Word, and the Word was with God, and the Word was God... And the Word became flesh and dwelt among us, and we have seen his glory, glory as of the only Son from the Father, full of grace and truth.
> – John 1:1, 14, ESV

God, Who was in the beginning and ever existing, became flesh. This is truly a great mystery. God became a man to have a dwelling place *among* men. The word for "dwelt" in the Greek literally means, "*to pitch a tent*" for residing. This word is a clear reference to the tabernacle in the Wilderness, in the Good Land. God had commanded Moses to build a tabernacle, where He dwelt on earth in the "Tent of Meeting" for forty years. The temple replaced the tabernacle after Israel entered the Good Land. In John 1, the apostle referred to Jesus in the flesh as the reality of the tabernacle.

Jesus is God residing in the flesh. Wherever the flesh of Jesus goes, God goes. This verse doesn't say "and the Word became *man*. . ." but "the Word became *flesh*" (John 1:14, emphasis added). The word "flesh" is used to denote man is fallen, corrupt, and sinful. Jesus didn't become like the original Adam created by God; rather, He became associated with fallen man, putting on flesh. This flesh described by Paul is "*where nothing good dwells*" (Rom. 7.18) — it is sinful (Rom 8:3).

Just as the tabernacle (where God resided) in the Old Testament was full of God's glory, Jesus, Who is the real tabernacle of God, is full of God's glory. Inside His flesh, a fallen body of man, is the glory of God; therefore, Jesus is full of grace and truth. The incarnation of God, Jesus Christ, is full of grace and truth for man's ultimate enjoyment and participation. This is a mystery that cannot be fully explained. God became a real man, had a real birth, and had a real, physical body. This is an essential point of the Christian faith.

Yet without Sin...

> For we do not have a high priest who is unable to sympathize with our weaknesses, but one who in every respect has been tempted as we are, yet without sin.
>
> – Hebrews 4:15, ESV

> For what the law could not do in that it was weak through the flesh, God [did] by sending His own Son in the likeness of sinful flesh, on account of sin: He condemned sin in the flesh.
>
> – Romans 8:3

Because Jesus put on a flesh like man's flesh, with all its weaknesses and temptations, He can fully sympathize with fallen man. He experienced the same temptations as any man, because of His fallen body — the flesh — that He put on as a man. But Jesus didn't succumb to any of its temptations. He was without sin in the core of His nature; He lived His entire life on earth without sin.

Jesus was without sin — this is paramount — for He became the "perfect sacrifice" (Hebrews 8:12; 9:9, 12-15; 10:1-7, 10-14, 17, 22; 11:24-26; 12:2-3; 13:11-13; Leviticus 11:23-47). If Jesus Himself possessed sin, He would have needed to die for His own sin. Jesus cannot be a substitute to die for man's sin (He is our propitiation for sin — 1 John 2:1-2). Man was judged by God to die for sin — the penalty for our sin was paid by the blood of Jesus — God's wrath was satisfied (Rom. 5:6-10; 6:23). If Jesus as a man had sin, then He would be under the same judgment of death/wrath as every other person who has lived on this earth. The only reason Jesus could die for man's sin was because *He was sinless.*

Romans 8:3 states Jesus put on the *"likeness of sinful flesh."* The flesh put on by Jesus was somehow the same as man's sinful flesh, but it was also something different. It was "like" the sinful flesh in every way, yet, without sin. If it were exactly as man's sinful flesh, it would mean Jesus also possessed sin; therefore, what Jesus put on was *in the likeness of* sinful flesh — somehow very close, but not exactly. Although He didn't have sin, still as a man with flesh, Jesus aged, and he grew tired. He needed to sleep, eat, drink, and breathe, and like any human being, He could die . . . *and He did.*

A good picture of the likeness of the "flesh of sin" (i.e., "sinful flesh") is the story of the brass serpent in Exodus 21:4–9. The Israelites were bitten by poisonous serpents and were dying because of the poison the snakes injected into them. Moses prayed to God to save them. God answered by telling Moses to make a serpent out of brass and lift it up on a pole. Whoever would just look at the brass serpent on the pole would be saved. In other words, Jesus, if you would, "captured the flesh of sin in His own body on the tree" — yes, He nailed our flesh to His cross! (Col. 2:14; Gal. 3:13).

John interpreted the brass serpent in Exodus to be Jesus in John 3. Jesus has had the likeness and form of the serpent who bit the Israelites, but He didn't possess the nature and the poison of the serpent. This is a good example of a type of Christ. Although Jesus put on flesh, it was only in the "likeness of sinful" flesh. His nature was not one of sin; He was sinless — yet, *"For He made Him who knew no sin [to be] sin for us, that we might become the righteousness of God in Him"* (2Cor. 5:21).

A Common, Everyday Man

Jesus grew up living a common human life with parents and siblings and worked as a carpenter.

> And the Child grew and became strong in spirit, filled with wisdom; and the grace of God was upon Him.
>
> – Luke 2:40

> Is this not the carpenter, the Son of Mary, and brother of James, Joses, Judas, and Simon? And are not His sisters here with us?" So they were offended at Him.
>
> – Mark 6:3

As a man, Jesus experienced birth, was a baby, had a childhood, and grew up with half-brothers and sisters. He worked in His trade as a carpenter. He had to obey human parents, and when he was about to die, He expressed concern for them. Jesus lived and experienced humanity in every way; yet, without sin.

The Bible does not record much concerning Jesus' life before He started His ministry at about thirty years of age.[11] It was likely uneventful, but He probably experienced every facet of humanity since He is man.

Why didn't God just come to earth as a full-grown man from the outset? He could have arrived in the form of a man like He did multiple times in the Old Testament. However, He needed to be born of a human virgin to be an authentic man with a genuine human nature.

This was God's desire and purpose from the very beginning: to join Himself to man, to be part of man and be one with man.

Jesus Died as a God–Man

... who, being in the form of God, did not consider it robbery to be equal with God, but made Himself of no reputation, taking the form of a bondservant, and coming in the likeness of men. And being found in appearance as a man, He humbled Himself and became obedient to death, even the death of the cross.

– Philippians 2:6–8

"And I, if I am lifted up from the earth, will draw all peoples to Myself." This He said, signifying by what death He would die.

– John 12:32

These verses speak of God becoming man and dying as a man. Jesus Christ did not use His supernatural power to escape death; rather, he suffered the most excruciating death: crucifixion. God's judgment on mankind was death; therefore, only the death of a sinless man could redeem man from God's judgment. God didn't just take away sin or forgive man's sin without requiring payment for sin. God's demand on man was fully satisfied by the death of the sinless man, Jesus Christ.

His death is referred to as a vicarious death (done for another) because Jesus became a propitiation (or "satisfaction" – He satisfied God's judgment and took away the penalty of sin, which is death) for man's sin: Jesus died instead of man (We receive God's pardon for sin through the death of Jesus). As a result of the death of the Son of Man, Jesus can draw all people to Himself. Without His death, man cannot come to God. But with His death, humanity can all be drawn and come to God.

... to shepherd the church [ekklesia] of God which He purchased with His own blood.

– Acts 20:28

> How much more will the blood of Christ, who through the eternal Spirit offered himself without blemish to God, purify our conscience from dead works to serve the living God.
>
> – Hebrews 9:14, ESV

> And he did not enter with blood of yearling goats and of calves, with his own blood he entered the holy place one time and has achieved eternal redemption.
>
> – Hebrews 9:12

Although He died as a man, Jesus is also God; therefore, God shed His own blood, since He joined man by taking on Himself the form of a man. God is not flesh and blood, so it was not possible for Him to shed His "own blood" *unless* that blood is the blood of Jesus.

When Jesus shed His blood, God shed His blood. Jesus Christ as a man offered Himself up to God by the shedding of His blood. He did this through the eternal Spirit within Him, as God; therefore, His blood is eternally effective. His blood's eternal value has redeemed every person from sin throughout time and space — past, present and future. This is the meaning of "eternal redemption."

Jesus Is the God–Man for Eternity

After Jesus' resurrection and ascension, He remained a man and will be the God–Man for eternity.

> But he, being full of the Holy Spirit, gazed into heaven and saw the glory of God, and Jesus standing at the right hand of God, and said, "Look! I see the heavens opened and the Son of Man standing at the right hand of God!"
>
> – Acts 7:55–56

When Stephen was being stoned to death, the writer of Acts says he was "*full of the Holy Spirit*" and that he "*saw the glory of God in heaven.*" Stephen saw Jesus, the "*Son of man standing at the right hand of God.*"

The right hand of God is figurative, alluding to power and authority. It symbolizes the One with God's power and authority to carry out His plan: Stephen saw a Man (i.e., the God-Man) while he was being stoned.

This echoes Peter's sermon in Acts 2:36, where Peter proclaimed Jesus in resurrection and ascension was made Lord and Christ.

Since Jesus' resurrection and ascension, He has remained bodily in the heavens; He is still a man. He didn't give up His humanity after His crucifixion; rather, He brought humanity into the Godhead for eternity. God is no longer only divine, but also human. Jesus Christ is the Son of Man with all of God's authority and power.

> And he showed me a pure river of water of life, clear as crystal, proceeding from the throne of God and of the Lamb.
> — Revelation 22:1

In this last chapter of the entire Bible unveiling a scene in eternity, there is one throne of God and the Lamb. The Lamb refers to Jesus, who came as a man to be the Lamb of God to take away the sin of the world.

Jesus will continue to be the Lamb for eternity. The Lamb indicates His humanity and that Jesus came to be man. Jesus with humanity will continue into eternity. Just as it would be silly to see a literal lamb on the throne, neither should believers picture two persons with two bodies occupying one throne. God and the Lamb are one person (Note: *The throne of God and the Lamb*" — Rev. 22:3), both divine and human. God and man, divinity and humanity, are fused together in the Godhead for eternity. God is on the throne of the universe, but there is a man also now on the throne, for eternity — the God-Man!

Today's world tends to depreciate humankind, making man the enemy of the environment and the cause of all problems. If given a choice, it seems worldly people today would prefer the existence of animals, or even plants, even if detrimental to man! But the reality is man is uplifted to the highest position in the universe. God loved humanity to the point of coming into complete, inseparable union with humanity. God Himself became man and brought man into God.

> For He has not put the world to come, of which we speak, in subjection to angels. But one testified in a certain place, saying: "What is man that You are mindful of him, Or the son of man that You take care of him? You have made him a little lower than the angels; You have crowned him with glory and honor; and

set him over the works of Your hands. You have put all things in subjection under his feet." For in that He put all in subjection under him, He left nothing [that is] not put under him. But now we do not yet see all things put under him. But we see Jesus, who was made a little lower than the angels, for the suffering of death crowned with glory and honor, that He, by the grace of God, might taste death for everyone.

– Hebrews 2:5–9

The writer of Hebrews states the coming kingdom is not subjected to angels, but to man. Though man was created in his physical make up to be lower than the angels, God ordained man to have dominion – to have everything subject to him – in the coming kingdom. Though this does not seem to be the situation presently, "*but we see Jesus.*"

He is the man that has everything subjected under His feet. He is the man Who went through death and is now crowned with glory and honor. Jesus Christ Who was made in His physical being lower than the angels so that He could suffer death; and was in resurrection crowned with glory and honor. He is the fulfillment of God's original intent in creating Adam: that man would have dominion over the whole earth. Jesus is the man ruling and reigning for eternity according to God's eternal purpose – He, Jesus, is the Last Adam:

> "But Jesus, who may be called the last Adam, is a life-giving Spirit." (Holman)

> For the scripture says, "The first man, Adam, was created a living being"; but the last Adam is the life-giving Spirit."
> – 1 Corinthians 15:45
> (Good News Translation)

The Importance of Believing Jesus Is a Man

Believing that Jesus is a man is an essential part of the faith; otherwise, it is a spirit of the antichrist to reject that God, in Christ (the Messiah), has put on the flesh.

> By this you know the Spirit of God: Every spirit that confesses that Jesus Christ has come in the flesh is of God, and every spirit that does not confess that Jesus Christ has come in the flesh is not

of God. And this is the spirit of the Antichrist, which you have heard was coming, and is now already in the world.

– 1 John 4:2–3

The spirit within any man that confesses by the Spirit of God that Jesus Christ came in the flesh, that He is a real man, is of God. Denying that Jesus is God in the flesh reflects the spirit of the antichrist (or Antichrist – the final Antichrist). This is a clear, essential tenet of the Christian faith – belief that Jesus is a man and continues to be a man.

If Jesus is not (**still**) a man, no virgin birth could have occurred, and therefore, no "perfect" shedding of blood for redemption – no faith in the imputed righteousness found in God alone. Union with God for any man would not be possible, and no fulfillment of God's eternal purpose for man to have dominion.

Let's now circle back to the question at the beginning of this chapter: *Who is Jesus?* Jesus is in every way God and in every way man. He is the complete God and a perfect and genuine man for eternity. God and man are united, fused/merged into a perfect union in one person for eternity.

This joining together did not produce a third nature; rather, God is still God and man is still man – always the Son from eternity past to eternity future but as the Creator God, He took upon Himself the "form of a man" (the pinnacle of His creation, man) and is now "the Man in the Glory!" However, they (God and Man) now live and abide within one another, a wonderful mystery!

At that day you will know that I am in My Father, and you in Me, and I in you.

– John 14:20

…that they all may be one, as You, Father, are in Me, and I in You; that they also may be one in Us, that the world may believe that You sent Me.

– John 17:21

Since Jesus is a man that has been accepted into the Triune God, every believer is now also included in their eternal fellowship. It is in the true nature of the Trinity – the Father, Son and Holy Spirit – that all believers are made eternally one (John 17:21).[12]

4

Jesus Christ – His Work to Fulfill God's Plan

Jesus is the name of the person Who is God, Who became man. Christ, the Anointed One, is commissioned by God to do God's will and fulfill God's eternal purpose.

This chapter will consider His work of crucifixion, resurrection, and ascension. Although these three events happened almost 2,000 years ago, the understanding of these events will affect people tremendously in our present time, and the result of understanding can wonderfully affect every believer's daily experience with the Lord. The believer's proper experience depends completely upon what Christ has accomplished and not upon their own accomplishments.

Overview of His Major Work

His Crucifixion

For most people of this world, death is tragic, sad, and has a finality about it. But the death of Jesus Christ on the cross was the beginning of a New Creation. Believers celebrate His death. Why? Because the work of the cross is the power of God able to deliver mankind from all that is negative in this universe. It is the ultimate freedom for those who truly understand and believe Christ's full accomplishment on the cross; it brings believers forgiveness of sins, destroys the devil, releases believers from a life of self that keeps them in bondage, and releases Jesus' reproducing life.

His Resurrection

Two major tenets of faith that give humanity salvation are the death *and* resurrection of Jesus Christ. When Jesus resurrected, He didn't just come back with the same physical body; He came back with a wonderful physical and *spiritual* (i.e., "glorified") body that can indwell all those who would believe in Him. After the resurrection, the disciples could touch him; He even ate food affirming He was physical. He also appeared and disappeared at will. Though physical, He also became the Life-Giving Spirit Who could indwell His ever-expanding number of followers (1 Cor. 15:45). What's more, something amazing happened when He resurrected. Jesus brought humanity into divinity; man was brought into God. At that point, Jesus was more than the only begotten Son of God; He also became *the firstborn among many brothers* (Rom. 8:29). It is important to embrace the richness of this miracle; to appreciate the greatness of Jesus' resurrection. The Son took on the image of His Own creation, man; then, through His death and resurrection He brought "man into God!"

His Ascension and Outpouring

To most Christians, the ascension of Jesus Christ was just a historical fact. Not many realize how this work of Christ affects them today. His ascension — together with the outpouring of the Spirit — is what makes all of His people a part of the Christ (i.e., the "Messiah" or "Deliverer"). Now they share in His anointing and commission to fulfill God's purpose on earth. Today, Christ as the Head of His One Body, is on the throne in the heavens praying for believers; and Christ as the Body is on this earth with His authority and power continuing and spreading His gospel and building work (viz., "*I will build my Ekklesia*" — Matt. 16:18). How wonderful — believers are the continuation of Christ's work on the earth!

Jesus Christ Crucified on the Cross

> Then he released Barabbas [a murderer] to them; and when he had scourged Jesus, he delivered **Him** to be crucified.
> — Matthew 27:26

Crucifixion refers to Jesus Christ's death upon the cross. At His crucifixion, Jesus literally died as a substitute for a murderer who deserved death; the murderer (Barabbas) was freed, and Jesus died in his place. Through the Eternal Spirit, all believers who are deserving of death are released as a result of Jesus Christ's substitutionary death.

> For Jews request a sign, and Greeks seek after wisdom; but we preach Christ crucified, to the Jews a stumbling block and to the Greeks foolishness.
> — 1 Corinthians 1:22–23

Christ's crucifixion was a stumbling block to the Jews, possibly because Jesus did not perform any miracles to save Himself. Jews in the First Century sought after miraculous signs — for the promised Messiah would be a "miracle worker." Thus, they concluded Jesus could not possibly be the Son of God, because He let Himself die by such an excruciating death. The Greeks, priding themselves in rhetoric, considered Jesus foolish for not being wise enough to talk Himself out of crucifixion; therefore, to the Greeks, Jesus' crucifixion was "foolishness."

Jesus, a Qualified Substitute

Jesus was able to die as the Lamb of God to take away the sins of the world (John 1:29), because He was without sin (Heb. 4:15). He was qualified to be an adequate substitute so mankind would not have to die (1 Pet. 3:18), but instead man could receive forgiveness of sins (Matt. 26:28).

> The next day John saw Jesus coming toward him, and said, "Behold! The Lamb of God who takes away the sin of the world!"
>
> – John 1:29

What wonderful news! Men no longer need to be under the weight of guilt and sin's penalty, with its condemnation — the wrath of God upon sinful man was sufficed by the perfect sacrifice of the man, Christ Jesus. Jesus Christ took away the sins of the entire world. At the time of His crucifixion, though it was noon, the sky became dark as God forsook the Man, Jesus, Who came under judgment for all the sins of mankind. A divine mystery: The eternal fellowship the Father had always had with the Son was in time and space broken on that cross when *God made Him who knew no sin to be sin on our behalf, so that in Him we might become the righteousness of God* (2 Cor. 5:21).

The sin of the world was laid on Jesus Christ when He was crucified; therefore, God judged Him and departed from Him. Jesus Christ took on the sins of humankind, and thus God's judgment came upon Him for all of man's sins; therefore, man (male and female) is delivered from God's judgment, from the penalty of sin (death), and the guilt of sin. Guilt and shame can be debilitating and unbearable to a person to the point where psychotherapy is needed. But one who believes in the death of Christ for his or her sins will experience release from the depression of guilt and shame.

> For we do not have a High Priest who cannot sympathize with our weaknesses, but was in **all points** tempted as we are, **yet without sin.**
>
> ~ Hebrews 4:15

Jesus Christ could die instead of man because He was sinless. As a man without sin, He was not under the judgment and condemnation of God. If Jesus had also committed sin and broken God's law, then He Himself would have needed to die according to God's righteous judgment. He would not have been able to die for man's sin. But because He was without sin, He could die on behalf of sinful man. This is called "vicarious death" which is "efficacious" for man.

> For Christ indeed has once suffered for sins, [the] just for [the] unjust, that he might bring us to God; being put to death in flesh, but made alive in [the] Spirit.
>
> ~ 1 Peter 3:18, DBY

> For this is My blood of the New Covenant, which is shed for many for the remission of sins.
>
> ~ Matthew 26:28

Due to Jesus Christ's vicarious death, men with the faith of Jesus Christ, who were once unrighteous, are now made righteous. They have boldness to come to God. Unrighteous men would be afraid and ashamed to come before God, but believers can have full confidence to be in God's presence to build a relationship with God. The death of Jesus Christ is full payment to suffice God's righteous demand in judging the consequences of sin — "*death passed upon all men for all have sinned and come short of the glory of God*" ...

> Therefore, just as through one man sin entered the world, and death through sin, and thus death spread to all men, because all sinned . . . . For as by one man's disobedience many were made sinners, so also by one Man's obedience many will be made righteous.
>
> ~ Romans 5:12, 19

Therefore, God is obligated to forgive all of man's sins. He is obligated because man no longer owes Him for his sin — God's demand for justice has been executed and satisfied through the death of the Man, our Lord Jesus — our DEBT has been "paid in full!"

Jesus' Death Destroyed the Devil

> Inasmuch then as the children have partaken of flesh and blood, He [Jesus Christ] Himself likewise shared in the same, that through death He might destroy him who had the power of death, that is, the devil.
>
> – Hebrews 2:14

What wisdom! Our Lord used death, the very power of His enemy, to destroy the devil. God did not taint His holy hands to destroy a created being (Satan); rather, He used the devil's own schemes and power to crucify Jesus, which ultimately destroyed him. Satan is destroyed not in the sense he no longer exists, but rather his power is rendered ineffective through the death of Jesus, the Man.

The word "*destroyed*" in the Greek is "*katargeo*" which means, "to be idle, inactive, or inoperable." Satan has been defanged. He is harmless to believers because his power is no longer active or operable. Even though he still exists, all he can do now is deceive and accuse. It is all smoke and mirrors.

If a person falls under Satan's deception or accusation, it would affect their lives; however, once that person exercises his faith in Jesus Christ, the smoke retreats, and everything becomes clear: He is already victorious in Christ, and Satan is just a liar.

Jesus Terminated the Old "I" with All of Its Problems

> Knowing this, that our **old man** has been crucified with [Jesus Christ], that the body of sin might be annulled, that we should no longer serve sin.
>
> – Romans 6:6, DBY

The old man is the fallen sinful man — the cause of all man's problems such as anxiety, jealousy, greed, depression, hatred toward others, and the inability to forgive. Most of the problems in the world today are not because of Satan, but man's own actions expressing his fallen character. There is no need to look further than oneself. A person may ask himself, "How many people did you hurt or deprive of what is rightfully theirs in the last year?" Maybe this person didn't commit murder, but he might have wished a particular person would disappear. Multiply that by six billion people on earth, and it becomes obvious why the corrupt world situation is what it is today.

The good news is that as a result of Christ's death, this old man with all his difficulties died with Him. The reality is this: Believers are no longer bound as slaves to serve sin. The old man is dead, and there is no more need for the body of sin. Believers are no longer enslaved to their fallen character or nature — the old man. There is freedom from the fallen man because he is dead and buried. The body of sin is annulled. The Greek word for "annulled" is the same word that refers to Satan's destruction: *katargeo*. The body of sin is unemployed, inactive, or no longer needed because the person needing that body is dead and buried with Jesus Christ.

> I have been crucified with Christ; it is no longer I who live, but Christ lives in me; and the life which I now live in the flesh I live by faith in the Son of God, who loved me and gave Himself for me.
> — Galatians 2:20

The "I" who was crucified with Christ is the old man in Romans 6:6. The old "I" no longer lives, but instead a new "I" lives with the indwelling Christ. When believers are born anew, Christ comes into them to live *in* them, and the life they used to live without Christ is over. They are now completely freed from all the problems that were attached to the old "I" that was without Christ. They and Christ now live as one, a New Creation (Gal. 6:15).

The life that believers live today is by or in the faith of the Son of God. Without faith, it might seem that the old man is fully alive, and Christ is not living in the believer. But with the eyes of faith, the truth can be realized: The old "I" is no more, but Christ is the One living in believers. The life lived by believers in their physical bodies today is a life lived together with Jesus Christ. Jesus Christ's believers have the same life lived out and expressed in their daily living. Faith that can realize this is strengthened whenever believers appreciate the love of the Lord who died for them. Whenever a believer sincerely says to the Lord: "Lord Jesus, thank You for Your love and thank You for dying for me; I love You, Lord," immediately, in their experience, the Lord living in them is real and the old "I" is gone.

Jesus' Death Released His Generating Life to Bear Much Fruit: Other Believers

> But Jesus answered them, saying, "The hour has come that the Son of Man should be glorified. Most assuredly, I say to you, unless a grain of wheat falls into the ground and dies, it remains alone; but if it dies, it produces much grain."
> – John 12:23–24

Jesus Christ's death was a wonderful death, likened to the death of a seed. A seed's life is within its kernel. "Life" in a seed cannot be released unless it has gone through death. The result of the release of life in the seed is the reproduction of many more seeds; those seeds duplicate the original seed which died. A seed is the best analogy of resurrection life. Anything other than a seed will die once buried, and its death is terminal. But because there is resurrection life in a seed, the only way for it to grow, flourish, and reproduce is through burial and "death." Amazingly, that is exactly what resurrection life needs . . . death. Through death, there is more life . . . *abundant* life.

Like physical plants, Jesus' death reproduced other sons of God (seeds) who bear His exact image and likeness. The reproduced seeds are the same in form, shape, function and even DNA as the Seed (Jesus) Who was buried. Jesus is no longer the only divine and human person. Now believers are like Him, human, yet sharing in his divine nature (2 Peter 1:4), the sons of God. Therefore, the Bible can say that the New Man is created in the image of Christ: This is the destiny of every believer (Rom. 8.29) . . . they will be like Jesus Christ when they see Him again at His second coming (1 John 3:2).

This is the positive goal of the Lord's death. As a Seed, the Lord not only died for sin in order to destroy Satan, He died to bear much fruit. He died to reproduce Himself in millions and millions of people, so that God the Father would have many sons.

> Foolish one, what you sow is not made alive unless it dies.
> – 1 Corinthians 15:36

Unbelievers are skeptical of the Lord's resurrection. They foolishly question how a person can die and come back in resurrection. But the fact is, nature has been declaring resurrection in the form of the sowing of seeds and the growth of plants and trees from the beginning of time. Humanity has been enjoying and daily benefiting from the physical death and resurrection of plants through the supply of food, through useful material such as lumber, and through the beauty of the botanical kingdom.

Jesus said in John 11:25, "*I am the resurrection and the life*." Jesus is the real resurrection life. Plants are a physical picture of the real resurrection life in the universe. God wants to manifest resurrection life everywhere to benefit mankind for His physical sustenance and enjoyment, so that man may know and receive the real resurrection life of Christ. Every time men and women look at the beauty of the botanical kingdom or take a bite of their favorite bread, they should remember to receive Jesus Christ in resurrection.

Jesus' Death Abolished the Ordinances that Divided People

> For He is our peace, who has made both one, and has broken down the middle wall of enclosure, having annulled the enmity in his flesh, the law of commandments in ordinances, that He might form the two in himself into one new man, making peace; and might reconcile both in one body to God by the cross, having by it slain the enmity;
>
> – Ephesians 2:14–16, DBY

The Jews and the Gentiles were not at peace. The main reason for this enmity or hostility (even hatred) between the two peoples had to do with "*the law of commandments contained in ordinances*." These ordinances refer to the way of living the Jews were to abide by according to these divinely given ordinances. These ordinances included such major items as keeping the Sabbath day (cannot work on that day); having a diet that consisted of "clean" foods (as an example, pork and shrimp are "unclean"), and rituals surrounding religious "feasts." It is because of these ordinances that Jews were distinct and kept separate from the Gentiles (Nations) – hostility arose as a result between the two. Peter even said it was unlawful for a Jew to come near a non-Jew (Acts 10:28 – "*You know how unlawful it is for a Jewish man to keep company with or go to one of another nation*.").

Under such circumstances, it is not possible for the Lord to have His One Body consisting of all people. Therefore, in order to have One Body of all people, specifically a coming together of Jews and Gentiles, He needed to abolish all the hatred that kept the two people separate. On the cross He *"put to death the enmity"* or hatred caused by these laws relating to lifestyle, ritualistic, and ceremonial observances, for the sole purpose of joining the two people (Jews and Gentiles) into One New Man, One Body. By nailing to the cross the "enmity contained in ordinances," He eliminated the hatred, the animosity, and brought peace so that people can be joined together in His One Body. This is clearly needed for the fulfillment of His prayer in John 17.

In John 17:20 and 21, the Lord prayed not just for His disciples, who were all Jews, to be one, but for all those who would believe through their words, that they all may be one. Those that believe through their words clearly include Gentiles — those who would be "called out from the nations." So, in the Lord's Prayer He already foretold of Jews and Gentiles becoming one in order that the world will believe in Jesus. After that prayer, Jesus went to the cross to nail and abolish all the hatred, the enmity, contained in ordinances kept by the Jews which had made them separate; thus, now, all His people could become one according to His prayer.

Religious strife can be considered the most hostile form of division among peoples, because how a person acts and lives is through "God-given" commands (even Islam, Buddhism, Hinduism are all divided). Therefore, if Jews and Gentiles can be one, then it is an easier matter for the other races with all their other differences to be one in Jesus Christ. The topic of the law will be discussed in more detail in this text.

Jesus Christ Resurrected

> But the angel answered and said to the women, "Do not be afraid, for I know that you seek Jesus who was crucified. He is not here; for He is risen, as He said. Come, see the place where the Lord lay. And go quickly and tell His disciples that He is risen from the dead.
>
> – Matthew 28:5–7

Jesus' Death and Resurrection Are the Basis of the Gospel

The death and resurrection of Christ are foundational elements of the gospel; receiving both by faith is both essential and necessary for salvation.

> Moreover, brethren, I declare to you the gospel which I preached to you, which also you received and in which you stand, by which also you are saved, if you hold fast that word which I preached to you — unless you believed in vain.
>
> For I delivered to you first of all that which I also received: that Christ died for our sins according to the Scriptures, and that He was buried, and that He rose again the third day according to the Scriptures.
>
> – 1 Corinthians 15:1–4

> That if you confess with your mouth the Lord Jesus and believe in your heart that God has raised Him from the dead, you will be saved.
>
> – Romans 10:9

Paul in 1 Corinthians 15:1–4 presents the gospel in a nutshell: Jesus Christ died for the sins of all people, He was buried, and He resurrected on the third day. This is the faith of Jesus Christ that saves people. What simplicity! Believers trust that Jesus is both God and man, and that he died for their sins and was raised from the dead. This alone is what saves people, and it is the uniting faith of all believers. Why should there be so much arguing and infighting among Christians, when there is such simplicity of faith? The human mind tends to complicate things, and it is in these unnecessary complications that division surfaces among believers. In both of the above portions of Scripture, what it means to be "saved" is simply defined: believing the message of Jesus Christ, who died for man's sins and was resurrected.

Jesus, the Life-Giving Spirit

Jesus breathed into His believers in order to minister the indestructible life within His believers.

Thus also it is written, "The first man Adam became a living being; the last Adam [Jesus Christ] became a life-giving spirit."
– 1 Corinthians 15:45

The phrase, "The first man Adam" in 1 Corinthians 15:45 referred to the Adam God created in Genesis. However, Paul also referred to the "last Adam," Jesus Christ. As the "last," Jesus ended the old creation in Adam. In His resurrection, He became a life-giving Spirit to give His believers the divine, eternal, and indestructible life, thus making them a New Creation (2 Cor. 5:17). In resurrection, Jesus Christ took on a wonderful, spiritual form. In this form, He can now enter into His believers — into the spirit of each person — and give life to them. Life is something within a person and not outside a person. For Jesus to indwell a person, He must be the life-giving Spirit.

And having said this, He [Jesus Christ] breathed into [them], and says to them, Receive [the] Holy Spirit (lit. the "Holy Breath").
– John 20:22, DBY

This is the fulfillment of the promised Spirit, the Comforter mentioned in John 14, and the Living Water in John 7. Before resurrection, Jesus could only be *with* people, but after resurrection Jesus could breathe Himself *into* His believers. They, in turn, could receive the Holy Spirit.

The Greek word for "Spirit" is *pneuma*, which is the word for air. The Holy Spirit became the breathable air to the believers. Jesus could breathe the Spirit into them, and they could in turn receive the Spirit as breath. This mirrors the record in Genesis when God created Adam and animated him by breathing into his nostrils. Here, the New Creation came into being and the corporate new man was generated by another breath. This time in John 20:22 believers breathed and received the actual Holy Spirit.

…who [Jesus Christ] has been constituted not according to law of fleshly commandment, but according to power of indissoluble life.
– Hebrews 7:16, DBY

The life that He is ministering to His believers as the Priest of God is the "indissoluble," or indestructible life. No matter the obstacle, even death, nothing can destroy this life in the believer. The greater the challenges or deeper the problems, the more victorious this indestructible life shines forth. Resurrection is not just an event which happened to Jesus Christ 2,000 years ago. The same resurrection life is now in His believers. If that is their life, how can any difficulties cause them to lose heart or depress them? Since resurrection life overcomes our ultimate difficulty — death — believers can rely on the resurrection life in them to go through trials with strength and joy.

> Examine yourselves as to whether you are in the faith. Test yourselves. Do you not know yourselves, that Jesus Christ is in you? — unless indeed you are disqualified.
> — 2 Corinthians 13:5

Being "in the faith" means to believe that Jesus Christ is both God and man who died for sin and resurrected on the third day. By this simple faith, believers are approved by God. And not only this: Jesus Christ Himself also comes in to indwell man. Even while this is true, it is "unbelievable." No wonder man (male and female) needs to have the gift of faith from God in order to believe! Notice that 2 Corinthians 13:5 does not say *the Spirit* is in the believer, but the *very person Jesus Christ* is in them! Jesus Christ Himself is in each one of His believers, because He and the Spirit are one in the same person.

Jesus Became the Indwelling Comforter

As the indwelling Comforter (the Spirit of Truth), Jesus makes real to believers all things of Christ.

> And I will beg the Father, and He will give you another Comforter, that He may be with you forever, the **Spirit of Truth**, whom the world cannot receive, because it does not see Him nor know Him; but you know Him, for He abides with you, and shall be in you. I will not leave you orphans, I am coming to you.
> — John 14:16–18, DBY

The phrase "another Comforter" in John 14:16 is referring to the "Spirit of Truth" in John 14:17. As the Comforter in the flesh, Jesus abides *with* or physically with His disciples, but as "another Comforter," He abides *in* them. The Spirit of Truth is simply Jesus coming in another form. That is the reason He said, "*I am coming to you.*"

Today through His death and resurrection, no matter the time or place, Jesus continually comforts believers as the Spirit within them. The world is full of conflicts. It seems that wars and unprovoked attacks are increasing globally, even in the name of religion. Individually, it seems people today experience more anxiety, uncertainty, and unrest within their souls. Truly, the Comforter is needed; He needs to be present and available. The good news is that Jesus Christ, as the reliable Comforter, brings true comfort and He exists within every believer. Whenever comfort is needed, all believers need to do is turn to Him. He is never far away. He is available 24/7 to comfort each one of His believers from within them.

> But when He is come, the Spirit of Truth, He shall guide you into all the truth: for He shall not speak from himself; but whatsoever He shall hear He shall speak; and He will announce to you what is coming. He shall glorify Me, for He shall receive of mine and shall announce it to you. All things that the Father has are mine; on account of this I have said that He receives of mine and shall announce it to you.
>
> – John 16:13-18, DBY

Truth in John 16:13–18 is God (Jesus Christ, the Spirit) and all His attributes such as love, light and mercy. This is the eternal and universal truth.

This truth also includes everything that Jesus obtained, attained, and accomplished through His incarnation, crucifixion, resurrection and ascension. These wonderful life elements include such things as redemption, forgiveness of sins, and justification; they transform believers into the image of Jesus Christ, Who is both God and man, Who became both Lord and Christ. This is the unsearchable riches of Christ that the Spirit of Truth is guiding believers into. It is the Spirit of Truth Who makes all that Christ is, including all the things of the Father, true or real to believers in their understanding and experience.

The fact is this: The crucifixion of Jesus Christ has solved all problems. The old man, which is the source of man's troubles, has been nailed to the cross and buried with Christ. But in the believers' daily situations, they may not have such experiences. They may feel very much trapped in negativity and in the "death" of the world. It is at such a time that they need the Spirit of Truth (lit. "reality") to intervene. If they would start to pray and call upon the name of the Lord Jesus, the Spirit of Truth in them would be activated. He would guide them into the reality of their old man's crucifixion and burial and into the reality of being in their resurrection and ascension in Christ. It is the Spirit of Truth Who makes all the unseen realities accomplished by Jesus Christ real to believers, guiding them into all truth. This is reality.

It is unimaginable how rich and how wonderful are the many items into which the Spirit of Truth desires to guide believers. The Spirit's job is to be such a guide. Believers only need to be open to Him and turn to Him.

Jesus Brings Humanity into God

Through these things, Jesus brought humanity into God, so that mere men could become sons of God. As a result, they became His duplication.

> ...concerning His Son Jesus Christ our Lord, who was born of the seed of David according to the flesh, and declared to be the Son of God with power according to the Spirit of holiness, by the resurrection from the dead.
>
> – Romans 1:3

The reference to "His Son" in Romans 1:3 refers to Jesus' divinity as the Son of God. The phrase "*born . . . according to the flesh*" refers to His humanity. In His resurrection, Jesus — not just in His divinity but also in His humanity — was declared (appointed or marked out as) the Son of God. Romans 1:1 references this as the gospel of God: It is concerning such a One. He is the gospel, the good news.

> Now when they had fulfilled all that was written concerning Him, they took Him down from the tree and laid Him in a tomb. But God raised Him from the dead. And we declare to you glad tidings — that promise which was made to the fathers. God has fulfilled this for us their children, in that He has raised up Jesus. As it is also written in the second Psalm: 'You are My Son, Today I have begotten You.'
>
> – Acts 13:29-33

It is abundantly clear when at Jesus' birth He was *already* the Son of God. He didn't need resurrection to be begotten of God. He was already the "only begotten Son" (John 3:16). He existed in eternity as the Son with the Father (See chapter 2 concerning His person).

However, in verse 33, Luke (the writer of Acts) says that it was at the day of resurrection Jesus was begotten of God. Something transpired within Jesus on that day of resurrection! Before resurrection, Jesus' humanity was still flesh, susceptible to weakness, hunger, thirst, and even death. On the day of resurrection, however, His humanity was uplifted to the highest place. As a man, He was begotten of God. By incarnation, God was brought *into man*. By resurrection man was brought *into God*. Now, Jesus' divinity and even His humanity exist in God. Divinity and humanity are now joined, mingled, and blended in a perfect union in the same person. How wonderful!

> For whom He foreknew, He also predestined to be conformed to the image of His Son, that He might be the firstborn among many brethren.
>
> – Romans 8:29

Before death and resurrection, Jesus was the "*only begotten*" (John 1:18; 3:16), but after resurrection, He became the "firstborn" (Rom. 8:29). The word "only" in John 1:18 and John 3:16 is derived from the Greek word *monogenēs* and means that Jesus is unique and there is no other. "Firstborn" in Romans 8:29 comes from the Greek word *prōtotokos*, derived from the root word *prōtos* meaning, "first in any succession of things or persons." Thus, "firstborn" indicates there are others to follow. Many brothers will come after Jesus.

At His resurrection, all of Jesus' believers were begotten in resurrection with Him (1 Pet. 1:3). When Jesus' humanity was begotten of God at resurrection, believers were included with Him. Today, just as He is the firstborn Son of God with divinity and humanity, His believers too are sons of God with humanity and divinity (in the sense of participating in the "divine nature" – we speak NOT of "little gods" but as sons and daughters of the Living God). This is God's purpose: to reproduce many sons "*to be conformed to the image of his Son*" (Rom. 8:28–29; see also Eph. 1:5).

> Most assuredly, I say to you, unless a grain of wheat falls into the ground and dies, it remains alone; but if it dies, it produces much grain.
>
> – John 12:24

Christ is the "grain of wheat" Who fell into the ground and died, albeit on the cross. The "much grain" is Christ's increase in resurrection. Believers are the grains who were produced through His death and resurrection. The many grains produced in resurrection are the same as the first grain (Jesus) Who was planted through death. How amazing so many brothers produced through Christ's death and resurrection, exactly like Him, are true believers — the very image of the firstborn Son of God partaking in both His humanity and divinity.

Jesus Christ Ascended

> Now when He had spoken these things, while they watched, He was taken up, and a cloud received Him out of their sight. And while they looked steadfastly toward heaven as He went up . . . this same Jesus, who was taken up from you into heaven, will so come in like manner as you saw Him go into heaven."
> — Acts 1:9–10a, 11

The Crucified Jesus Made Lord and Christ

> Let all the house of Israel therefore know for certain that God has made him both Lord and Christ, this Jesus whom you crucified.
> — Acts 2:36 ESV

At birth, Jesus was already both Lord and Christ (Luke 1:43, 2:11). As the Son of God, surely, He was the Lord. And as Christ, He was appointed to fulfill God's purpose through incarnation and crucifixion. Why then was it necessary for Jesus to be made *both* Lord and Christ after His ascension? The reason is just as His humanity was declared the Son of God, in ascension His humanity was made both Lord and Christ. He is both Lord and Christ not only as God, but also as a man. There is a man today that is Lord over all! And God needs man. Therefore, this Man was anointed for the ultimate fulfillment of God's eternal purpose.

> ...who, being in the form of God, did not consider it robbery to be equal with God, but made Himself of no reputation, taking the form of a bondservant, and coming in the likeness of men. And being found in appearance as a man, He humbled Himself

and became obedient to death, even the death of the cross. Therefore God also has highly exalted Him and given Him the name which is above every name, that at the name of Jesus every knee should bow, of those in heaven, and of those on earth, and of those under the earth, and that every tongue should confess that Jesus Christ is Lord, to the glory of God the Father.

– Philippians 2:6–11

In Philippians 2:6–11, Paul presented a clear narrative concerning Jesus' incarnation, crucifixion, resurrection, and ascension. It was after this process, as a man, Jesus was exalted above all names.

It is this divine and yet lowly human Who is now ascended wherefore believers confess: *"Jesus Christ is Lord."* Jesus, at the end of this process (starting from Philippians 2:6), is different from when He started. In the beginning of this process He was God, the Son, Who became man. At the end of this process, He was (and currently is) a man Who is called Lord with everything under His feet.

The One Who was exalted by God was and is today a Man – there is a MAN IN THE GLORY; otherwise, Jesus didn't need God to exalt Him. He was "made a little lower than the angels" but now is *"crowned with glory and honor"* (Heb. 2:7-9) having tasted death for every man; therefore, this Man is highly exalted!

Jesus Intercedes and Saves Believers to the Uttermost

Now He who searches the hearts knows what the mind of the Spirit [is], because He makes intercession for the saints according to [the will of] God.

Who is he who condemns? It is Christ who died, and furthermore is also risen, who is even at the right hand of God, who also makes intercession for us.

– Romans 8:27, 34

How wonderful for believers to have Jesus at the right hand of God interceding for (or praying strongly for) them through every trial and circumstance. This is one of Jesus' full-time jobs; through His intercession, believers will be saved to the uttermost through each trial (Heb. 7:25), and God's purpose will be fulfilled in them. When the Lord prays for His people, He may not be praying for what they think they need. Typically, when believers pray they are praying for their own interests at heart, but Jesus prays for His people according to the will of God. Should God listen to prayers of the believers according to their own interests or listen to the prayer of Jesus according to God's will? Many times, when Christians' prayers are not answered, it is because their prayers are conflicting with the will of God. Believers should thus "amen" all His intercessory prayers on behalf of all His followers and submit to God's will. It is certain God's will is for every one of His people to be saved to the uttermost.

Jesus Was Made Head to Transmit to His Body (to Believers) All He Is, All He Has Obtained and All He Has Attained

> ...and what the surpassing greatness of His power towards us who believe, according to the working of the might of His strength, [in] which He wrought in the Christ in raising Him from among [the] dead, and He set Him down at His right hand in the heavenlies, above every principality, and authority, and power, and dominion, and every name named, not only in this age, but also in that to come; and has put all things under His feet, and gave Him [to be] head over all things to the assembly, which is His body, the fullness of Him who fills all in all.
>
> – Ephesians 1:19–23, DBY

The power of Jesus is toward those who believe. This power toward believers is the same power that raised Christ from the dead — resurrection power. This all-transcending power also raised Jesus to the heavens, to the highest position in the universe. Everything is subdued under his feet by this all-subduing power.

Believers' eyes need to be opened to see what tremendous and wonderful power has been given to them. Now Jesus is the Head of the ekklesia, the Body of Christ. As His body, all His believers are certainly under the constant supply and transmission of this power. Under and attached to the assembly's ascended Head, how can believers create excuses to be weak?

Satan is a liar. All the power of Christ is at the believer's disposal to be experienced.

His Spirit Outpoured to Complete His Work on Earth

By pouring out His Spirit, Jesus gives believers the power and authority to speak His words to complete His life-giving ministry.

> When the day of Pentecost had come, they were all together in one place. And suddenly a sound came from heaven like the rush of a mighty wind, and it filled all the house where they were sitting. And there appeared to them tongues as of fire, distributed and resting on each one of them. And they were all filled with the Holy Spirit and began to speak in other tongues, as the Spirit gave them utterance.
>
> – Acts 2:1–4, RSV

> Being therefore exalted at the right hand of God, and having received from the Father the promise of the Holy Spirit, he has poured out this which you see and hear.
>
> – Acts 2:33, RSV

In John 20:22, after Jesus' resurrection, He breathed into his disciples. At that point, His disciples had already received the Holy Spirit as the breath within; however, on the day of Pentecost, the Spirit was described as a "mighty, rushing wind" (Acts 2:2). A mighty or rushing wind is very different from a breath. A "breath" is necessary for life, whereas a mighty wind can accomplish a lot of work. Wind can move a ship and generate electricity through a turbine. Therefore, the outpouring of the Spirit on the day of Pentecost was to empower believers for the working of His ministry to spread the gospel for the building up of His Body — His ekklesia.

This is the fulfillment of the promise given by the Lord in Luke 24:49, when He told His disciples to wait to be clothed with "*power from on high*" so that they could go forth to all nations to preach in His name.

Then, Luke spoke of "*tongues as of fire*" in Acts 2:3. Tongues are a symbol of speaking and indicate God's work of preaching the gospel to all nations and spreading the truth for building up the Body will be mainly accomplished through *speaking*. Jesus is the speaking Spirit. Just as the apostles started to speak the gospel immediately after receiving the out-poured Spirit on the day of Pentecost, this same poured-out-Spirit has reached all His believers enabling each and every one to go forth to speak with power and authority — and thus fulfill the ekklesia's commission.

> And Jesus coming up spoke to them, saying: All power has been
> given Me in heaven and upon earth. Go therefore and make
> disciples of all the nations, baptizing them to the name of the
> Father, and of the Son, and of the Holy Spirit; teaching them to
> observe all things whatsoever I have enjoined you. And behold, I
> am with you all the days, until the completion of the age.
>
> — Matthew 28:18–20, DBY

According to Matthew, believers are to spread the good news to minister Christ to people in order that many may be immersed and be brought into the fellowship with the entire Triune God. Then they are to continue to teach these new believers the entire counsel of God (Acts 20:26–27) as unveiled in the Scriptures.

The Lord with all His authority is surely with believers as they go, stepping out in faith to do this. Believers are to continue this ministry until the end of this age when the Lord returns. As believers go, the Lord is with them, with all the power that He has obtained and attained. Only by going to fulfill such a commission are believers in the position to experience "all power" that has been given to the Lord. If believers just stay home and care for their own interests, they will not experience this power because this power is specifically for the carrying out of God's eternal purpose.

Believers Share in His Anointing to Be the Continuation of Christ on Earth

> Now He who establishes us with you in Christ and has anointed
> us is God,
>
> — 2 Corinthians 1:21, DBY

When people heard and received the gospel from the first apostles, they were immediately established together in Christ. Initially, some apostles were specifically sent to preach the gospel. However, whenever anyone hears and believes the gospel, even today, those new believers become the same group of believers as the apostles, established in Christ.

Not only so, but God has anointed the *entire group* in Christ. This anointing is the commissioning by God to fulfill His purpose on earth. Since believers are in Him, they presently share the same anointing as Jesus Christ to carry out His work of ministering. Anyone who believes into Christ through the preaching of the gospel will join all other believers as they unite with the early apostles into one, in Christ. No matter how new the believer, upon belief, this person immediately receives the same anointing or commission as the early apostles to preach the gospel and teach the truth in order to accomplish God's purpose. No Bible school, seminary, or special calling is necessary to have this anointing; rather, this anointing comes with the initiation of faith in Jesus Christ.

> For as the body is one and has many members, but all the members of that one body, being many, are one body, so also is Christ.
> – 1 Corinthians 12:12

"Christ" in 1 Corinthians 12:12 does not just refer to Jesus, but also His One Body. According to most Christians' understanding, this verse should say, "so also is the church," where there are many members. They would associate the many members to the church or assembly, and not to Christ. The Scriptures reveal it is Christ who has many members. This cannot refer to the individual Jesus Christ, but rather the corporate Christ – with Jesus as the Head and His believers as the many members of His One Body.

Again, Christ means "the anointed one," intended to fulfill God's purpose. Since believers are now members of Christ and share in the same anointing as Jesus Christ as the Head, they naturally share in His commission to accomplish God's purpose. As His body in this day, believers are the continuation of Christ on earth commissioned to do God's will, mainly by speaking – ministering Christ to others. This results in salvation for sinners and growth and building for other believers.

According to 1 Corinthians chapter 12, the Spirit's anointing upon all believers produced many kinds of gifts. Some of these gifts of the Spirit can manifest themselves supernaturally such as healing, speaking in a different dialect, interpretation of tongues, and performing miracles. Other gifts may come across more naturally such as a word of wisdom or knowledge, but even then some words can only be attributed to a supernatural speaking directly from the Spirit.

In Romans 12 there is another list of gifts for the building up of the Lord's Body. These gifts are also given to every believer simply based on their faith in Christ. The gifts listed in Romans 12 all seem very human and normal rather than supernatural; yet, they are all powered by the supernatural grace of the Holy Spirit. They don't come across as miraculous; yet, there is a joy, resilience, strength, and kindness manifested that can only be attributed to receiving the gift from the Spirit. The anointing has come upon the Body in order for each member to function, to teach, exhort, provide financial support, show mercy, love and honor others, feed an enemy, and more. All these manifestations are based on the anointing every member has received in order to further the building up of God's ekklesia to both reach those having not yet believed and to edify those already in the Body of Christ.

Therefore, the gifts given by the Spirit are not provided for believers to miraculously receive help for themselves. Divine healing and other miracles are not for selfish interest. All the gifts of the Spirit are given with the expressed purpose for the building up God's ekklesia, His eternal purpose. All believers have received such an anointing to complete God's purpose on earth!

5

GOD, MAN, AND SATAN

God created man, male and female, with the ultimate purpose of man becoming His sons with His image and likeness, having His eternal life and divine nature. Equally as important, man would be able to defeat His enemy, Satan. This was God's purpose and pleasure. Satan came to deceive man, so instead of man eating of the Tree of Life, man ingested the tree of the knowledge of good and evil. Thus, man became aligned with Satan and Satan's desire to be God — to exist without God or in place of God. Man became utterly corrupted and fallen, so much so that God even regretted creating man. This chapter technically would not be considered truth since the focus of this chapter is concerning man and not Jesus Christ. However, it may be considered *healthy teaching* since understanding the fallen state of man should cause a person to turn to Jesus Christ for salvation.

Satan Wanted to Overthrow God and Be God Himself

Lucifer, which means, "light bearer," was the highest angel leading worship to God. Though he was God's leading angel[13], he wanted to overthrow God to *be God himself* — thus becoming God's enemy. The prophets Isaiah and Ezekiel reveal how Lucifer fell from God's favor:

> How you are fallen from heaven, O Lucifer, son of the morning! How you are cut down to the ground, you who weakened the nations! For you have said in your heart: 'I will ascend into heaven, I will exalt my throne above the stars of God; I will also sit on the mount of the congregation On the farthest sides of the north; I will ascend above the heights of the clouds, I will be like the Most High.'
>
> – Isaiah 14:12–14

Thus says the Lord Jehovah: Because your heart is lifted up, and
you have said, I am a god, I sit in the seat of God, in the heart of
the seas, and you set your heart as the heart of God.

. . .Thus says the Lord Jehovah: You, who seal up the measure
of perfection, full of wisdom and perfect in beauty, you were in
Eden, the garden of God. Every precious stone was your covering:
. . . The workmanship of your tambours and of your pipes was
in you: in the day that you were created were they prepared. You
were the anointed covering cherub, and I had set you so: you
were upon the holy mountain of God; you did walk up and down
in the midst of stones of fire. You were perfect in your ways, from
the day that you were created, till unrighteousness was found in
you By the abundance of your traffic they filled the midst of you
with violence, and you have sinned; therefore have I cast you as
profane from the mountain of God, and have destroyed you, O
covering cherub, from the midst of the stones of fire. Your heart
was lifted up because of your beauty; you have corrupted your
wisdom by reason of your brightness.

– Ezekiel 28:2b, 12b–17, DBY

Lucifer was the only angel whose beauty was described in detail in the
Bible — as one covered in precious stones (Ezek. 28:13). He was the utmost
measure of perfection, full of wisdom and perfect in beauty (Ezek. 28:15).
There was nothing in the universe like him. He had and still has authority
to roam freely through the very inner sanctum of God. He may have been
more beautiful than God in appearance.

For certain, Lucifer considered himself wiser than God. This would
be the assumed reason why he thought that he should be on the throne of
God. On top of this, he was crowned the highest of angels with musical
celebrations before the throne of God — even so, he apparently led in the
worship of God. He was the anointed cherub — the head of the angels who
protected God's glory and led creation in adoration, or worship of God
(Rev. 4:8). At a certain point (perhaps as he was considering God's glory
and leading the adoration of God), he began to compare himself with
God. Lucifer looked at his own beauty and wisdom and thought that he
should replace God. In fact, he should *be* God. He then rebelled with a large

contingent of angels under his authority (one-third of the "stars of heaven" – Rev. 12:4), and he became Satan — an adversary and enemy to God.

Man Was Created to Fulfill God's Purpose and to Give God Pleasure

God's will and pleasure was to produce many sons that would be the fullest expression of Himself. Unlike all other creatures fashioned after their own kind, man is fashioned after God's kind.

> . . . having predestined us to adoption as sons [sonship] by Jesus Christ to Himself, according to the good pleasure of His will.
> – Ephesians 1:5

In the beginning, in eternity past, hidden within God is His will to produce many sons. His pleasure was not just to have the only begotten Son within Himself, but as the eternal Father, to also reproduce many sons for His glory and pleasure.

The English word "adoption" does not accurately translate the original Greek word *huiothesia* which Paul used in Ephesians 1:5. The Greek word *huiothesia* is a compound word made up of "son," an offspring by birth, and "appoint" or "set in place."

The English word "adoption" is merely a legal procedure, without the actual birth of a son. *Huiothesia*, however, clearly indicates believers are indeed sons by birth. With God's life, they *also* have a place in maturity or patrimony — a legal standing — to be God's appointed sons. This is the Father's will. How great and wonderful God is, Who has begotten millions upon millions of sons who are not just babies but have the maturity to take their appointed place for the entire universe to behold and glorify the Father in His many sons. This is God's pleasure and glory. A human father can identify with this in a minuscule and limited scale for earthly fathers enrich their patrimony.

Let me share a personal testimony. I (the author) am a father of four children, and they were definitely my pleasure. It was enjoyable to be with them and do things with them as they were growing up. Now that they are grown and are all married with careers that are contributing to society, I am proud of them. They are my glory displaying my achievement. Magnify this by infinity, and a sense of the immensity of God's pleasure and glory in His many mature sons, then in measure you can begin to appreciate this.

> And God made the beast of the earth according to its kind,
> cattle according to its kind, and everything that creeps on the
> earth according to its kind. And God saw that it was good. Then
> God said, "Let Us make man in Our image, according to Our
> likeness; let them have dominion over the fish of the sea, over
> the birds of the air, and over the cattle, over all the earth and over
> every creeping thing that creeps on the earth."
>
> – Genesis 1:25–26

Genesis 1:25–26 describes every creature in the water, in the air, and
on land as made according to "its kind" (Gen. 1:25). Each was fashioned
according to its own species. However, when it came time for God to
make man He said, "Let Us make man in Our image and according to Our
likeness" (Gen. 1:26).

When God fashioned man, His three-oneness (His Triune nature, or
the Trinity) was revealed; this is reflected in the use of the pronoun "Us"
in Genesis 1:26. It seems creating man was of such utmost importance a
conference within the Godhead was necessary – a joint decision had to be
made. Man was not made according to "its kind" but *according to God's own
image and likeness*, according to *God's kind*. Man was made very distinct and
different from all other creatures. Clearly before man there was nothing like
man. Man was uniquely formed at that point, after God Himself.

> So God created man in His own image; in the image of God He
> created him; male and female He created them.
>
> – Genesis 1:27

God's character and nature are clearly expressed in the vast expanse of
the universe and in the minute details of creation. However, human beings
express God on a much higher plain.

Man's ability to be inventive (to imagine and to create), along with
his ability to express sacrificial love, and to set goals and to have purpose
beyond just existence, clearly expresses God in man in a much more specific
and excellent way than the rest of creation. Man expresses God's very inner
being, His attributes – even His personality; other creatures cannot do

this. Although scientists have concluded that human-like creatures were in existence for hundreds of thousands of years (or longer) before man, most anthropologists and scholars agree — man's language and culture is associated with modern humans who have only been in existence within the last 10,000 years.[14]

Man is special. Man has a unique purpose which took a conference within the Godhead of the Father, Son, and Spirit to design. This was indicated when God said: "*Let Us make man in Our image.*" It is also important to recognize "man" is both "male and female." In God's view man is a pair including both male and female. He does not have a preference between the sexes. Just as God consists of Father, Son and Spirit with distinct roles, but not one more important than the other — for He is ONE PERSON — so too when God created man, He viewed male and female together as "man." Therefore, this should be kept in mind throughout this book that whenever "man" or even "sons of God" is mentioned, it includes both male and female.

> Beloved, now we are children of God; and it has not yet been revealed what we shall be, but we know that when He is revealed, we shall be like Him, for we shall see Him as He is.
>
> — 1 John 3:2

If man with God's image and likeness would have eaten the Tree of Life, signifying the very life and nature of God, then man (men and women) literally would have become God's children. Man would have the psychological faculties and the physical ability to express the life and nature of God.

In the New Testament, when men receive Jesus Christ, they are born of God to be His children (John 1:12–13). Right now, believers do not *appear* like children of God, but one day everyone will see believers revealed in the glory of their Father God. Their physical body will even be a body of glory like the Lord Jesus' body in resurrection. In eternity, all creation will recognize we humans have become "the sons of the Living God." Man, with God's divine eternal life and nature, expresses God's attributes, fullness, and glory.

God's Purpose: Man Would Be the One to Defeat His Enemy, Satan

> Then God said, "Let Us make man in Our image, according to Our likeness; let them have dominion over the fish of the sea, over the birds of the air, and over the cattle, over all the earth and over every creeping thing that creeps on the earth."
> ~ Genesis 1:26

In Genesis 1:26 God declares created man will have dominion "*over all the earth.*" This means dominion should already include all earthly creatures. However, God then says, "*and over every creeping thing.*"

Why would God single out "*every creeping thing,*" distinct from all the other creatures already included on the earth? It seems they are not part of the earth, but an addition to other creatures on the earth; Genesis 1:26 is referring to Satan with all his followers, the fallen angels and demons.

> And the LORD God said to the woman, "What is this you have done?" The woman said, "The serpent deceived me, and I ate." So the LORD God said to the serpent: "Because you have done this, you are cursed more than all cattle, and more than every beast of the field; On your belly you shall go, and you shall eat dust All the days of your life. And I will put enmity between you and the woman, and between your seed and her Seed; He shall bruise your head, and you shall bruise His heel."
> ~ Genesis 3:13–15

Even after man ate of the forbidden fruit, God still prophesied that a man born of a woman would defeat Satan (the serpent), with a crushing blow to the head. Even though the Devil did his best to cause man to sin, bringing man to a fallen state, God never gave up His purpose: to use lowly man to defeat His enemy.

This also means God will do something to preserve man. God will not let him become extinct due to sin. Remember, God said when man eats of the tree of the knowledge of good and evil, "*you shall surely die.*" It was after God made this promise Adam named his wife "Eve," which means, "life" or "living," because he understood she would live.

Satan Is Not Afraid of God, but Is Terrified of Man

Satan walks freely in God's presence, according to Scripture, and unafraid. He challenges God and accuses God's people, as in the example of Job:

> Now there was a day when the sons of God came to present themselves before the LORD, and Satan also came among them. And the LORD said to Satan, "From where do you come?" So Satan answered the LORD and said, "From going to and fro on the earth, and from walking back and forth on it." Then the LORD said to Satan, "Have you considered My servant Job, that there is none like him on the earth, a blameless and upright man, one who fears God and shuns evil?" So Satan answered the LORD and said, "Does Job fear God for nothing? "Have You not made a hedge around him, around his household, and around all that he has on every side? You have blessed the work of his hands, and his possessions have increased in the land. "But now, stretch out Your hand and touch all that he has, and he will surely curse You to Your face!" And the LORD said to Satan, "Behold, all that he has is in your power; only do not lay a hand on his person." So Satan went out from the presence of the LORD.
>
> ~ Job 1:6–12

Satan was free to come and go before God. He was bold to even challenge God concerning Job. Because Satan wrongly accused God of "buying" Job's love and worship by providing Job with many physical blessings, God allowed Satan to cause Job to suffer much loss. Satan's access to heaven's portal shall be terminated when he and his ilk are cast to the earth where Christ's final victory shall assail the Evil One on that day:

> So the great dragon was cast out, that serpent of old, called the Devil and Satan, who deceives the whole world; he was cast to the earth, and his angels were cast out with him. Then I heard a loud voice saying in heaven, "Now salvation, and strength, and the kingdom of our God, and the power of His Christ have come, for the accuser of our brethren, who accused them before our God day and night, has been cast down."
>
> ~ Revelation 12:9–10

Until the time of the Lord's second coming when he is cast out from God's presence, Satan will continue to wander freely before God, and accuse God's people day and night. It seems that has been his full-time job since his power was destroyed through the cross of Christ. The condemnation within believers that speaks failure, or lies that God has given up on them, causes weakness, discouragement, and even depression. But these condemnations are accusations from the Devil. In those moments believers should look to the blood of Christ shed for them and testify of their faith in Christ in order to overcome the accuser (Rev. 12:11).

God Ordained Man to Be the One to Destroy Satan

> Now when the tempter came to Him, he said, "**If You are the Son of God**, command that these stones become bread." But He answered and said, "It is written, 'Man shall not live by bread alone, but by every word that proceeds from the mouth of God.'" Then the Devil took Him up into the holy city, set Him on the pinnacle of the temple, and said to Him, "If You are the Son of God, throw Yourself down. For it is written: 'He shall give His angels charge over you,' and, 'In [their] hands they shall bear you up, lest you dash your foot against a stone.' "Jesus said to him, "It is written again, 'You shall not tempt the LORD your God.'"
>
> – Matthew 4:3–7

When Satan came to tempt Jesus Christ, his first two attempts aimed at seducing Jesus were to do something miraculous — like God. Notice both temptations started with the phrase, "*If you are the Son of God.*"

Even though Jesus IS the Son of God, He was ordained to defeat Satan as a man. Jesus' reply to Satan was that of a man — He, though God took the position of a man, stating that man was to live by God's Word. Furthermore, man should not tempt the Lord His God! Jesus did not fall for Satan's temptations. He resisted doing anything supernatural, as God could readily have done.

It is interesting to note when Satan tempted Adam and Eve by telling them the same thing: They would "*be like God*" if they ate of the tree of knowledge of good and evil. Similarly, Satan tempted Jesus into taking a stand to demonstrate He was God. Adam and Eve failed, but Jesus succeeded by staying in the position of a man to defeat God's enemy, Satan. Adam, though man, was defeated by his desire to be like God, to be independent from God. Jesus, though God, was victorious by depending on God as a man.

> But we see Jesus, who was made a little lower than the angels, for the suffering of death crowned with glory and honor, that He, by the grace of God, might taste death for everyone. . . . Inasmuch then as the children have partaken of flesh and blood, He Himself likewise shared in the same, that through death He might destroy [inoperative] him who had the power of death, that is, the Devil.
>
> – Hebrews 2:9, 14

In his physical attributes and mental capabilities, man was created a "little lower" than the least of the angels. Angels are much more powerful than man; while the top angel's *rebellion* was an attempt to become God and rule over everything, *God's* desire was for lowly man to defeat Satan and be placed in the very position Satan coveted. Satan was in direct opposition to God's plan; thus, Satan detested man, for he knew this "man" was designed in the very image of God to defeat him. Thus, Satan's goal was to kill every single human being on planet earth if possible — terminating God's ultimate plan and purpose in ridding the universe of man. He used the ultimate weapon he possessed — death — the crucifixion of Jesus (who, likewise, was "*made a little lower than the angels*"). Satan must have thought he had won, putting to death God Himself! Alas! Satan was foiled.

Apparently, he didn't know the death of this sinless God–man would be his very undoing. He didn't know the power of the true resurrection Life of God. Resurrection life cannot be tested and proven, until it is put to death. God needed Satan's power of death to manifest His resurrection life!

Jesus Christ came as the lowliest of men; was put to death by the Devil, and subsequently resurrected and ascended. He was crowned with glory and honor *as a man*. The Devil was made inoperative, defeated by his own schemes and weapons, while the MAN he killed became the One at the pinnacle — the position that Satan desired. This is absolute "poetic justice"!

Man – A Vessel to Ultimately Contain and Become One with God

> Does not the potter have power over the clay, from the same lump to make one vessel for honor and another for dishonor? What if God, wanting to show His wrath and to make His power known, endured with much longsuffering the vessels of wrath prepared for destruction, and that He might make known the riches of His glory on the vessels of mercy, which He had prepared beforehand for glory, even us whom He called, not of the Jews only, but also of the Gentiles?
>
> – Romans 9:21–24

A beautiful image throughout Scripture is God as the master potter, and His people as clay. For example, in the prophetic Scriptures Isaiah declared, *"You are our Father; We are the clay, and You our potter; And all we are the work of Your hand"* (Isaiah 64:8). Paul draws from this potter–clay imagery in Romans 9:20–24. God created man to be a vessel, to contain the *"riches of His glory"* (Rom. 9:23). "Glory" is the very expression of who God is. When a "clay vessel" contains the riches of His glory, the vessel itself will also *express* God's glory. What a waste if a vessel does not contain what it was made to contain! What mercy! Believers have received the riches of God's glory in Christ Jesus. God is still enduring and waiting for more vessels to be filled with His riches. These riches can't be earned; no one deserves them. Believers only need to be open to hear, receive, and be filled with His riches.

> For we do not preach ourselves, but Christ Jesus the Lord, and ourselves your bondservants for Jesus' sake. For it is the God who commanded light to shine out of darkness, who has shone in our hearts to give the light of the knowledge of the glory of God in the face of Jesus Christ. But we have this treasure in earthen vessels, that the excellence of the power may be of God and not of us. We are hard-pressed on every side, yet not crushed; we are perplexed, but not in despair.
>
> – 2 Corinthians 4:5–7

As believers hear the good news of Jesus Christ, God's light shines into their darkened hearts — they receive light from the knowledge of

Jesus Christ. At that very moment, Jesus Christ Himself becomes the treasure indwelling these earthen "vessels." Without this treasure, earthen vessels are almost worthless. One day they will become dirt again. The highest treasure in the universe cannot be bought or earned; for He only can come inside and make these earthen vessels glorious. Possessing this treasure provides an unlimited supply of God's energy and power within the believer. When believers are hard-pressed, or perplexed by challenges, they can draw from this power to triumphantly persist. Not only so, but during their own problems, they can still provide love, support, and eternal life to those around them because they are able to share these riches within them to others.

This Human Vessel, or "Container" Has Three Parts – Body, Soul and Spirit

- Body – To contact and interact with the physical world
- Soul – Composed of the mind, emotions and will, to relate with the psychological world
- Spirit – To fellowship with and relate to God

> And the LORD God formed man of the dust of the ground, and breathed into his nostrils the breath of life; and man became a living soul.
> – Genesis 2:7, KJV

> And the very God of peace sanctify you wholly; and I pray God your whole spirit and soul and body be preserved blameless unto the coming of our Lord Jesus Christ.
> – 1 Thessalonians 5:23

The whole, human person consists of three distinct parts: body, and soul, and spirit. The body is composed of elements made from the earth. The physical body can relate to the physical world – the body is a vessel which needs to consume material food in order to live. Food ingested provides energy and becomes the very constituent or fabric of the human body.

Man, then, became a living soul. The word *soul* in Greek is *psyche*, which is the origin for the English word "*psyc*hology." Knowledge, consideration, love and hate, purpose, and the need for accomplishment – these items are present in the psychological world. The human soul hungers after these things. Therefore, for the soul to "eat" it desires to ingest such things as knowledge and various causes in the world. What was once outside a person becomes part of that person's soul, their personality. Whether knowledge of football or engineering, environmental sciences or social causes, once ingested, this external knowledge will energize and bond with the person's soul. As a result, it becomes hard to distinguish whether the person's thoughts, loves, and purposes reflect who they really are, or whether he or she is emulating someone or something else having an influence upon their soul.

The essence which animates the soul is from the breath of God. The original word for "breathe" and "breath" is also translated "spirit" (from the Greek word *pneuma* from whence we derive the word *pneumatic* or that which is powered by air). Therefore, it was the very breath of God that formed the spirit within man to animate man. Thus, the spirit of man was derived from the breath (or Spirit) of God. Although man did not actually receive the Spirit of God into himself at creation, the spirit of man, in man, was attuned to and akin to God's Spirit — man had the "capacity" to perceive the "things of God's Spirit." Such a potential — a relationship, a receiving, or a union — could be made with God through man's spirit. Man's spirit was formed at creation as a vessel to have a relationship and the capacity to contain the very Life and nature of God!

Only man has this potential to be in fellowship with the Spirit of the Living God — animals and plants, although they have mental capabilities or "built-in" patterns of the soul with feelings, etc., they are NOT made in God's image with the capacity for FELLOWSHIP with God. We carefully note the following:

> We know that the whole creation has been groaning together in the pains of childbirth until the present time. Not only that, but we ourselves, who have the first fruits of the Spirit, groan inwardly as we wait eagerly for our adoption as sons, the redemption of our bodies . . .."
>
> — Romans 8:22-23
> Berean Study Bible

The universe is groaning and travailing until "*Christ be formed in you!*" (Gal. 4:19). Indeed, all "others" may groan and travail — but they cannot be in fellowship with the living God!

The human spirit is the innermost hunger, even when men or women are well fed both physically and psychologically, and though they may continue learning, accomplishing goals and experiencing loving relationships, there will remain a sense of emptiness, a "void." This is the hunger for a connection with God. Not understanding this yearning, men and women are driven to abusive behaviors or insatiable cravings to fill the void that can only be filled by God Himself.

Man Fell by Eating the Wrong Tree and Became Joined with Satan.

Man chose to eat the tree of the knowledge of good and evil and was therefore rejected from the Tree of Life.

> Then the serpent said to the woman, "You will not surely die. For God knows that in the day you eat of it your eyes will be opened, and you will be like God, knowing good and evil." So when the woman saw that the tree was good for food, that it was pleasant to the eyes, and a tree desirable to make one wise, she took of its fruit and ate. She also gave to her husband with her, and he ate. Then the eyes of both of them were opened, and they knew that they were naked; and they sewed fig leaves together and made themselves coverings.
>
> – Genesis 3:3–7

Satan raised doubt within man — God was withholding something good from him. Satan tempted man, deceiving him to believe if he ate of the tree of the knowledge of good and evil, "[he would] *be like God knowing good and evil*" (Gen. 3:4) . . . surely then, man thought, he would choose the "good over the evil" because he would know the difference. Alas! His disobedience utterly "disabled" him from doing that which was "good" — thus, as Paul states:

> I know that nothing good lives in me, that is, in my flesh; for I have the desire to do what is good, but I cannot carry it out.

> For I do not do the good I want to do, instead, I keep on doing the
> evil I do not want to do.
>
> ~ Romans 7:18-19
> Berean Study Bible

The truth is, God *did* want man to be like Him, but not in that way! God wanted man to depend on Him for life. He wanted man to be like Him, not just in image and likeness, but also with His life and nature. Satan wanted to be like God but *without* God and *independent* from God. He wanted to replace God. Satan's deceptive goal was to make man like himself: like God, but *without* God.

Satan wanted man to do this without eating the Tree of Life — without depending on God by partaking of Him — ingesting Him as the Tree of Life. Man fell into this temptation and ate of the tree of the knowledge of good and evil.

This tree, encompassing such positive words as "knowledge" and "good," is a deceptive cloak resulting in death because of its satanic nature. By ingesting this tree, what constituted Satan (such as sin and death) became man's constitution.

> Then the LORD God said, "Behold, the man has become like one of Us, to know good and evil. And now, lest he put out his hand and take also of the tree of life, and eat, and live forever."
>
> So He drove out the man; and He placed cherubim at the east of the garden of Eden, and a flaming sword which turned every way, to guard the way to the tree of life.
>
> ~ Genesis 3:22, 24

Though man's life and nature became corrupted with sin and death, God could not allow man to continue in such an infected state forever; therefore, God kept man away from the Tree of Life. Man was no longer able to partake of God in this fallen corrupted state. Man was driven away and guarded from the Tree of Life.

Sin Entered One Man, Causing Death to All Men

Therefore, just as **through one man** [Adam] sin entered the world, and death through sin, and thus death spread to all men, because all sinned —

For if by the **one man's offense death** reigned through the one…

For as by **one man's disobedience** many were made sinners.
– Romans 5:12, 17a, 19

For **as in Adam** all die.
– 1 Corinthians 15:22

When Adam ate of the tree of the knowledge of good and evil, what he ingested was sin and death; the poison fruit of satanic life and nature entered into man. It was like the DNA of man became contaminated and corrupted. Subsequently, sin and death passed on from one generation of men to another.

What is sin? The original Greek word for "sin" is *hamartia*, which literally means, "missing the mark." The "mark" was the Tree of Life — God desired to be life to man. By missing this mark man partook of the tree of death, which includes sin. Satan set up a false dichotomy: good and evil.

Satan enticed man to focus on good and evil. Whether man does good or evil, he nonetheless bounces back and forth within the tree of death, totally missing the real mark, which is life. The real choice is not between good or evil, but between life and death.

The result of man's disobedience brought death — he chose the wrong tree, and thus, sin entered into the human race . . .

Therefore, just as sin entered the world through one man, and death through sin, so also death was passed on to all men, because all sinned and have come short of the glory of God.
Rom. 5:12 – Berean Study Bible

Man Became One with God's Enemy, Possessing His Life, Nature and Expression

You are of your father the devil, and the desires of your father you want to do. He was a murderer from the beginning, and does not stand in the truth, because there is no truth in him. When he speaks a lie, he speaks from his own resources, for he is a liar and the father of it.

— John 8:44

Serpents, brood of vipers! How can you escape the condemnation of hell?

— Matthew 23:33

In this the children of God and the children of the devil are manifest: Whoever does not practice righteousness is not of God, nor is he who does not love his brother.

— 1 John 3:10

In both John 8:44 and Matthew 23:33, the Lord Jesus condemns fallen people when speaking particularly to the Pharisees (the religious people of Jesus' time). He declares their father to be the Devil. In Matthew 23:33, Jesus called the Pharisees "vipers," alluding back to Satan, the chief serpent. Satan was the first murderer, and deception is his nature.

In 1 John 3:10, the apostle notes there are only two groups of people: the children of God (those with God's life and nature), and the children of the Devil (those with Satan's life and nature). Today men express this fallen nature in many ways: selfishness, anger, violence and covetousness. This is the sin nature in humankind today. Parents all over the world consistently teach their young children to be honest, to share, and not to be selfish. Nevertheless, no matter how much parents try, children growing up all over the world get angry, become deceptive, and are selfish. This is the sin in humankind developing from within them as they grow and mature. When sin is expressed by hurting others or oneself, those *actions* are recognized and called "sins" (Rom. 4:7).

Man's Entire Condition Became Hopeless

> . . . in which you once walked according to the course of this world, according to the prince of the power of the air, the spirit who now works in the sons of disobedience, among whom also we all once conducted ourselves in the lusts of our flesh, fulfilling the desires of the flesh and of the mind, and were by nature children of wrath, just as the others.
>
> . . . that at that time you were without Christ, being aliens from the commonwealth of Israel and strangers from the covenants of promise, having no hope and without God in the world.
>
> – Ephesians 2:2–3, 12

This portion of Scripture refers to believers before having faith in Christ. Prior to belief, those in Christ were a real mess, completely under satanic influence. Their nature had degenerated into one born under God's judgment; they were people truly without hope. Their destiny was (and continues to be today) under God's wrath and judgment.

Man's Spirit Is Deadened and Has No Contact with God

> Jesus said to him, "Let the dead bury their own dead, but you go and preach the kingdom of God."
>
> – Luke 9:60

> And you He made alive, who were dead in trespasses and sins... even when we were dead in trespasses, made us alive together with Christ (by grace you have been saved).
>
> – Ephesians 2:1, 5

"The dead" in Luke 9:60 obviously did not refer to those who were physically or psychologically dead. Thus, if people were not dead in body and soul, the only thing Luke could have been referring to was to man's spirit. As a result of the fall, the spirit of man became dead. In God's eyes, fallen man was *already* dead and one with His enemy: death.

Faith in Christ makes believers' spirits alive. This concept is referenced in other places in Scripture, in phrases such as "the new birth," "being born again," or "being regenerated." This new birth (enlivening) happens in the spirit of man with the receiving and entering of the Spirit of the Living God.

Man's Soul Is Vain and Darkened, Driven by a Perverted Love

> This I say, therefore, and testify in the Lord, that you should
> no longer walk as the rest of the Gentiles walk, in the futility
> [vanity] of their mind, having their understanding darkened,
> being alienated from the life of God, because of the ignorance
> that is in them, because of the blindness of their heart.
>
> *— Ephesians 4:17–18*

> For men will be lovers of themselves, lovers of money, boasters,
> proud, blasphemers, disobedient to parents, unthankful,
> unholy, unloving, unforgiving, slanderers, without self-control,
> brutal, despisers of good, traitors, headstrong, haughty, lovers of
> pleasure rather than lovers of God.
>
> *— 2 Timothy 3:2–4*

Man's soul, due to the fall, was damaged. People's minds — the leading
part of their psychological being — became darkened and full of vanity.
Though men can be very intelligent, however, in relation to God, they
are ignorant and blind. Additionally, man's fallen self-centered "love" is
focused on his ego. Even when doing something good, man's love is tainted
with a selfish motive. He (or she) is ready to cause harm to others for self-
gratification. Man's entire being is alienated and separated from God.

Man's Body Is the Corrupted Flesh Where Sin Dwells

> But now, it is no longer I who do it, but sin that dwells in me. For
> I know that in me (that is, in my flesh) nothing good dwells; for
> to will is present with me, but how to perform what is good I do
> not find. For the good that I will to do, I do not do; but the evil I
> will not to do, that I practice.

> I find then a law, that evil is present with me, the one who wills to
> do good. For I delight in the law of God according to the inward
> man. But I see another law in my members, warring against the
> law of my mind, and bringing me into captivity to the law of sin
> which is in my members. O wretched man that I am! Who will
> deliver me from this body of death?
>
> *— Romans 7:17–19, 21–24*

Man's body, once created pure and good, became the dwelling place of sin and death. In God's eyes the body became flesh — a derogatory word for the body — where nothing good dwells. It is like the original God-created DNA became corrupted with sin and death through the ingestion of the tree of death. The human body became a body of sin and death (flesh) forcing man to practice evil. But, since God created man good, there is still good in the soul of man and even a longing to agree with God's laws. However, this desire is simply not strong enough to overcome the enslavement of sin, no matter how much good is in a person's mind. Man's "good" is no match for the power of sin and death, the nature of God's enemy.

God Regretted Making Man, Condemning Man under His Righteous Judgment

> The LORD saw that the wickedness of man was great in the earth, and that every intention of the thoughts of his heart was only evil continually. And the LORD regretted that he had made man on the earth, and it grieved him to his heart.
> — Genesis 6:5–6, ESV

> ...being filled with all unrighteousness, sexual immorality, wickedness, covetousness, maliciousness; full of envy, murder, strife, deceit, evil-mindedness; they are whisperers, backbiters, haters of God, violent, proud, boasters, inventors of evil things, disobedient to parents, undiscerning, untrustworthy, unloving, unforgiving, unmerciful; who, knowing the righteous judgment of God, that those who practice such things are deserving of death, not only do the same but also approve of those who practice them.
> — Romans 1:29–32

> But in accordance with your hardness and your impenitent heart you are treasuring up for yourself wrath in the day of wrath and revelation of the righteous judgment of God.
> — Romans 2:5

It seemed the risky venture of creating man was a failure. How great must God's grief have been, seeing man — the desire of His heart — now filled with His enemy's rebellious spirit! What was in man was continually evil. God's heartache and disappointment were intense enough for Him to regret creating man. There is no record of God regretting the creation of Satan; yet, He regretted creating man. Why is this?

The stronger and deeper the love is, the more devastating the disappointment of losing the object of this love. It seemed all was lost. The man God desired for His own pleasure and purpose was completely ruined and corrupted. Man, destined to be the sons of the Living God, became children of evil; instead of defeating His enemy, man joined himself with Satan and **became** God's enemy.

God had no choice according to His righteousness but to judge and condemn man, His heart's love and desire. It seems the entire creation was witness to what appeared to be Satan's triumph over God. It appeared Satan was wiser than God — was he qualified to replace God?

Calling on the Name of the Lord!

> And Adam knew his wife again, and she bore a son and named him Seth, "For God has appointed another seed for me instead of Abel, whom Cain killed." And as for Seth, to him also a son was born; and he named him Enosh. Then men began to call on the name of the LORD.
>
> – Genesis 4:25–26

Adam and Eve bore two sons: Cain and Abel. Cain murdered Abel out of jealousy and anger. Adam then **begat** another son, Seth. Seth had a son and called his name Enosh. The name "Enosh" means mortal, a word associated with sickness and disease. Seth realized early on in this second-generation mankind's condition was sick, frail, weak and mortal. It is at this point, when men realized their fallen condition, that Scripture says men began to call upon the name of the Lord (Gen. 4:26). From then on until today, calling on the name of the Lord brings salvation to men.

> For there is no difference of Jew and Greek; for the same Lord of all is rich toward [Gk. into] all that call upon him. For everyone whosoever, who shall call on the name of the Lord, shall be saved.
>
> – Romans 10:12–13, DBY

When any person realizes he or she is fallen and in a poor, sick and dying state, this person has the choice to call upon the name of the Lord Jesus. In Romans 10:12–13, the word for "call" in the original Greek is the word *epikaleō*, which means, "an audible calling out to invoke the Lord Jesus."

Human beings need to come to such desperation wherein they audibly call on the name of the Lord Jesus. He answers with the richness of His life, peace, joy, and so much more. Calling out to the Lord Jesus brings the Lord's riches into a person and saves the person from their fallen condition. His riches and salvation are for whoever calls, without prejudice.

6

GOD'S FULL AND WONDERFUL SALVATION

The unique way of salvation is by grace through the faith of Jesus Christ. God's salvation is not so simple. It must conform to His righteous requirements and can only be accomplished by His life. This chapter will explore the key terms relating to God's complete salvation: grace, faith, redemption, justification, reconciliation, sanctification (both positional and dispositional), regeneration, feeding, renewing, transformation, conformation and glorification. The result of this wonderful salvation is mankind (male and female) able to express God as His sons in fullness.

God's Full Salvation for Man Is by Grace Through Faith

> . . . even when we were dead in trespasses, made us alive together with Christ (by grace you have been saved)…For by grace you have been saved through faith, and that not of yourselves; it is the gift of God, not of works, lest anyone should boast.
> – Ephesians 2:5, 8–9

These verses are clear and definitively state humankind's salvation is purely by grace through faith. In fact, just to make sure there is no misunderstanding, Paul included a contrast to illustrate it is not possible to work for salvation: how can man, being dead in sins, work? If there were any effort on man's part at all, it would have opened the door for boasting.

This chapter will expand upon how rich, high, and complete God's salvation is. The popular concept of salvation is understood to be going to heaven, rather than hell, after death. This kind of simplistic concept is not only common among Christians but in pagan religions as well. It's time to appreciate God's full salvation and bring fallen man from the absolute hopelessness of death (see Chapter 5) to something glorious, far beyond imagination.

Faith which brings a believer into saving grace is a gift from God. There is nothing man can do to receive this gift, other than to be open and listen to the good news of Jesus Christ whereby man receives faith.

Faith Enables Men to Receive the Invisible Things of Christ

Faith is a gift from God, which enables men to substantiate and receive the invisible things concerning Jesus Christ, and what He has accomplished.

> Simon Peter, bondman and apostle of Jesus Christ, to them that have received like precious faith with us through the righteousness of our God and Savior Jesus Christ.
>
> – 2 Peter 1:1, DBY

> Looking unto Jesus, the author and finisher of our faith.
>
> – Hebrews 12:2

These verses reveal faith was something believers received. It did not originate from them; rather, the author – or originator – was the Lord Jesus Christ. This precious faith believers received was the same faith which has been given to and received by believers throughout time, everywhere. No believer ever "worked-up" their own faith; this simply was not possible. Man only needs to receive and thank the Lord for this wonderful gift.

> Now faith is [the] substantiating of things hoped for, [the] conviction of things not seen.
>
> – Hebrews 11:1, DBY

Most people think faith is something they can manipulate for their best interests. If they want something to come to pass, faith can make it happen. The harder one believes, the more likely the event can occur. They believe it is the power of faith which causes something a person wants to materialize.

However, this is contrary to the definition of faith according to the Bible. Real faith enables the receiver of this gift to realize or substantiate what is already there. Faith is the proof or conviction of things not seen. In other words, the items are already there, but it is faith which enables a person to realize it. Faith proves to people it already exists.

For example, colors surround everyone. However, if a person is blind (or even colorblind), they will not be able to realize those colors. The same can be said of sound. If a person is deaf, music is simply not real to them. Likewise, God in Jesus Christ is very real: His death, resurrection and Lordship of all is true. But to the faithless, these items of truth are mere fairytales. Once faith is received, however, everything concerning Jesus Christ is substantiated, proving His reality.

Grace Is the Believer's Enjoyment of the Lord Jesus

As believers rejoice in Jesus, He works in them to fulfill His good pleasure. Grace came into existence with the Lord Jesus, and He affords real joy, pleasure, sweetness, rejoicing, and enjoyment to His children:

> For from his fullness we have all received, grace upon grace. For the law was given through Moses; grace and truth came [into being] through Jesus Christ.
>
> – John 1:16–17, ESV

The concept of grace in the Christian Scriptures is profound. It is much more than just a favor given or being kind to a person – being "gracious." The common definition among believers of "unmerited favor" does not truly unveil the meaning of this word. The grace of Jesus Christ did not come into existence until Jesus was manifested in the flesh. Jesus brought grace as defined in the New Testament. The Greek word for "grace" is *charis*, which means, "That which affords joy, rejoicing, pleasure, and enjoyment" (Thayer's).

This kind of rejoicing and enjoyment simply did not exist before the coming of Jesus Christ. When a person receives Him, Jesus affords wave upon wave of joy and enjoyment, hence "grace upon grace." Grace is always fresh, a constant surging of enjoyment toward those who believe. Without Jesus, humankind simply is not afforded real joy, rejoicing, pleasure, and enjoyment.

While the law given by Moses was demanding, requiring, and condemning – grace came into being through Jesus Christ. While believers cannot fulfill the law and are under the curse of the law, Jesus Christ came to be their joy, rejoicing, and enjoyment. What a contrast! Why wouldn't everyone receive such a wonderful Jesus who originated grace for all men?

While the Law of Moses demands; the grace of our Lord Jesus Christ supplies us His very Life to accomplish that demand!

> Let us therefore come boldly to the throne of grace, that we may obtain mercy and find grace to help in time of need.
> – Hebrews 4:16

The throne of God to which believers come is not the throne of a judge, a commander, or even a king. Rather, the One on the throne, the God-man Jesus Christ, *is* grace supplying believers joy, rejoicing, and enjoyment. Interestingly, upon approaching this throne there is only one thing to find: *grace*. And that is exactly what is required for all the help every person needs.

What do all men pursue? In the end, it is just happiness. People pursue things like money, health, fame, relationships, drugs, and sex because they desire enjoyment. Since happiness is the result of what men pursue, grace is exactly what they need no matter what situations they may find themselves. A person's finances or health might be deteriorating; yet, in Christ they find themselves happy, full of joy, rejoicing, and finding enjoyment. If they are truly joyful, they have achieved their pursuit and are satisfied. This is the reason believers in the present experience of grace can stand firm, no matter what challenging situations arise. This is the Lord Jesus–this is grace in action.

> The Lord Jesus Christ be with your spirit. Grace be with you. Amen.
> – 2 Timothy 4:22

When a person receives *the faith* of Jesus Christ, Jesus — as the Spirit — joins to the believer's spirit. He resides in the core (or the seat) of their being, their spirit. Since He is with them, grace is also with them. No Jesus, no grace; with Jesus, with grace.

If grace is simply Jesus, then why use the word grace? Why say, "Saved by grace" and not just, "Saved by Jesus"?

The reason has to do with the fact that grace speaks of Jesus being the believer's present joy and reason for rejoicing and enjoyment. He is experiential, and His experiential salvation depends on the experiences of Christ as the believer's joy and enjoyment. The believer may be "saved," but if he or she is depressed, anxious or feels condemned, in that person's experience, salvation is far away. But as soon as they come to the throne of grace and find Jesus, He affords the believer joy, rejoicing and enjoyment. They are then practically and experientially saved from all things which trouble.

Jesus Works in Believers to Both Save and Fulfill God's Will

> . . . who has saved us and called us with a holy calling, not according to our works, but according to His own purpose and grace which was given to us in Christ Jesus before time began.
> – 2 Timothy 1:9

Here again, Paul clearly states people are saved not according to their works, effort, or labor, but according to the Lord's purpose and grace. The joy, enjoyment, and pleasure supplied by the Lord Jesus to believers doesn't stop there. While they are enjoying Him, something else is transpiring: *Salvation.*

Salvation, on one hand, is once for all. On the other hand, it is a life-long process. Unlike mere joy and rejoicing as an end, grace is much more. The more believers enjoy Jesus, the more they are saved according to His purpose. The result of grace is not just salvation benefitting the believer but enables them to become a people who bring God pleasure, according to His eternal purpose.

> . . . through whom also we have access by faith into this grace in which we stand, and rejoice in hope of the glory of God. . . . For if by the one man's offense death reigned through the one, much more those who receive abundance of grace and of the gift of righteousness will reign in life through the One, Jesus Christ. . . . so that as sin reigned in death, even so grace might reign through righteousness to eternal life through Jesus Christ our Lord.
> – Romans 5:2, 17, 21

Faith is the only way to realize and take hold of grace – the source that will always afford joy, rejoicing, and enjoyment. Because of faith, a believer simply cannot be removed from grace. It is in this grace believers remain and stand.

Faith makes a believer righteous before God. It is the abundance of grace causing them to *reign* in life. Complete salvation in the Lord's eternal life is through the joy, rejoicing, and enjoyment of the Lord Jesus Christ.

Therefore, enjoy Him!

> ...a thorn in the flesh was given to me, a messenger of Satan to torment me so that I would not exalt myself. Concerning this, I pleaded with the Lord three times that it would leave me. But he said to me, "My grace is sufficient for you, for my power is perfected in weakness." Therefore, I will most gladly boast all the more about my weaknesses, so that Christ's power may reside in me. So I take pleasure in weaknesses, insults, hardships, persecutions, and in difficulties, for the sake of Christ. For when I am weak, then I am strong.
> – 2 Corinthians 12:7-10 CSB

> And Nehemiah continued, "Go and celebrate with a feast of rich foods and sweet drinks, and share gifts of food with people who have nothing prepared. This is a sacred day before our Lord. Don't be dejected and sad, for **the joy of the LORD** is your strength!"
> – Nehemiah 8:10, NLT

Satan sent a messenger to trouble Paul in his flesh. He didn't say specifically what his trouble was. He called it a weakness. Some say this thorn is persecutions or hardships since it is hard for them to imagine an apostle like Paul would have weaknesses. However, being persecuted is not a weakness. In fact, he delineated his "weaknesses" from persecutions, insults, calamities, hardships and needs. This means according to Paul his weaknesses were separate and different than those other named items.

This thorn from Satan must have been tantamount to some form of shame — perhaps exposing what Paul considered a major deficiency in his walk with the Lord, since he desperately wanted to have it removed. It was there to prevent him from boasting. In any case, it was directly from Satan and in his flesh. Paul was extremely troubled. He had healed many people physically; and he had delivered people from demonic possession. Notwithstanding, he is now besieged and unable to be healed or delivered after praying earnestly and repeatedly. Some Christians may suggest: If you have faith, you can overcome everything. Paul certainly must have been one of the giants of faith; still, here he was unable to rid His "thorn in the flesh" brought by Satan.

Paul was suffering in his current circumstance. He prayed to the Lord to change it. The Lord's answer was, *"My grace is sufficient for you."* The Lord did not take away his thorn, didn't heal or deliver him; rather, He asked Paul to take His grace in it. The Lord afforded enjoyment and pleasure to Paul in the midst of his struggle with his weaknesses. This should have been sufficient salvation for him. While Paul enjoyed God, the Lord's strength was manifested in his weaknesses. In the same way, when we believers just enjoy Him, He can then work to save, to work out our salvation.

Often Christians are focused on a salvation that gives them deliverance from all personal troubles related to their health or the ability to overcome sin. This one-dimensional emphasis has caused unnecessary doubt and stumbling. One may start to think: "Shouldn't I be delivered from any attack from Satan. After all there must be something deficient with me spiritually if I can't cast out this Satanic thorn." It may also lead to condemning others: "This trouble and failure in his life means he has a problem with God; he must not be a good Christian."

However, God left Paul with this thorn and told him to keep taking grace. Grace is still available, maybe even more so when a person recognizes he has a problem. Although he is weak or has failed in some way, grace is available. Grace is available and brings in the joy of the Lord. The Lord's desire is for us to seek His grace even during being distressed by Satan. No matter the thorn and no matter the weakness, the Lord's grace is here to be our enjoyment and pleasure.

During Nehemiah's time, the people of God were dejected due to their hard situations. Nehemiah's charge was for them to eat and drink and share their enjoyment with others. This joy in the Old Testament is grace for us today. The joy of the Lord activates His strength to save. One can say outside of enjoying and being joyful in the Lord, salvation in our daily experience does not work. To be saved daily, the believer must enjoy Him daily.

This verse in Nehemiah also affirms fellowshipping with believers is where grace is found. There was joy when those who returned to Jerusalem shared their food and drink in celebration with those who were lacking.

Many times, those under attack of the enemy experience weakness and failure — thus, they are inclined to stay by themselves ("I just need to be alone with the Lord"). They isolate themselves from fellowship. However, the grace of the Lord is in the fellowship of His Body. Go and share your experience of Christ and receive Christ from others. The Lord has prepared a feast for His followers in the presence of the enemy! (Psalm 23:5).

Redemption Based on Righteousness with the Blood of Jesus

> Christ has redeemed us from the curse of the law, having become a curse for us (for it is written, "Cursed is everyone who hangs on a tree").
>
> – Galatians 3:13

The words "*redeem*" or "*redemption*" have two meanings: to pay a price to purchase something, and to pay a ransom in order to secure a release. Man broke God's command by eating the forbidden fruit in the Garden of Eden; he then continued to break God's laws as embodied in the Ten Commandments from Sinai to the present. This unleashed God's judgment and brought the curse according to the Law. God had to judge man according to the righteous requirements of His law. If after man broke God's law he was not judged according to the law, then God would have also broken His own law by *unrighteously* forgiving man. Man's curse is fully based on the law, and redemption is therefore a legal or judicial matter. The payment is based on the law.

Consider the following illustration: Say a man breaks the law by stealing from another person, and he is caught. The thief is then brought before a judge to determine guilt and punishment according to the law. If the thief happens to be the judge's son, that judge cannot arbitrarily forgive his son just because he loves him; if he did, he would be an unrighteous judge and the victim might not receive due restitution. The judge must sentence his son according to the extent of the law; that includes full payment back to his victim. This is the "curse of the law" for his crime. After the sentencing, if the son spent all his money and could not pay back his victim, he would continue under the "curse" until the debt is paid. The judge then, as his father and out of love, could pay the debt for his son. When the debt was fully paid, his son would no longer bear the curse of his crime.

This is what is meant by redemption based on righteousness. The demand for the price of death must be paid according to righteousness. Yet, it was God's love to send His only begotten Son to pay the price of death on man's behalf.

> Not with the blood of goats and calves, but with His own blood He entered the Most Holy Place once for all, having obtained eternal redemption.
>
> – Hebrews 9:12

The judgment for breaking God's law is the curse of death. God's law would not have been satisfied unless man died. Man's sin was a capital offense. What an unbearable price and punishment! Goats and calves cannot die in man's stead to pay off God's judgment. That is like a thief owing someone a billion dollars and trying to pay the debt off with an apple. Since the sentence was death for man, a *sinless* man, who wasn't under the curse of death, had to die. Jesus Christ paid that price and the ransom to release man from this curse of death. Because Jesus is both God and man, He legally could obtain eternal redemption. As a man, He has human blood to die for man's sins; as God, His blood has eternal value and is thus able to pay for the sins of all of mankind, throughout time and space. Only a pure and spotless offering could suffice God's holiness — and that was HIMSELF!

> . . . knowing that you were not redeemed with corruptible things, like silver or gold, from your aimless conduct received by tradition from your fathers, but with the precious blood of Christ, as of a lamb without blemish and without spot.
>
> – 1 Peter 1:18

All fallen men are living in a way that is vain or aimless, whether their manner of life is worldly (living for the riches and glories of this world), fleshly (desiring shameful things of their passion) or even religious (practicing religious traditions from their forefathers). These lifestyles are worthless and empty — as king Solomon said: *"Chasing after the wind"* (Ecclesiastes 1:14).

Money, fame, possessions or religious rituals can never release man from vanity and emptiness; only the blood of Jesus Christ can do this. When a person receives and believes *into* Jesus Christ, his life becomes full and purposeful.

Forgiveness and Cleansing of Sins

> . . . in whom we have redemption through His blood, the forgiveness of sins.
>
> – Colossians 1:14

> ...and without the shedding of blood there is no forgiveness of sins.
>
> – Hebrews 9:22, ESV

Since Christ paid the highest price by His death, it satisfied man's debt under God's judgment; therefore, sins are forgiven. According to the illustration above, when judgment required paying back stolen money (plus any penalty according to the law) was paid, the thief was no longer guilty. Rather, he received a full pardon.

Man's debt to God according to His judgment was death; therefore, Jesus Christ needed to die in order to pay off man's debt under God's judicial sentence. Now, the believer's past, present, and future sins are forgiven through simple faith in Jesus Christ.

> ...then He [God] adds, "Their sins and their lawless deeds I will remember no more."
>
> – Hebrews 10:17

God's memory is wonderful. When man sins, God cannot forget until judgment is paid in full. However, once it is paid, He cannot remember sin at all. To Him, it is like the believer has never sinned — we all have passed "from death into Life" ("*Truly, truly, I say to you, he who hears My word, and believes Him who sent Me, has eternal life, and does not come into judgment, but has passed out of death into life*" (John 5:24--Jubilee Bible 2000). After coming to faith in Christ, believers also need a memory like God's, in order to forget about their sins. Believers can stand with confidence and boldness before God, because in God's eyes, believers in Christ have never been sinners.

> But if we walk in the light as He is in the light, we have fellowship with one another, and the blood of Jesus Christ His Son cleanses

us from all sin . . . If we confess our sins, He is faithful and just
to forgive us our sins and to cleanse us from all unrighteousness.
                                                    – 1 John 1:7, 9

The blood of Jesus can cleanse all people from even the *stain* of sin. If a
person spilled grape juice on another person's shirt, they could genuinely
be forgiven for the accident. However, there might still be a stain left from
the juice as a reminder of the spill. What if the stain of sin remained to
remind believers of their past sins? That would be terrible! The blood of
Jesus is so efficacious even the stain of sin is gone. There is no reminder of
past, present or future failures. Believers simply receive His cleansing by
confessing sin (admitting sin by repeating back to God what He is revealing
to their conscience) for both forgiveness and cleansing. What a release to be
freed from bearing the burden of a guilty conscience.

Justification – Righteous Before God
God approves believers based on His standard of righteousness. This is
called "justification."

> . . . being justified freely by His grace through the redemption
> that is in Christ Jesus, whom God set forth as a propitiation by
> His blood, through faith . . . to demonstrate at the present time
> His righteousness, that He might be just and the justifier of the
> one who has faith in Jesus.
>
>   – Romans 3:24–26

To "justify" someone means to declare (or approve of) him or her as
righteous, or right. In this case, according to Romans 3:24–26, the "approver"
or the "declarer" is God. In ancient biblical times, "propitiation" was the
action of propitiating or appeasing a god, spirit, or person. In the case of
Christ, the blood of Jesus appeased God's demand for judgment. Justification
can happen for a believer because the blood of Jesus acts as propitiation.
It has appeased God's demand for judgment to be rendered – and that
judgment is the sentence of death. Since man's standard of righteousness is
often quite low, it is easy for men and women to consider one another to be
"righteous." But God's standard of righteousness is higher than the heavens.
Therefore, it is amazing God would declare man righteous through faith

in Christ! In God's evaluation, believers are as righteous as He is. In fact, their righteousness is based on and is a manifestation of His righteousness. Because He is righteous, He is *required* to justify His children and declare they are as righteous as He.

Say a judge fines a person $10,000 for a crime according to the law. After the entire amount of the fine is paid off including penalty and interest, if the judge comes back and asks for more money from the person, that judge would be considered unrighteous. Since the debt has been paid in full, the judge, according to righteousness, should then declare the person to be righteous; this one should owe nothing else. Jesus Christ has paid off mankind's debt of sin in full through His death; therefore, God, according to His righteous judgment, is required to justify all those having the faith of Jesus; otherwise, He would be unrighteous.

> ...knowing that a man is not justified by the works of the law but by faith in Jesus Christ, even we have believed in Christ Jesus, that we might be justified by faith in Christ and not by the works of the law; for by the works of the law no flesh shall be justified.
> – Galatians 2:16

This justification believers have received from God is not because of any effort to fulfill God's law. In fact, a person could try their utmost to follow God's laws and requirements, but they cannot be justified (forgiven, obtain salvation). So, give up trying and just accept and enjoy what Jesus Christ has done! Trying to please God through endless effort to fulfill His laws will only guarantee being kept *under* the curse of the law, since one can never fulfill all His requirements. The only way to immediately fulfill all of God's demands is through faith in Jesus Christ.

Reconciliation – Mutual Love and Respect

Once a person puts their faith in Christ, the requirement for sin's punishment is satisfied and they become reconciled to God.

> For if when we were enemies we were reconciled to God through the death of His Son, much more, having been reconciled, we shall be saved by His life. And not only that, but we also rejoice

in God through our Lord Jesus Christ, through whom we have now received the reconciliation.

– Romans 5:10–11

Fallen men were not just sinners – they became God's enemies. Due to the hostility between God and man, reconciliation was and still is needed. If a friend steals from another friend and gets caught, even if the person pays back everything, the likelihood is high that they will no longer be friends. Reconciliation is needed.

The death of Christ not only paid off man's debt to God, justifying those who believe before Him, but Jesus Christ also *reconciled* people to God. Those who believe are no longer enemies but can carry on an intimate relationship as if the offense never happened. No wonder believers rejoice! In Christ, there is mutual love and respect between God and man.

Sanctification – Made Holy

Not only are believers justified and reconciled to God, they are also "sanctified" (or made holy). This means those in Christ are separated out of humanity before God in their position.

> To the church [ekklesia] of God which is at Corinth, to those who are sanctified in Christ Jesus, called to be saints, with all who in every place call on the name of Jesus Christ our Lord, both theirs and ours.
>
> – 1 Corinthians 1:2

The moment a person believes and calls on the name of Jesus Christ the Lord, they are immediately sanctified and called "saints."

The words "sanctified" and "saints" are derived from the same Greek word *hagos*, which means "holy."

Holy means something separated for God. Since faith brings people into Christ Jesus, believers immediately become holy – not because of their condition or behavior, but simply because of their new position in Christ.

> Woe to you, blind guides, who say, 'Whoever swears by the temple, it is nothing; but whoever swears by the gold of the temple, he is obliged to perform it.' Fools and blind! For which is greater, the gold or the temple that sanctifies the gold? . . .

> Fools and blind! For which is greater, the gift or the altar that
> sanctifies the gift?
>
> — Matthew 23:16–17, 19

In the Old Testament, the gold or the animal to be offered to God, became holy simply by changing its location or position from outside the temple to its place within the temple, or from wandering in the field to being on the altar. Even though the nature or characteristics of the gold or the animal didn't change, once the position was changed, then it was made holy. What we are talking about here is "positional" in location.

This is the same with believers who are now holy in their *position* in Christ. Even though their character is very much the same as before they believed. The fact they have believed *into* Jesus Christ sanctifies them . . . and from henceforth they are called *saints*. What sets them apart, sanctifies them, is being "placed into Christ" Who is their very holiness — a "saint" is simply one "set apart" by their newly obtained salvation wrought in Christ.

The Organic Salvation by the Life of Christ

Jesus became the Life-giving Spirit indwelling and working in believers. This is what salvation is based on: the organic life of Christ.

> For if when we were enemies we were reconciled to God through
> the death of His Son, much more, having been reconciled, we
> shall be saved by His life.
>
> — Romans 5:10

This verse, Romans 5:10, lays out the believer's complete salvation in two parts: The first part is accomplished through His death, and the second is accomplished by His life.

Jesus' death for redemption fully accomplished forgiveness, cleansing, justification and reconciliation. This part is what is known as the "positional" or "judicial" side of salvation. However, there is a more wonderful side of His salvation that is *within* the believer; this is known as the "dispositional" or "organic" side of salvation.

Faith in Jesus Christ brings His very divine, eternal life into the believer's inner being. His life is now saving people organically.

Consider now, item by item, what this "*saved by His life*" means to the believer. This knowledge is wonderful because these daily experiences are full of real enjoyment.

Regeneration – The New Birth of Divine Life

When a person, through faith, believes into Jesus Christ, they receive the Spirit of God.

> But as many as received Him, to them He gave the right to become children of God, to those who believe in [Grk. **into**] His name: who were born, not of blood, nor of the will of the flesh, nor of the will of man, but of God.
>
> – John 1:12–13

The immediate inner transaction which happens when someone first comes to faith in Jesus Christ is a new birth (or being born anew, "*born from above*"). Many refer to this as being "born again" or regeneration. This new birth is of God. This is the birth which brings in His life and nature, giving believers the right or authority to become the children of God. There are no steps to climb to achieve this. All that is needed is for the person to receive Him, to believe *into* His name. A person's pet dog is a dog because it's born of a dog. It is impossible to be an offspring of anything other than from what animal or human originated that birth. Likewise, believers are sons of man because they are born of man, but at the same time they are children of God because they are born of God.

> Jesus answered, "Most assuredly, I say to you, unless one is born of water and the Spirit, he cannot enter the kingdom of God. That which is born of the flesh is flesh, and that which is born of the Spirit is spirit. Do not marvel that I said to you, 'You must be born again [Grk. anew].'"
>
> – John 3:5–7

The only way for a person to enter a kingdom is if that person has the life of that kingdom. For example, only plants are in the botanical kingdom; only animals can be in the animal kingdom. The only way to enter the human kingdom is to be born human. Following this line of thought, the only way to enter the kingdom of God is to be born of God — born of the Spirit of God.

"Water" in John 3:5 in context should refer to baptism, which was what John the Baptist did when he introduced Jesus Christ. The water of baptism means the end and burial of the old creation, making it possible for a person to arise as a new creation by being born of the Spirit. The first birth was of the flesh; therefore, man is flesh. The second birth is of the Spirit. When the Spirit of God enters and joins with man's spirit, the innermost part of a person's being — their spirit — then that man is born of the Spirit.

> Whoever believes that Jesus is the Christ is born of God, and everyone who loves Him who begot also loves him who is begotten of Him.
>
> — 1 John 5:1

What Does the New Birth Feel Like?

The only requirement to initiate this salvation wrought by the new birth is belief in Jesus as the Christ (viz., the Messiah or Deliverer), the eternal Son of God, and that He resurrected from the dead. How wonderfully simple!

How do people feel when they have this new birth? Experiences can vary from person to person. People may experience various levels of joy, peace, strength, and fulfillment. Sometimes this occurs immediately when they pray and call on His name in faith to receive the Lord Jesus. Or, this experience may come months later. In any event, sooner or later, it is inevitable the new birth will be a powerful life-changing experience. One clear indication new birth has occurred is the innate sense of love new believers have for all other believers of the Lord Jesus Christ, regardless of socio-economic differences, skin color, or ethnic diversity

Feeding – Food for Growth

As newborn babes, believers need continual feeding to grow into salvation.

> . . . newborn babes desire earnestly the pure mental milk of the word, that by it ye may grow up to salvation, if indeed ye have tasted that the Lord is good.
>
> — 1 Peter 2:2, DBY

Birth is simply the initiation of our new life in Christ. Every life at birth starts as a babe, and every babe needs to grow. This is the same for believers at their spiritual birth. Immediately, there is a deep desire for milk in order to grow. The salvation we receive is a *growing* salvation. The more believers grow, the more they are saved in their daily experience.

For example, even as a believer, a person may struggle with losing their temper. Or, they may experience anxiety or even bouts of depression. These are external signs believers need to grow out of these symptoms of death through their daily salvation experiences. As believers ingest the pure milk of the Word, this new life in them will grow and save them from their temper and anxiety. This is the "much more" saving in His life Paul speaks of in Romans 5:10. The Lord is so good when believers taste His Word and grow in this manner.

> . . . and not holding firmly to the Head, from whom all the body, being supplied and knit together through the joints and ligaments, grows with God's growth.
> — Colossians 2:19, HNV

Religious practices, outward laws, and various philosophies distracted the recipients of this letter sent to the Colossians; therefore, they were NOT holding firmly to Jesus Christ, the Head. Paul encouraged the Colossians to come back and hold fast to the Head from which the entire Body of Christ finds its source. As believers are supplied by the Head in the Body, they can grow with God's growth.

According to this verse, spiritual growth is the very increase of God in man. As believers experience more and more of God, they grow up more and more. A believer's growth is not measured by a change in outward behavior or increasing in mere biblical knowledge absent the knowledge of Jesus Christ; growth is measured from the increase of *God within the believer* (i.e., "God's growth").

Dispositional Sanctification

Dispositional sanctification is the process of being made holy. By partaking of God's holy and divine nature, a believer's entire being is being sanctified.

Now may the God of peace Himself sanctify you completely; and may your whole spirit, and soul, and body be preserved blameless at the coming of our Lord Jesus Christ.

– 1 Thessalonians 5:23

Paul's writing concerning sanctification – being made holy – is also inwardly directed. It starts from a believer's human spirit and spreads into his soul. This results in the ever-increasing God of peace growing in each believer day by day until the Second Coming of Christ. God Himself comes into a believer's spirit through the new birth, makes their spirit alive, and then spreads His holiness into that person's soul – eventually affecting his body through glorification! Their entire being is made holy. In the entire universe only God is holy; therefore, only by God growing and increasing in believers can they be completely sanctified.

. . . by which have been given to us exceedingly great and precious promises, that through these you may be partakers of the divine nature, having escaped the corruption that is in the world through lust.

– 2 Peter 1:4

How wonderful! Believers in Jesus Christ are partakers of the divine nature. The word "divine" literally refers to God. The divine nature is God's nature. As human beings with a human nature, believers have the capacity to partake of His divine nature. Believers are both human and divine in this sense.

The Greek word for *partake* is κοινωνός (transliterated as *koinōnos* - Strong's G#2844) and is the masculine noun form matching its feminine counterpart which we're all familiar with, *koinōnia* (Strong's G#2842) which, again, we all know is "fellowship." However, the masculine, as Strong's brings out, has an emphasis upon the person . . . whereas *koinōnia* emphasizes the "relational aspect of fellowship." In other words, *koinōnia* is between and/or among one another--relational; whereas, *koinōnos* stresses a person's intimate relationship/fellowship with God's divine nature. Regardless, this is the very "fellowship" within the Triune God into which the Son has brought us – the very fellowship He had/has with the Father *"before the foundation of the world"* (John 17:24; 1 John 1:3-7).

God's nature includes such items as unconditional love, perfect righteousness, unfathomable mercy, and genuine humility. As believers partake, these items also become the believer's true nature.

It is this divine nature that makes believers holy. The more they partake/participate in the divine nature, the more it affects their character . . . since a person's character expresses his or her nature. This partaking of the divine nature influences the person's character: *dispositional sanctification*. This means believers have escaped positionally into Christ through His death, so now they may partake in His divine life. By this partaking, they also escape the corruption of their fallen nature.

> Do you not know that the unrighteous will not inherit the kingdom of God? Do not be deceived. Neither fornicators, nor idolaters, nor adulterers, nor homosexuals, nor sodomites, nor thieves, nor covetous, nor drunkards, nor revilers, nor extortioners will inherit the kingdom of God. And such were some of you. But you were washed, but you were sanctified, but you were justified in the name of the Lord Jesus and by the Spirit of our God.
>
> ~ 1 Corinthians 6:9–11

All fallen people have a sinful nature and have committed at least one of these offenses. Some have habitually lived out their fallen nature – without restraint. Believers have been known to exhibit one or more of these characteristics. That is why it is so important one's nature or character is washed, sanctified, and justified by the Spirit.

Notice here, unlike judicial redemption (accomplished through the Lord's blood), this washing, sanctifying and justifying is through His Spirit. A person's disposition or character is within them. Only the Spirit of God indwelling a person can change that person's character. When believers are sanctified in this way, it doesn't necessarily mean they will never fail and fall into sin again. It does mean; however, they no longer habitually express their fallen nature to be then labeled as a certain type of sinner (viz., "*such were some of you*"). This is the meaning of dispositional sanctification: God's nature is saving believers from inward corruption.

Renewing of the Mind

As the Spirit penetrates the believer's mind, their logic and reasoning begin to change to the mind of Christ.

> And do not be conformed to this world, but be transformed by the renewing of your mind, that you may prove what [is] that good and acceptable and perfect will of God. For I say, through the grace given to me, to everyone who is among you, not to think [of himself] more highly than he ought to think, but to think soberly, as God has dealt to each one a measure of faith.
>
> – Romans 12:2-3

People live and are guided by the way they think. What is important to them in their thinking is what they will pursue and how they will work things out. Therefore, a believer's mind needs renewing; otherwise, their thinking will be no different from the people of this age, and it will conform (lit. "squeeze") them into the mold of this world (cosmos). However, if the believer's thinking is changed through renewal, then their experiences, goals, and the way they live will follow. For example, if a person thinks God hates them and wants to punish them, their experiences in life will reflect that belief. Those life experiences would be drastically different if they considered God's love for them — He wants the best for them and counts them as righteous in Him. Or, if a person thinks money is the most important pursuit in life, they will live differently than if they thought *God* should have the preeminence in their life. Changing one's thinking is central to the changing of one's character.

In understanding this section of Romans, the *"renewing of the mind"* is in relation to how we think of other members in the Body. The saints in Rome were divided because those associated with one group thought they were the "chosen" and superior to those in another. Therefore, those with a renewed mind would not think of themselves more highly than they ought to think since all believers are in the one Body of Christ. This subject will be discussed more thoroughly in a later chapter of this book.

> Let nothing be done through selfish ambition or conceit, but in lowliness of mind let each esteem others better than himself. Let each of you look out not only for his own interests, but also for

the interests of others. Let this mind be in you which was also in Christ Jesus.

– Philippians 2:3–5

Reading His Word and receiving the knowledge of Jesus Christ renews the believer's mind and transforms it into His mind – His way of thinking. The minds of immature believers will be focused on selfish ambitions or religious duties, but as they open themselves up to read the Word concerning Jesus, they enter fellowship with Him, and their thinking begins to change – to be renewed. As a result of such a renewing of the mind, they spontaneously start to look out for the interests of others – to genuinely and unselfishly care for others; they do not consider themselves better than anyone else.[15]

... and be renewed in the spirit of your mind.

– Ephesians 4:23

The Word of God is also Spirit. It does not just pass on information, knowledge and logic for the mind. God's Word is living and full of the Spirit. This powerful Spirit works in the renewing of the mind. Logic is not the only thing changing. The Spirit in the believer's spirit penetrates and expands throughout their whole inner being. Therefore, it is called *the spirit of your mind*. The more a believer's mind is renewed, the more he or she will be affected by the Spirit; the more the Spirit affects the believer's mind, the more he or she is renewed. For this reason, when believers approach the Bible, they should try to understand its logic, and pray with their "*spirit*" to allow the Holy Spirit to guide them into the reality of all things concerning Christ. This brings in the renewing of the mind.

Indeed, commencing the reading of the Scripture – the Word of God – with one's unrenewed mind is akin to when Jesus confronted His persecutors:

You search the Scriptures, for in them you think you have eternal life; and these are they which testify of Me. **But you are not willing to come to Me that you may have life.**

– John 5:39-40

Staring these religious zealots in the face was The Truth – not the hollow words upon the printed page, if you would. Jesus said: *The words that I speak to you are Spirit, and are life* (Tyndale — John 6:63b). In order to ingest that which is Spirit, one must exercise or use the renewed human spirit. The J. B. Phillips "free New Testament translation" of 1 Corinthians 2:14-16 captures the essence of this profound understanding:

> *But the unspiritual man simply cannot accept the matters which the Spirit deals with — they just don't make sense to him, for, after all, you must be spiritual to see spiritual things. The spiritual man, on the other hand, has an insight into the meaning of everything, though his insight may baffle the man of the world. This is because the former is sharing in God's wisdom, and 'Who has known the mind of the Lord that he may instruct him?' Incredible as it may sound, we who are spiritual have the very thoughts of Christ!*

Transformation

Through this life process of metamorphosis, believers are being changed from their old form to that of Christ.

> And do not be conformed to this world, but be transformed by the renewing of your mind, that you may prove what is that good and acceptable and perfect will of God.
>
> – Romans 12:2

The result of the renewing of the mind is transformation. The Greek word for *transformation* is the origin of the word "*metamorphosis*," meaning a profound change in form from one stage to the next in the history of an organism (e.g., from that of a caterpillar to that of a butterfly).[16] Believers are simultaneously going through a transformation because the DNA of the life of Jesus Christ is in their very being. Transformation is part of the history of Christ's organic salvation within all believers. As they eat and drink (partake) of Him for growth and as their minds are renewed by the Spirit (and the knowledge of Him), a transformation takes place in their being.

On the one hand, the world conforms people to a certain way of thinking and living through external influences such as advertising and fashion. On the other hand, believers are being transformed by His indwelling Life according to the divine "DNA" from within.

> But we all, with unveiled face, beholding as in a mirror the glory of the Lord, **are being transformed** into the same image from glory to glory, just as by the Spirit of the Lord.
>
> – 2 Corinthians 3:18

Into what are believers being transformed? Paul says they are being transformed into the image of Jesus Christ, whom they are beholding – we are likened to a mirror beholding and then reflecting whatever the mirror views. An "unveiled face" is a face which has turned from trying to "outwardly" keep God's law and now simply beholds the Lord.

By beholding (and reflecting) Jesus, believers are continually being transformed into the Lord's image, so they transcend, love, forgive, endure, rest, and rejoice as He does — they are being transformed into what they are beholding: The Lord Jesus! They express Him in life, nature, and character. He is expressed through them in their living, actions . . . and even their *reactions*. This is happening *from glory to glory*.

It has everything to do with His indwelling, life-giving Spirit working in and through His believers.

Conformed and Glorified

The last step in the believer's salvation will happen when even their bodies will be *transfigured* into a glorious body to fully express God.

> For whom He foreknew, He also predestined to be conformed to the image of His Son, that He might be the firstborn among many brethren. Moreover, whom He predestined, these He also called; whom He called, these He also justified; and whom He justified, these He also glorified.
>
> – Romans 8:29–30

This is the result of transformation: believers are conformed to the image of God's Son. Their spirit is joined to Him and becomes one Spirit/spirit — "*he that is joined to the Lord is one Spirit/spirit*" (1 Cor. 6:17). No distinction is made of this "spirit" — divine or human — it can be understood to be both! The Greek word for "joined" is Strong's G#2853 κολλάω and is used in the marriage of a man and a woman ("*cleaving unto*" – Matt. 19:5; 1 Cor. 6:16-17 – i.e., "one in relationship" – their distinction is maintained but they are "viewed" as inseparable – "one flesh" as per Mark 10:8).

The believer's mind becomes the mind of Christ; his soul is fully in His image, and his body is glorified — *"like unto His glorious body"* (Phil. 3:21). Conformation and glorification are the end of God's full salvation for each individual follower of Jesus. His organic/living salvation having begun in the believers' spirit continues through daily salvation experiences wrought within the soul culminating in the Lord's return with the glorification of one's entire being, including the physical body. What a wonderful salvation!

> . . . who will transform our lowly body that it may be conformed
> to His glorious body, according to the working by which He is
> able even to subdue all things to Himself.
>
> — Philippians 3:21

Even though today Jesus Christ is in the believer and their inner character is being transformed, their physical body is still lowly in humiliation due to sin and death in the flesh. Because the believer's body is still flesh, it is susceptible to disease, aging, indwelling sin, and eventually death. No matter how much their disposition has become an image of Christ, their bodies remain the same until the day of glorification.

On that day they will transfigure into a "butterfly" (metaphorically). In reality, and much more magnificently, they will have a body like Jesus' glorious body. That glorious body will discard the body of flesh, and not only be freed from sin and death, but be one filled with and expressing the glory of God. This is the final subduing of all things fallen, originating from Adam. This is salvation to the uttermost – HOW WONDERFUL!

7

THE OIKONOMIA (ECONOMY) OF GOD

The Greek word for economy, *oikonomia,* was prominently used in the New Testament to describe a mystery relating to God's will, pleasure, and eternal purpose. Without a full understanding of this word and the concept of *oikonomia,* it would be very difficult to have a complete understanding of what God is doing to fulfill His purpose. That is why the apostle Paul determined to bring light to this idea of *oikonomia.* All believers should not only participate in the *oikonomia* of grace, but they should take active responsibility for carrying out and furthering God's *oikonomia.*

Oikonomia and the Mystery of God's Eternal Purpose

Understanding *oikonomia* is critical to understanding the mystery of God's eternal purpose. The definition of this Greek word is "household management." *Oikonomia* is a word rich in meaning. Translators have used various English words for *oikonomia* in the New Testament, depending on context: administration, dispensation, plan, stewardship, and economy.

"Household management" in the first century described the proper administration needed to effectively grow a household. The following scenario uses the translated words (underlined) to describe *oikonomia:* a rich father who desired to build up his family would have an <u>administration</u> specifically to <u>dispense</u> food to multiple generations of his children scattered in his vast land so that they might be fed and grow to increase his household. The <u>steward</u> would be the one dispensing — he would be responsible for carrying out this <u>plan</u>.

The anglicized word for *oikonomia* is *economy.* Contemporary usage for this word is the production, distribution and consumption of goods. If any part of this chain is weak, the entire economy suffers. A growing economy equals a strong nation.

Oikonomia is composed of two words: *oiko* means "house," and *nomia*, derived from the Greek root word *nomos* which means "law"; therefore, *oikonomia* literally means "house-law."

Law (*nomos*) comes from the primary word *nemo* meaning, "*To parcel out, especially food or grazing to animals*" (www.biblestudytools.com/lexicons/greek/nas/nomos). It seems counterintuitive that law, which is so strict and demanding, comes from a word meaning the parceling out of food. In God's view, His laws have an underlining purpose: *to feed*.

God's original intention in establishing law was not something for His children to keep, but rather to give them food. Interestingly, the very first command from God was to eat: "*of every tree of the garden you may freely eat*" (Gen. 1:26).

Food was dispensed through the law since the entire law included the offerings and the eating of those offerings. When a commandment was broken, in order to fulfill the law, an offering had to be made accompanied by the consumption of the offering. Righteousness, according to the law, was made possible by these offerings; when the offerings were made for sins and trespasses, a portion was to be eaten. In the New Testament, Jesus Christ is the real offering; thus, believers partake and eat of Him as the Lamb of God.

Therefore, Paul could say in Philippians 3:6 concerning the righteousness, which is in the law, he was blameless. However, Paul admitted in Romans 7 he could not keep the law but instead practiced evil. Then how could he say he was blameless in the law? This is because Paul also *made sacrifices* according to the law, in order to be *forgiven* according to the law.

From the view of distributing food, the more the moral law was broken, the more offerings were needed — resulting in enjoyment and nourishment from consuming the offerings.

This concept should be applied to believers in the New Testament. Every time there is conviction of sin or failure, believers should turn to Jesus Christ to enjoy Him as their redemption and their food for strengthening. Therefore, Paul could say in Romans 5:20, "*where sin abounded, grace abounded much more.*" It seems clear that *oikonomia,* or *house-law,* has everything to do with the distribution of food for the household.

God's Economy Is How He Accomplishes His Will and Eternal Purpose

God makes known to His children His mysterious will, which is to head up all things in Christ. He accomplishes this through His economy.

... having made known to us the mystery of his will, according to. his good pleasure which he purposed in himself into the **administration** [oikonomia] of the fullness of times; to head up all things in the Christ, the things in the heavens and the things upon the earth.

–Ephesians 1:9–10a, DBY

God has a will – a purpose – according to His good pleasure. Human beings also set purposes and life goals which are according to *their* pleasure or to what is pleasing to them. God's ultimate purpose, however, is to head up all things in Christ. Everything in the entire universe will be summed up in Christ as the head. As seen in Chapter 3, this Christ in eternity is both God and man. God's purpose is that everything will have Jesus Christ as the Head. Believers will not be able to really grasp the depth and height of what this means until eternity.

While this won't happen in completeness until the future, God's economy (*oikonomia*) is needed during this span of time before eternity. Therefore, before time is filled up (or over with), God's economy is needed among men. It is God's economy which accomplishes what He desires. It fulfills His purpose of heading up all things in Christ. Therefore, God's economy is God's way (method or plan) to accomplish His ultimate will.

These verses clearly show the prominence of God's economy (*oikonomia*) in relationship to His will, purpose, and pleasure. Consequently, understanding God's economy is critical in realizing God's ultimate purpose. Believers who do not understand the concept of God's economy may easily become entangled with non-essential doctrines, thereby becoming subservient to outward religious regulations or hypes.

Next, let's prayerfully consider the following verses in coming to terms with a fuller grasp of God's economy.

Stewards Dispensing Grace—the Riches of Christ

Stewards in God's economy dispense grace (the riches of Christ for every believer's enjoyment) with a vision of building up the Body of Christ – God's household. An example of a steward in the New Testament is the apostle Paul. Paul received the *oikonomia* (stewardship, dispensation, administration) of the grace of God, so he could then dispense this grace to believers.

> . . . (if indeed you have heard of the administration [oikonomia]
> of the grace of God which has been given to me towards [Greek:
> into] you, that by revelation the mystery has been made known
> to me, . . .
>
> — Ephesians 3:2–3, DBY

Paul wrote concerning God's economy having been given to him —
it was the economy of grace. He understood he was to be a steward in
administering and dispensing this grace to people.

Grace is the spiritual food believers need for sustenance and for spiritual
growth. Grace was given to Paul so he might be a "dispenser of grace" into
humanity. God's entire economy is an economy of grace. Grace as the
product, which arrived and was made available through Jesus Christ (John
1:17), is to be distributed to all believers to enjoy all the riches of Christ,
thereby growing up into mature believers by receiving grace. The entire
chain of God's economy is grace — its supply is unlimited because its eternal
source is Jesus Christ.

All humanity demands and seeks grace (pleasure and enjoyment).
Therefore, stewards are needed to distribute grace to *all* men.

Revelation Concerning the Mystery of Christ

The first item dispensed to all believers is revelation concerning the
mystery of Christ — joint heirs, joint body and joint partakers. This is
God's household.

> . . . that by revelation the mystery has been made known to me,
> . . . the mystery of the Christ, which in other generations has
> not been made known to the sons of men, as it has now been
> revealed to His holy apostles and **prophets** in the power of the
> Spirit, that they who are of the nations should be joint heirs, and
> a joint body, and joint partakers of His promise in Christ Jesus
> through the glad tidings.
>
> — Ephesians 3:3–6, DBY

God unveiled His mystery to Paul, and in turn Paul wanted to pass it
on to other believers. Paul's desire was for others to understand God's will
which had been kept in secret since the beginning of creation. This is also
part of the stewardship of grace: to unveil the *result* of God's economy. God

wants joint heirs, a joint body, and joint partakers. This is manifested in joining the nations (aka, the Gentiles) with Israel to become one household, one family of God.

The first item Paul addresses in Ephesians 3:6 has to do with believers as "joint heirs" in this mystery; confirming God as the Father is after a family. This family is destined to include many mature children (heirs). This concept is completely consistent with Paul's use of the word *oikonomia*. Recall the original use of this word related to building up the household of the patriarchs. Therefore, *God's* economy of grace culminates with the proliferation and maturity of His household, His offspring.

This mystery is also about a body expressing Him, whose partakers enjoy Him. Note the word "*partakers*" is also consistent with *oikonomia*, since those who share in this mystery are the beneficiaries of *oikonomia*. Today, it is through these glad tidings (or the gospel) wherein grace is dispensed by partaking. For eternity, believers will continue to enter and participate in this grace — the Tree of Life and the river of life (Rev. 22:1–2).

The "mystery of the Christ" being joint heirs, one body, and joint partakers unveils the dispensing (administration) of the Trinity to His previously divided people. They are now one as joint heirs of the Father, the one Body of the Son, and joint partakers of the promised Spirit.

Dispensing the Unsearchable Riches of Christ for All Men

> ...of which I am become minister according to the gift of the grace of God given to me, according to the working of His power. To me, less than the least of all saints, has this grace been given, to announce among the nations the glad tidings of the unsearchable riches of the Christ.
>
> — Ephesians 3:7–8, DBY

A minister is one who serves food. The food that Paul served was grace. Grace is the enjoyment of the unsearchable riches of Christ. The gospel (glad tidings, or the good news) is simply making available or unveiling the unsearchable riches of Christ. The gospel is much more than believing in Jesus so one does not "go to hell" but instead one "goes to heaven."

Consider an item of the good news: the Lord's love. How *unsearchably* rich is His love! For eternity, believers will not be able to fathom its depth.

The Scriptures describe Jesus' person, character, and function using many different symbolic images: He is the rock, shepherd, door, corner stone, top stone, morning star, first fruit, bridegroom, captain, bread of life . . . and much more. Each one of these items will take eternity to appreciate.

His work on the cross, His resurrection, His ascension, and His enthronement to be both Lord and Christ are also *unsearchably* rich. Believers can appreciate the riches of Jesus Christ are inexhaustible, so too is the gospel (glad tidings). Jesus is our abundant grace. His intention is to distribute or dispense His grace — this is God's economy.

God Desires All Men to See and Participate in His Economy

God's desire is for all men to see and participate in this economy or dispensation; therefore, Paul was charged to enlighten all to see the *oikonomia* of the mystery.

> . . . and to enlighten all with the knowledge of what is the administration [oikonomia] of the mystery hidden throughout the ages in God, who has created all things.
>
> – Ephesians 3:9, DBY

As one who had received God's *oikonomia*, Paul was able to enlighten others to the understanding of this *oikonomia* — revealing its mystery. It is interesting to note God's *oikonomia* is a concept needing enlightenment — akin to the enlightenment believers receive at the time of salvation. Clearly, it is essential for all believers to see and understand God's economy as soon as they come to faith in Jesus Christ.

Believers who have been enlightened concerning God's economy, like Paul, will want all people to understand and participate in God's economy. However, unlike Paul's heavy burden for this, the amount of teaching and speaking among believers today concerning this knowledge of God's *oikonomia* is miniscule. Readers should ask themselves how many times they have heard of God's *oikonomia* in the last year. Such knowledge is critical for believers to be able to stay the course — living out His divine life and being equipped to serve God and humanity. Though this topic is critical and essential for God's eternal purpose, why is it that such a topic has been hidden from most believers with such little emphasis spent in general Christian discourse today?

God's Purpose for the Ekklesia: To Glorify God and Shame His Enemies

God's eternal purpose in having a built-up ekklesia is designed to bring glory to God and shame to His enemies.

> ...in order that now to the principalities and authorities in the heavenlies might be made known through the assembly [ekklesia] the all-various wisdom of God, according to the eternal purpose, which he purposed in Christ Jesus our Lord.
>
> – Ephesians 3:10–11, DBY

The end result, or the outcome of God's economy is the building up of His household – the ekklesia – through which the all-various wisdom of God will be made known to all heavenly beings. This is especially true for Satan and all the angels who have followed His rebellion. As described in much more depth in an earlier chapter, it was not possible for God to manifest *His* manifold wisdom without an adversary who was called the, "sum of all wisdom." The more complex the problem, the more wisdom is needed to solve the problem. The loftier the purposes and goals, the more wisdom will be displayed when the purpose is finally accomplished.

After the creation of man (male and female), Satan entered the scene to fully corrupt man by injecting man with sin and death. This manifestation of satanic life and nature resulted in corrupting the image of God – man. All of humanity became God's enemy. Man was condemned under the righteous judgment of God. Humanity once loved and desired by God but now His own image and likeness was contaminated to the core of his DNA. It was in this dismal and seemingly hopeless state God intervened to restore His image, man. God's recovery work through Jesus Christ didn't just rescue man back to his created state, but it went far beyond. In God's economy, man was born anew with divine life and became a partaker of the divine nature. It was God's pleasure to have many sons – a family – and ultimately the household of God with man. This household, His ekklesia, is the culmination of His manifold and extensive wisdom at its pinnacle. This is the ultimate outcome of God's economy.

Christ in You the Hope of Glory

To Complete the Word of God Dispenses Food

The food dispensed is the completing of the Word of God; this is not simply announcing something objective about Christ, but the Christ Who needs to be *consumed* to become the *indwelling* Christ. This is the steward's struggle, but necessary for growing the members of God's family — the metaphors used here are subjective and depict how God's economy operates and/or is dispensed.

> Now, I rejoice in sufferings for you, and I fill up that which is lacking of the tribulations of Christ in my flesh, for His body, which is the assembly [ekklesia]; of which I became a minister, according to the dispensation [**oikonomia**] of God which is given me towards you **to complete the word of God**, the mystery which has been hidden from ages and from generations, but has now been made manifest to His saints; to whom God would make known what are the riches of the glory of this mystery among the nations, which is Christ in you the hope of glory: whom we announce, admonishing every man, and teaching every man, in all wisdom, to the end that we may present every man perfect [mature] in Christ. Whereunto also I toil [labor], combating [striving] according to His working, which works in me in power.
>
> – Colossians 1:24–29, DBY

Paul's words in Colossians 1:24 may seem strange, to *"rejoice in suffering,"* but some human experiences readily may be identified with this idea: a mother giving birth or raising a family, for example.

Women suffer greatly in childbirth, but they also rejoice in their suffering knowing her baby is coming. A father also rejoices in his labor, which gives him the ability to provide for and raise his family.

Paul, too, rejoiced in the suffering related to God's economy (the raising up of God's household, the ekklesia). He rejoiced in his suffering for believers. This suffering is not at all related to the sufferings of Jesus Christ for redemption, which is fully completed with no lack. However, what still lacks are *stewards* in God's economy, willing to suffer to fulfill their commission of God's *oikonomia*. Paul was such a minister according to God's *oikonomia* given to him for believers.

His commission as a steward was to **complete the Word of God** by unveiling and making manifest God's mystery, "*Christ in you, the hope of glory.*" His stewardship (*oikonomia*) was to dispense Christ in a way that would be consumed and ingested by believers becoming "*Christ in* [them]." As a faithful steward, Paul labored and toiled to take every opportunity to announce and teach "Christ in you, the hope of glory." Yes, these are "economic terms" with profound spiritual meaning — God is in the business of distributing the riches of Christ into us and from us to others!

Paul may have spoken on many topics. One can collect a number of subjects from his letters, but don't lose focus on what he considered to be the completion of the word of God and what he struggled to announce: "*Christ in you, the hope of glory.*" If this point is missed or glossed over, then the heart of Paul is ripped out. A believer may think, "Okay, I've got it, Christ is in me. Now let's move on to study such and such."

No! There is no moving on from this. In fact, all topics of the Scriptures should end or result with "*Christ in you, the hope of glory.*" Paul continued to announce this. This was his struggle: how to communicate "*Christ in you, the hope of glory*" in a way that would really stick, enabling believers to experience growth. His goal was to labor on behalf of each of God's children so that they would be perfected — mature as God's household, His ekklesia.

Teach to Lead People to God's Economy

This is why anything believers teach, which does not directly lead to God's economy is a distraction, a deviation preventing believers from growing to maturity.

> . . . that you might enjoin [charge] some not to teach other doctrines, nor to turn their minds to fables and interminable [endless] genealogies, which bring questionings rather than God's dispensation [**oikonomia**], which is in faith.
>
> – 1 Timothy 1:3–4, DBY

Even during the time of the Apostle Paul, believers were distracted by many miscellaneous teachings, doctrines, fables, genealogies and keeping of laws. The question believers should always ask in order to evaluate any

"Christian" teaching is whether it supports God's economy. If it does, then it is healthy teaching. If it does not, then at best it is a distraction from God's plan. Therefore, understanding God's economy (how it works) is of utmost importance. Without this understanding, believers will not have a reference point to discern various teachings and practices among God's people today . . . "rabbit trails" leading to multiple distractions from God's economy abound!

It is important to recognize teachings which distract--which are not necessarily non-scriptural or heretical. Certain teachings can be related to discussing leadership, miraculous gifts, baptism, creationism, or holiness. None of these are bad topics, in and of themselves. However, if these teachings do not further God's economy by unveiling the riches of Christ for all believers to partake of His grace — for the growth of God's household — then these teachings are nonessential for building up the Lord's ekklesia, according to Paul's instruction to Timothy.

Apparently, there was a tendency in Ephesus to miss God's administration/economy; therefore, by the time John wrote the letter to them in Revelation (Rev. 2:1), they had lost their first (best) love for the Lord Jesus. Although they were upright to reject evil men and were even scripturally knowledgeable enough to try and expose false apostles, they were about to lose their testimony as a shining lampstand because Jesus Christ — their affection for Him — was not their focus. If an assembly is no longer shining forth Jesus Christ, then it is no longer an ekklesia — a true lampstand. How awful to be a gathering of Christians, and yet not be part of God's ekklesia because it does not shine forth Christ. It lacks real love for the Lord Jesus! How critical it is for a gathering of believers to stay focused on Jesus Christ, Who He is and what He has accomplished. To truly love Jesus is to love the receiving and dispensing of His wonderful unsearchable riches--this is God's economy!

A Privilege and a Responsibility

This economy (stewardship) has been given to believers as both a privilege and a responsibility.

> ...according as he has received a gift, ministering it to one another, as good stewards [oikonomos] of the various grace of God.
> — 1 Peter 4:10, DBY

The apostles are not the only ones who have received the responsibility of God's economy; every believer has received this gift and is charged to minister it one to another. As one in God's economy, believers are to minister these various graces of God to each other. These various graces are the unsearchable riches of Christ to be enjoyed every day as true expressions of their salvation.

Unfortunately, it is almost universally accepted, the job of ministry has been assigned to the clergy class such as pastors, ministers, and priests. God's stewardship, wherein God's will is to be fulfilled, is tremendously hindered because of this erroneous concept. For God's economy to advance — the number of God's stewards must exponentially increase.

> For if I preach the gospel, I have nothing to boast of, for necessity is laid upon me; yes, woe is me if I do not preach the gospel! For if I do this willingly, I have a reward; but if against my will, I have been entrusted with a stewardship [**oikonomia**]. What is my reward then? That when I preach the gospel, I may present the gospel of Christ without charge.
>
> — 1 Corinthians 9:16–18

Paul's attitude found it mandatory for anyone entrusted with God's *oikonomia* was to be responsible for dispensing Christ to others. Basically, he was saying he didn't have a choice; he had to do this service — fulfill this stewardship. The more a believer sees and enters God's economy, the more he or she will be compelled to be a minister of Jesus Christ and of His grace . . . that person will do this without charge. Paul's reward for being a steward was to be able to do this without charge, without anyone paying him or supporting him. How counterintuitive was his reward for the work of ministry being accomplished without compensation for his labor!

How different was his attitude from today's practice of hiring clergy to do the work of ministry? This demonstrates every believer who is normally working and caring for their family should also be stewards doing service based on necessity, not getting paid to minister Christ to others. To be able to minister freely without charge is in itself the reward.

> And the Lord said, "Who then is that faithful and wise steward
> [**oikonomos**], whom his master will make ruler over his
> household, to give them their portion of food in due season?
> "Blessed is that servant whom his master will find so doing when
> he comes. Truly, I say to you that he will make him ruler over
> all that he has. But if that servant says in his heart, 'My master
> is delaying his coming,' and begins to beat the male and female
> servants, and to eat and drink and be drunk, the master of that
> servant will come on a day when he is not looking for him, and
> at an hour when he is not aware, and will cut him in two and
> appoint him his portion with the unbelievers. . . . For everyone
> to whom much is given, from him much will be required; and to
> whom much has been committed, of him they will ask the more."
>
> – Luke 12:42–46, 48b

Every believer has been called to further God's economy by being
a faithful steward. Luke's use of the word "*steward*" in this parable is
consistent with its original meaning. This steward's goal was to take care of
the household. The function of such a person was to distribute and dispense
sustenance. However, Luke warns us, believers should not live selfishly; they
must care for other family members in God's household. According to this
parable, there are rewards or punishment (losses) associated with diligence
in carrying out the duties of dispensing food in the household of God.

One could argue whether this unfaithful steward in Luke 12:42–48 is
eternally saved or not, but this doesn't change the fact believers have a duty
to provide food for the building up of the household. There is a requirement
from the "master" to be a faithful steward, whether they provide a little
or much. It seems the more the Lord gives believers both physically and
spiritually, the more responsibility they have in caring for others in His
household. *Lord Jesus may those You have entrusted as faithful stewards in Your
economy embrace the responsibility of building up Your household!*

The One God Working as Three (Trinity)

> Blessed be the God and Father of our Lord Jesus Christ, who has
> blessed us in Christ with every spiritual blessing in the heavenly
> places, even as he chose us in him before the foundation of the

world, that we should be holy and blameless before him. He
destined us in love to be his sons through Jesus Christ, according
to the purpose of his will,

$$- Ephesians\ 1:3-5, RSV$$

In the first chapter of Ephesians, the letter where Paul described God's
oikonomia in vivid terms, the Triune (*three-one*) God was clearly displayed
and praised in three sections. This first section was a blessing to the Father.
The Father has a will and a purpose. His desire is to have many mature sons.
As seen in a previous chapter, the Greek word for "son" is a compound word
for both a son by birth and also a son with legal status; this means a "son" of
God has the maturity to fulfill the legal requirements to be an heir. It was
the Father's pleasure and will from the beginning of eternity to have such
sons. He did not want just one only begotten Son, but many sons.

The number of offspring in a household measures the greatness of a
father in biblical times. The Father God is the *real* Father, and He is full
of life — desirous that His riches be discharged, resulting in millions upon
millions of mature sons who can express His life and nature.

The Son Becoming the Head of All Things Realized through Oikonomia

In him [Jesus Christ] we have redemption through his blood, the
forgiveness of our trespasses, according to the riches of his grace
that he lavished on us in all wisdom and insight. He did this when
he revealed to us the secret of his will, according to his good
pleasure that he set forth in Christ, toward the administration
of the fullness of the times, to head up all things in Christ — the
things in heaven and the things on earth.

$$- Ephesians\ 1:7-10, NET$$

It is interesting to note that *oikonomia* is unveiled in this next section on
the Son (Eph 1:7–10). Jesus is the accomplisher by coming to mankind as
grace. Through His death, He accomplished redemption so believers would
have complete forgiveness and cleansing of sin. Through His resurrection,
the Father sent the Spirit of Promise to indwell His people wherein by His
abiding life all things are headed up in Him.

A Permanent Image Sealed into the Believers

The Spirit, through faith in Jesus Christ, becomes a permanent image sealed into the believer's being, giving believers a guarantee as sons in God's household of inheriting all that God is.

> In him you also, who have heard the word of truth, the gospel of your salvation, and have believed in him, were sealed with the promised Holy Spirit, which is the guarantee of our inheritance until we acquire possession of it, to the praise of his glory.
> – Ephesians 1:13–14, RSV

The riches of Christ were dispensed to believers in the hearing of the Word of Truth, which is the gospel. Believers should not think the gospel is just for unbelievers; rather, the entire truth concerning the person and work of Jesus Christ — together with His eternal purpose and the way to fulfill His purpose through His *oikonomia* — is the good news, the gospel. This gospel is for unbelievers as well as mature believers because this truth is inexhaustible. The more a person hears, the more they believe. The more they believe, the more the Spirit (through a believer's participation) imprints His permanent image on them.

When an item was sealed with a signet ring in ancient times, it left a permanent image of the seal on the item sealed. Not only so, but the ink or wax used for the seal was also transferred (or absorbed into) what was sealed, such as a piece of parchment. In the same way, at the very moment of faith, believers are sealed. The Spirit is permanently transferred into a believer's being. The believer now bears His image.

The more truth heard, and grace received, the more this image of the Spirit grows and becomes more pronounced in that believer.

This seal of the Spirit is also the believer's guarantee they will inherit all God is in fullness. They are certain to become fully mature heirs of God. All God is and has is theirs for eternity. What they are enjoying of God Himself today is just a pledge of an unimaginable amount to come. Understanding God's desire for heirs brings what has been discussed full circle — back to the Father's desire for sons. This is a beautiful portrait of the Triune God working together in His *oikonomia* to fulfill His will, purpose, and pleasure from eternity to eternity through what man today calls time.

God's Oikonomia: Love, Grace and Fellowship

God's economy for his eternal purpose was initiated by the Father's love, accomplished by the Son's grace, and made available for participation in the Spirit's fellowship

> The grace of the Lord Jesus Christ and the love of God and the fellowship of the Holy Spirit be with you all.
> ~ 2 Corinthians 13:14

God's *oikonomia* is summed up by Paul in 2 Corinthians 12:13, which echoes what has been previously discussed. Here, Paul leads with the Lord's grace, because Jesus said He is the way, and no one comes to the Father but through Him. The Lord's grace is the believers' entrance into basking in the love of God. The more believers appreciate the death and resurrection of Christ, the more they comprehend the significance of God's forgiveness, leading them to realize and enjoy His love. This grace and love instantly and perpetually transpires within the fellowship of the Holy Spirit.

Fellowship means participation – partaking with and subsequently sharing with others. This fellowship is not just for reaching individual believers, but every individual who participates also shares with others. If the love of God and the grace of Christ received by believers does not reach others, then the fellowship of the Holy Spirit is stifled. Just as the circle of fellowship within the Triune God Himself grew to include all His people, the practical circle of fellowship among believers also needs to grow. The fellowship of the Spirit is persistently seeking to expand, to include more partakers and dispensers of grace and love.

This is God's oikonomia.

God has already produced an unlimited supply of foodstuff; therefore, for believers to be in God's economy today means to identify, know, and enjoy real food which is Christ's person and work. This also includes distributing this abundant food to others, so they may also ingest, digest, and enjoy this heavenly food. Believers should enlighten others concerning God's economy, so they can be raised up as the next generation of distributors (ministers). The result of this cycle is the building up of God's family – this is His divine intent!

The spiritual food God has prepared is in this truth as defined and its riches outlined in this text. Paul was a steward of the grace of God, and the way he dispensed grace was through the preaching of the truth, the unsearchable riches of Christ. Grace and truth go together, since grace and truth came through Jesus Christ (John 1:17).

Paul preached truth as the gospel. When people received the truth of Jesus Christ, they were saved by grace. Believers initially received grace for salvation through hearing of the truth concerning Who Jesus is and what He has accomplished through His death, resurrection and ascension. The Lord Jesus entered their spirit as grace; therefore, Paul proclaimed, "the grace of the Lord Jesus Christ be with your spirit" (Phil. 4:23).

However, most believers may be short of grace because they stopped hearing, learning, and understanding truth. Their knowledge of the Son, Jesus Christ, may be lacking. They may have much Bible knowledge, but not concerning the truth. Most of today's teaching is in the realm of *didaskalia, various scriptural practices*; rather than the doctrine of Jesus Christ Himself — Who is the truth. Christians mostly come to the Bible to learn how to apply various teachings in their particular lifestyle. Yet, they have little appreciation of the truth, the knowledge of the Son of God. Therefore, no matter how much they learn and try to apply what they have learned, they are short of grace — real enjoyment, and pleasure of the Lord. In their daily experiences, they are short of the abundance of His salvation.

It is time to refocus on truth: the doctrine (*didache*) of Jesus Christ. God's economy is stalled without dispensing of this truth. Believers need to dive into truth, understand it, appreciate it, enjoy grace, and **dispense the truth** they have learned and understood to others so they too may enjoy grace through truth. If believers have little to say concerning the knowledge of Jesus Christ, then little dispensation (administering) of grace can occur How needful is this truth today!

8

THE OLD COVENANT AND THE NEW COVENANT (SECTION A)

T he matter of the Law is a source of challenge and confusion to many Christians. Some try to fulfill the Law and fall under its condemnation when they continually fail. Others maintain they no longer live under the Law — this too can be confusing. Do they mean they can steal from others and drive as fast as they want? Dishonor their parents – commit adultery?

Which part of the Law are Christians still under and which part are they not? If Christians are still under *some* form of the Law, then what is the difference between the Old Covenant and the New Covenant?[17] If Christians possess eternal life — no matter what they do, and are not under the Law's requirements — then by what standard will they be judged by God? Hopefully, this chapter will give clarity and answers to these questions.

What Is a Covenant?

In the Bible, the Law is central in the relationship between God and people, and between human beings in society. This relationship between people and God is defined in biblical terms by an Old Covenant and a New Covenant (2 Cor. 3:6, 14).

A "covenant" is an agreement made with an oath. God made such a covenant with Israel when He gave the Ten Commandments to Moses on Mount Sinai. That covenant was called an "Old Covenant" by Paul in 2 Corinthians 3:14, and the "first covenant" in a few verses in Hebrews (Heb. 8:7; 9:1, 15). The Ten Commandments are embodied in the Old Covenant. Basically, that first covenant was a bilateral agreement where there were binding conditions for both man (male and female) and God: if men fulfilled the Law of God as stated in the covenant, then God would bless them; if men broke the Law, curses would come on them. That first covenant didn't work out for man since man kept breaking the Law and was continually under the curse. Because of God's love for man, He first promised and then established a *New Covenant* which would be unilateral and unconditional: God declared He alone would do amazing things for man without man doing anything to earn those things. This chapter (Sections A and B) will mainly expound on these two covenants.

> "Behold, the days are coming, says the LORD, when I will make a New Covenant with the house of Israel and with the house of Judah — not according to the covenant that I made with their fathers in the day that I took them by the hand to lead them out of the land of Egypt. My covenant which they broke, though I was a husband to them, says the LORD. But this is the covenant that I will make with the house of Israel after those days, says the LORD; I will put My law in their minds, and write it on their hearts; and I will be their God, and they shall be My people. No more shall every man teach his neighbor, and every man his brother, saying, 'Know the LORD,' for they all shall know Me, from the least of them to the greatest of them, says the LORD. For I will forgive their iniquity, and their sin I will remember no more"
>
> ~ Jeremiah 31:31-34.[18]

These two covenants govern the relationship between God and man. This means how God treats people and judges them, and how man is to approach God and thus have a relationship with his Creator. By understanding these two covenants, a person can be released from the bondage of the law[19] into a life of freedom and joy in Jesus Christ. When believers are not clear about which covenant they are living under today, they will experience condemnation, confusion, disappointment, and ultimately spiritual death amidst moments of joy and victory in Christ. A believer will vacillate between the two until one day he or she finds clarity and understands the difference between the Old Covenant and the New Covenant in their relationship with God.

The Law and Morality

A major portion of the Ten Commandments is related to morality. It governs human interaction within a society. Moral laws relate to justice and judgment and are often translated as "ordinances" (i.e., "dogma") in the Bible.[20] These laws are based on God's holy nature. Their purpose is to promote and safeguard the welfare of human society. When Jesus came, He uplifted the moral law which governed human interactions.

This moral law is, at its core, embodied in the Ten Commandments with numerous statutes and ordinances (See Endnote No. 17). Think of the Ten Commandments as the frame; all auxiliary laws, statutes, and ordinances flesh out this frame. Though only the "frame" is considered — the Ten Commandments — a large portion of the Law provides the basis of morality for a civil society. If the first four commandments concerning God and the Sabbath are dismissed as "religious," the following six then form the foundation of a safe and healthy society, secular or otherwise. The fifth commandment says to "honor your father and your mother" (Deut. 5:16), and number seven commands God's people not to commit adultery (Deut. 5:18). Interestingly, both are the core of building up and protecting a healthy family unit. It is well accepted the breakdown of families is a key reason for a variety of societal woes, and vice versa — strong family units are foundational for a healthy society.

The rest of the Ten Commandments include the following: do not murder, do not steal, do not bear false witness and do not covet. These four, with their supplemental statutes and laws, are to control the actions stemming from evil desires.[21] If these acts or deeds can be controlled and prevented, then men can live together safely and harmoniously, and grow a society together for everyone's benefit. Regardless of whether a person is religious, fears God or not, these laws are meant to protect human beings from each other. Therefore, man, (including all Christians), will always be under such laws for an orderly society. Today's secular governments around the globe have set up laws to govern society which are like the moral laws under the Old Covenant. Therefore, everyone should be subject to the moral laws as described in the Bible if their goal is a safe and just society. Breaking these laws will bring negative consequences, and in many cases the lawbreaker will face legal prosecution, whether a Christian or not.

The famous and possibly greatest moralist and philosopher of China is Confucius. He lived about 1000 years after the giving of the Ten Commandments. One of the main focuses of his teachings was the importance of a strong family unit. His encompassing "golden rule" of morality toward each other in a civil society was: "What you do not wish for yourself, do not do to others." Interestingly Jesus presented a similar idea when He summarized the moral part of the Ten Commandments: love your neighbor as yourself. The difference is that Confucius taught from a negative point of view — *not* doing something *bad* to others. But Jesus' view was positive — *doing* something *good* to others.

The Old Covenant Law with its supplemental ordinances was mainly to control and prevent man from doing harmful things: man was not to murder or commit adultery, steal or bear false witness. A righteous person was one who did not commit these negative actions. But when Jesus came, He uplifted these moral laws to a divine level of sacrificial love with pure intentions of the heart. If anyone thought that it was even possible to fulfill the old Law, then the uplifted Law from Jesus was completely impossible to fulfill. There is no one before Jesus who would have dreamed of this standard of morality. If man could live anywhere close to Jesus' standard, human society would not only be safe, but it would also be a loving, caring, generous, joyful, and peaceful society, like nothing man has ever known.

Here are a few examples of the "uplifted" Law:

- The old Law said, "*An eye for an eye.*" This meant if someone blinded another in the eye, the injured person could blind him back as compensation. The new Law given by Jesus, however, requires the person to whom evil is done to turn the other cheek, walk the extra mile, and give if they are asked (Matt. 5:38–42).
- The old Law required people to love their neighbor and hate their enemy. The new Law requires people to love their *enemies* and bless those who curse them (Matt. 5:44).
- The old Law said, "*Do not murder.*" The new Law says not to be angry with someone without a cause (Matt. 5:21, 22).
- Again, the old said, "*Do not commit adultery.*" The new says to not even to look with lust at another person (Matt. 5:27, 28).
- The old says nothing about being anxious. The new says, "*Do not be anxious*" (Matt. 6:25).
- The old said to not bear false witness. The new says to speak grace to the hearer for building up (Eph. 4:29).[22]

Certainly, if men can treat each other in love and handle relationships such as described by Jesus' moral laws, then surely that would be a model society! Therefore, whether a Christian or not, everyone should consider the "expanded morality" according to Jesus and everyone should do their best to follow Jesus' moral laws.

It was impossible for men to keep the old law, but even more so the new law/commands. It doesn't mean people should not try. Just as people should do their best not to break the any of the Ten Commandments lest they end up in jail – indeed, they should do their best to care for their fellow human beings. The old Law (under the Old Testament/Covenant) mainly tries to control man's action, but the new Law (under the New Testament/ Covenant) goes deeper by changing the heart and soul of a person.

For example, it is one thing to not murder someone (which requires an action), but it is a whole different level of obligation to love an enemy – a matter of the heart. While men should do their best to keep the highest standard of moral Law/Code as described by both the Old *and* New Testaments, anyone who honestly tries will welcome the good news of the New Covenant. What is impossible to man is possible with the Life of God.

Ceremonial Laws

> Having abolished in the flesh the enmity, [even] the law of commandments [contained] in ordinances; that he might create in himself of the two one new man, [so] making peace . . ..
> – Ephesians 2:15 ASV

According to this verse and a similar one in Colossians 2:14, there is an entire body of law that was abolished when Jesus died on the cross. This body of law is what separated Jews from Gentiles. It is because of this body of law Jews could not co-mingle and eat with Gentiles (aka, "the nations" or "ethnos") – this caused their living habits to be kept at a distance from those among the nations. By abolishing this body of law (Eph. 2:15; Col. 2:14), Jews and Gentiles could become one in the New Man being created in Christ Jesus where there could be peace between peoples ("*So as to create in Himself one New Man from the two, thus making peace*" – Eph. 2:15b). This body of law is called "ceremonial laws."

Jesus Christ (the reality) fulfilled the Old Testament ceremonial laws (the shadow). In addition to moral laws under the Old Covenant, there are also statutes and ordinances relating to performing certain ceremonies, as well as regulations on daily living such as: animal sacrifices and offerings, the priesthood and its duties, rigidities surrounding the keeping of the Sabbath, dietary restrictions, and ceremonial adherence in keeping the annual feast days. This category of law in the Old Testament was a type, or a shadow, of the coming Christ; Jesus Christ is the reality of this entire category of law. For example:

> Therefore purge out the old leaven, that you may be a new lump, since you truly are unleavened. For indeed Christ, our Passover, was sacrificed for us. Therefore let us keep the feast, not with old leaven, nor with the leaven of malice and wickedness, but with the unleavened bread of sincerity and truth.
>
> – 1 Corinthians 5:7-8

Jesus Christ is the *real* offering to God; therefore, animal sacrifices are no longer needed. He is the *real* high priest and temple, so the high priest with the Levitical priesthood performing its duties is not needed. Jesus Christ is the *real* rest; therefore, the regulation regarding the Sabbath is gone. This is true for all the ceremonial laws not related to morality. In previous chapters, the topic of Jesus Christ as the reality and fulfillment of the Old Testament types and shadows has been covered more fully.

Believers in the New Testament have the liberty to either continue with these laws, or not. Some may choose to observe the Sabbath or continue with the Old Testament diet (which many people consider to be healthier than a diet containing "non-clean" food). Regardless of whether a Christian practices these regulations or not, no one should judge another over them (Romans 14 makes this abundantly clear). If believers continue to receive and fellowship with one another regardless of differences in living regulations, then they are non-issues and will not be a cause of division in the "Body of Messiah."

Therefore, whether Old Testament or New, all people should attempt to keep these moral laws to the best of their abilities, Christian or not. Keeping them will improve society and breaking them will cause negative personal and societal consequences. Some Christians may choose one set of biblical morals by which to live when in a society of believers and another standard while they are within secular society. However, let's be clear, the New Testament does not support this duality.

There is certainly something special within a community of believers, since there is responsiveness and reciprocation when the virtues of the highest morality are displayed. This highest morality is encapsulated in the superiority of the Lord's New Commandment: "*Love one another as I have loved you.*" Please notice when Jesus responded to the question concerning the greatest of the commandments — "*Thou shalt love the Lord thy God with all thy heart, and with all thy soul, and with all thy mind. This is the first and great commandment. And the second is like unto it, Thou shalt love thy neighbor as thyself. On these two commandments hang all the law and the prophets* (<u>Matthew 22:34-40</u>) . . . the emphasis was upon the individual's ability to perform — whereas Jesus' New Commandment was to love one another "*as I have loved you that you also love one another.*" The capacity or ability to love under the New Commandment is much higher but bears within its injunction the very love of Jesus *through* the believer.

At the same time, it should be the same divine love with which believers love and honor (considered *precious*) all people (1 Pet. 2:17). Certainly, it would take the same divine love to love one's enemies, and there is no separation given as to whether the "enemy" spoken of by Matthew is a Christian or a non-Christian. (This author does not promote believers to ignorantly love in a way which could possibly bring harm to himself and to his loved ones).

Ceremonial laws and regulations on living habits are completely voluntary depending on each person's preferences, local customs, and rules. For certain, whether a person observes these laws and regulations should not be a factor in their relationship with God. As far as God is concerned (in the New Testament), they are no longer mandatory as a reflection of one's holiness before the Lord and, most certainly, keeping of such laws and ordinances are NOT salvific (they do not save a person from their sins — salvation is through the shed blood of the Savior and belief in His provision).

The rest of this chapter will focus on the huge gulf of differences between relationships with God based on the Old Covenant versus those based on the New Covenant. The difference is night and day, death and life, blessing or cursing. It is part of the good news that all men should hear.

The Old Covenant – The Law

> Then the LORD said to Moses, "Write these words, for according to the tenor of these words I have made a covenant with you and with Israel." . . . And He wrote on the tablets the words of the covenant, the Ten Commandments.
>
> – Exodus 34:27, 28b

These verses clearly reveal the Ten Commandments were a covenant. This is a critical point to understand in order to follow the rest of the chapter. The Old Covenant was tied to the Ten Commandments with all its subsidiary statutes and ordinances. Here is a review of the Ten Commandments:

1. You shall have no other gods before Me.
2. You shall not make idols.
3. You shall not take the name of the LORD your God in vain.
4. Remember the Sabbath day, to keep it holy.
5. Honor your father and your mother.
6. You shall not murder.
7. You shall not commit adultery.
8. You shall not steal.
9. You shall not bear false witness against your neighbor.
10. You shall not covet.

These Ten Commandments are not the entire Law of the Old Testament (as we discovered in Footnotes Nos. 5 and 6), but rather they form the basis for a host of supplemental rules and ordinances relating to topics such as: marriage and family, times and seasons, diet, business practices, judicial procedures, property rights, criminal laws and restitutions, the priesthood and the Levites, tithing, the temple and sanctuary, sacrifices, and offerings. It is based on these laws that God made a covenant with Israel.

The Old Covenant Is Conditional

There is blessing to those who obey the Old Covenant Law and cursing for those who break it.

> You have seen what I did to the Egyptians, and how I bore you on eagles' wings and brought you to Myself. Now therefore, if you will indeed obey My voice and keep My covenant, then you shall be a special treasure to Me above all people; for all the earth is Mine.
>
> Then all the people answered together and said, "All that the LORD has spoken we will do." So Moses brought back the words of the people to the LORD.
>
> ~ Exodus 19:4–5, 8

Cursed is the one who does not confirm all the words of this law by observing them. And all the people shall say, 'Amen!'
> – Deuteronomy 27:26

Now it shall come to pass, if you diligently obey the voice of the LORD your God, to observe carefully all His commandments which I command you today, that the LORD your God will set you high above all nations of the earth.

But it shall come to pass, if you do not obey the voice of the LORD your God, to observe carefully all His commandments and His statutes which I command you today, that all these curses will come upon you and overtake you.
> – Deuteronomy 28:1, 15, KJV

The Israelites were slaves in Egypt for more than 200 years serving Pharaoh. Then God came to deliver them by sending various plagues to Egypt. His goal of delivering the Israelites was to bring them to Himself. After God carried them out on *"eagles' wings,"* He made a covenant with them by the giving them the Ten Commandments. The agreement was conditional: *"If you obey . . . then I will bless"* . . . *"If you do not obey . . . curses will come upon you."* From a contractual law perspective, this was considered a bilateral (or a conditional) agreement. God would do His part of blessing man or bringing curses to man depending on whether man obeys or disobeys His laws.

The worst part of this arrangement was grading or judging this bilateral contract was not based on a curve – or where sixty percent is a passing D grade. Judgment, according to this agreement, was based on man's agreement to keep all the laws. This means one hundred percent obedience to the Law, or the person has failed. If a person breaks just one of God's laws, they have broken them all (James 2:10). This may not seem fair now, but when this agreement was originally presented, Israel absurdly signed on and agreed to this conditional agreement. Israel didn't negotiate; it confidently said "yes," "amen," and "we will do it."

Israel was so weak that God needed to bring them out from slavery on eagles' wings, and yet proudly they (the Israelites) said they could do whatever God commanded them. Man's blindness, or pride, makes him think he can obey everything God commands. Ironically, when Moses came back from the mountain to give Israel the Ten Commandments, Israel was already breaking them: As Moses descended the mount, God's people were worshipping a calf made of gold. Throughout the Old Testament, Israel was cursed and under judgment again and again for disobeying God's law.

Works of the Law

It takes a lot of effort and energy to comply with the law; therefore, it is called "the works of the law."

> . . . yet we know that a person is not justified by works of the law
> . . . because by works of the law no one will be justified.
> – Galatians 2:16, ESV

> For by works of the law no human being will be justified in his sight, since through the law comes knowledge of sin.
> – Romans 3:20, ESV

According to Paul, fulfilling God's Law depends on man's effort and work. It does not come naturally. God's Law and man's fallen nature are not compatible; therefore, it takes a lot of effort to work at keeping God's Law. The problem is this — no matter how much men do their utmost to work at keeping God's Law, they will fail on at least one point. For certain, everyone fails with the tenth commandment, "*Do not covet.*" It is impossible for fallen people not to yearn for what others have! Just that one area of failure alone brings in the entire curse. So, if man is working on keeping God's Law, he is under a curse — he will never be justified.

Recall that "justified" means to be completely righteous before God. Since human beings cannot continue keeping all the Law, therefore, none can be justified, and none can be counted righteous.

The *"works of the law"* also means to be counted righteous depends on merit; it is a merit reward system--meritorious. If one can work hard enough to keep God's Law, then he can gain enough merit for God to reward him with justification or salvation. Many people may think they deserve merit from God just for making a good effort at trying harder, even if they can't keep the whole Law. But, according to these verses in Galatians and Romans, no matter how hard people try, they can never be justified.

Ephesians 2:9 states if works can save men, then they would be able to boast they have "earned" salvation. The religious law keepers in Paul's day (who in their own estimation had been doing a relatively good job in keeping the Law) had become judgmental about others whom they deemed to have failed in keeping the Law. Over time, a law keeper will either become disappointed, discouraged, and give up on God, or they will become proud and judgmental of people around them who are not up to their religious standards.

The Dreadful Results of Law Keepers

One of the main results of keeping the Law is being cursed.

> For all who rely on works of the law are under a curse; for it is written, "Cursed be everyone who does not abide by all things written in the Book of the Law, and do them."
> – Galatians 3:10, ESV

> "Cursed be anyone who does not confirm the words of this law by doing them." And all the people shall say, "Amen."
> – Deuteronomy 27:26, ESV

For the sake of society, man must continuously work at keeping the moral laws, but because he can't keep all of them, he falls under the curse. This is a Catch 22, a "damned if you do and damned if you don't" scenario. If a person does not care about God's blessing or cursing, then they will only use their effort to be a good citizen in society. However, once a person tries to live under the Old Covenant, they will want to please God and will desire to keep God's Law, in order to please Him and receive His blessings. This category of people living under the Old Covenant will always come up short and will continually fall under condemnation. How terrible to live in such a way, constantly having to work at keeping God's Law, but always falling short and coming under condemnation. What a dreadful religious life to live! The *law keeping life* is a cursed life — not because the Law in and of itself is cursed — because *"the Law is holy, and the commandment holy, and just, and good"* (Rom. 7:12) — but because of our inability to keep it and the consequent curse related thereto.

Indwelling Sin Is Revived and Results in Death

> What then shall we say? That the law is sin? By no means! Yet
> if it had not been for the law, I would not have known sin. For I
> would not have known what it is to covet if the law had not said,
> "You shall not covet." But sin, seizing an opportunity through
> the commandment, produced in me all kinds of covetousness.
> For apart from the law, sin lies dead. I was once alive apart
> from the law, but when the commandment came, sin came alive
> and I died. The very commandment that promised life proved
> to be death to me. For sin, seizing an opportunity through the
> commandment, deceived me and through it killed me.
> – Romans 7:7–11, ESV

Typically, people think the Law is supposed to control and eradicate
sin. It is ironic Paul would teach the "reviving" of sin because of the Law-
-the Law made sin alive! Previously, Paul was physically alive, going about
his business doing whatever he wanted. Paul could have even had some
spiritual admiration for God. Then, he became aware of the Law and wanted
to please God. At that moment, sin "came alive" and death in the sense of
incapacitation, condemnation, and defeatism arose. Paul died to any hope
of a relationship with God. It is not the Law's fault that "death" occurred for
Paul; it was sin taking advantage of the Law which brought death to him.
Sin deceived him, causing Paul to think he should use his best effort to keep
the Law — the works of the Law. Once he tried, due to sin, he found out he
couldn't fulfill the Law; therefore, his condition *after* becoming aware of
the Law was worse than his initial state *before* the Law. The very Law meant
for life (if man could keep it) turned out to be for death because of sin's
debilitating affect

Using Paul's struggle with coveting as an example: Paul didn't know
coveting was against God. So, he lived his life coveting this and that,
thinking it was normal. It didn't strike him coveting was wrong.

But one day, Paul learned in order to please God, he needed to abide
by God's commandments. He learned one of the commandments is "do
not covet." Because he had become religious and wanted to please God by
being a good law keeper, he wanted to stop coveting. Once that decision
was made, sin awakened. It came alive and overwhelmed his desire to stop

coveting. Paul's coveting became more pronounced. Now, aware of this sin, he could not stop himself from all kinds of coveting. This continuing defeat was spiritually killing him in the form of condemnation and despair. Therefore, whatever desire and hope he might have for a relationship with God was completely killed off.

Worse yet, the Lord had uplifted the standard of the commandments to a whole other level which included loving one's enemies. Alas! There are more (and a higher standard of) laws for religious Christians wanting to please God by way of the Old Covenant criteria. If Paul was killed by trying to fulfill the laws of the Old Testament then Christians who want to please God by fulfilling the laws in this manner, which would include those in the New Testament, will be killed ten times faster than Paul.

Minister of Death or Life

> ...who also made us sufficient as ministers of the New Covenant, not of the letter but of the Spirit; for the letter kills, but the Spirit gives life.
>
> ~ 2 Corinthians 3:6

Believers should ask themselves what kind of ministers they are or wish to be. What are they ministering — the New Covenant, the Spirit which gives life, or the Old Covenant which is the letter of the Law which kills? The letter of the Law referenced in 2 Corinthians 3:6 refers to the Old Covenant (2 Cor. 3:14) which relates to the works of the Law. If one's ministry is merely to tell people God's Law, teaching them they need to try to keep God's Law in order to reap God's blessings, such ministry will lead people to spiritual death. The letter of the Law ministered in such a way kills.

When believers read the Bible, "the letter," they also need to be mindful how they are approaching the Bible. Is it just the letter of Law to them, or will they turn their hearts to the Lord (2 Cor. 3:16) and receive the life-giving and life-transforming Spirit? Whenever they come to the Bible, believers need to look to Jesus in order to turn their hearts to Him. This is the way to be transferred out of the Old Covenant and into the New.

The Positive Purposes of the Old Covenant

What was God's purpose in giving the Law and making such a covenant with man? Was God a hater who wanted to punish man and make man miserable? Why would He propose such an agreement? Didn't He have the forethought wherein man would fail at keeping His Law?

Yes, God knew, but He didn't *force* man to sign such an agreement. A more relevant question may be: why was man foolish enough to sign up and agree to such a covenant with God? This question is still relevant today; there is something innate in man in which man thinks he is able to fulfill the Law — if he works hard enough at it.

Let's consider for a moment, from the Scriptures, God's purposes for giving the Law. First, it's important to understand the context leading up to this covenant (the commandments given). God called Abraham and his wife Sarah out of today's Iraq into the "good land," today's Israel. There in the good land Abraham begot Isaac and Isaac begot Jacob. Jacob bore twelve sons before God changed Jacob's name to "Israel."

Jacob and his twelve sons became Israel, which included twelve "tribes." Israel (Jacob) brought his entire family to Egypt because of a famine. It turned out one of Israel's sons — Joseph, whom his jealous brothers sold as a slave years earlier — became what would be equivalent to the prime minister of Egypt. Because of his position, Joseph was able to give his family (seventy souls) a portion of land in Egypt; thus, taking care of them during the famine. Israel (the twelve tribes) remained in Egypt for more than 200 years.

Initially, (because of Joseph) Israel was treated well. However, when Joseph passed away and as Israel's population grew, they lost favor with the Egyptians, eventually becoming slaves to that nation. By the time God called Moses to bring Israel out of Egypt, there were close to two million Israelites. After spending multiple generations in Egypt, the Israelites understood Egyptian culture and its gods. They had little knowledge of the God of Abraham, Isaac and Jacob (their patriarchs). It was for this reason Moses said to God, *When I come to the children of Israel and say to them, 'The God of your fathers has sent me to you,' and they say to me, 'What is His name?' what shall I say to them?"* (Ex. 3:13)

Israel didn't know the name of their God, the *true* God; that's how far the nation was removed from the knowledge of Him.

God, through Moses, rescued Israel from Egypt and its tyranny. He carried Israel out of Egypt on "eagle's wings," but the nation had absolutely no idea who God was. They did not know what He was like, or what His purposes were. It was within this context, after Israel had just crossed the

Red Sea, when God met Moses on Mount Sinai and gave Israel His covenant, the Ten Commandments.

God's Testimony of Who He Is

God had positive purposes in giving the Old Covenant. First, the Law testified as to God's identity or character:

> And he gave to Moses, when he had finished speaking with him on Mount Sinai, the two tablets of the testimony, tablets of stone, written with the finger of God.
>
> — Exodus 31:18, ESV

> The law of the LORD is perfect, reviving the soul; the testimony of the LORD is sure, making wise the simple.
>
> — Psalm 19:7, ESV

To man, the Old Covenant was the ten foundational commandments on how to behave; but to God, it was His testimony. The Law to man was a demand — a standard for man to live up to. But to God, the Law is a testimony of Himself. Without His testimony, man has little or no concept of who God is, what He is like, or what His character is like. After giving His testimony, man finally had a very good description of God. Stories of the Greek gods, for example, include testimonies which describe the gods being powerful, but also lustful, ambitious, angry, or deceitful — in a word: avaricious! Who is the *real* God, the true God, and what is He like? Mankind needed Him to reveal this. This is what it means regarding the Law being God's testimony.

Therefore, this is the detailed testimony God gave concerning Himself. One may say this is His formal introduction to man. Before His testimony, man could only guess what kind of character God possessed; but after His testimony, there was no doubt concerning His character. People can make their own judgment after such a testimony whether they will admire and adore such a God or belittle Him without respect. God's testimony is sealed in stone, by a covenant, written down for generations of humankind to know God's nature and character. He certainly gave a testimony wherein people can prove true or not from generation to generation.

Additionally, God would not give a law He could not fulfill Himself. What if God steals or He covets? Then He will have to sentence Himself to death for breaking the Law. That cannot be; therefore, whatever laws God gives He is certain to eternally fulfill. He will not break one of them . . . ever. Otherwise, God would not be righteous . . . He would not be qualified to judge.

The Law then is a description of God's nature, not His actions. A person's nature cannot change, but actions can. Eventually, the higher Law in the New Testament commands people to love their enemies. That is also a description of God's nature. Matthew, in Chapter 5, who spoke concerning the various expanded laws, ended his gospel with a command to "*Be perfect as your heavenly Father is perfect*" (Matt. 5:48). Matthew was speaking of the Father's perfect nature. "Being perfect" is not an "act" for God. It is Who He *is* — His innate, eternal attribute.

God's eternal plan was to have an unbreakable union or marriage with man for eternity. In the Old Testament, Israel represented the man with whom God joined Himself. Therefore, God called Israel His "wife" and His "bride" (Isa. 54:5–6; Jer. 62:5).

Later, we will review how the first three commandments are specifically likened to a marriage vow. However, first let's consider the fourth through the tenth commandments which can be considered His testimony to woo Israel to marriage by displaying what a good "husband" He will be. God was trying to impress His bride by giving His testimony so she would be drawn to Him, marry Him, and depend on Him as her husband.

4. Sabbath – God is a person who is at rest. He has done everything and prepared everything. He is not fighting, and He is not working. He is at rest for eternity, a peaceful God.

5. Honor your father and mother – God is a family man. He cares for family. As the Father, surely, He loves all of His children. Even within the Trinity, there is a "family" relationship between the Father and the Son: mutual honor. The Father honors all His children through His care and supply. Now, as sons of God we should reciprocate that honor back to the Father.

6. Do not murder – God treasures life. He is the author of life, and He loves life. Additionally, His anger is controlled and limited.

7. Do not commit adultery – God is faithful. Once He has joined Himself with someone, He will never break His bond with that

person. No matter if His elect strays, He will continue to be faithful to them for eternity.

8. Do not steal – God is self-sufficient. In fact, He is the only one in the universe who is. He does not steal because all things belong to Him.

9. Do not bear false witness – God is truthful. God cannot lie. Whatever He says is the reality, the truth. Man can bank on it.

10. Do not covet – God is fully satisfied not just in Himself but also in His eternal purpose which is His household (the bride, the body – the assembly). He does not covet anything outside of Himself.

What an amazing testimony of God, of His person, and His character! After such a testimony, man now knows who God is and what He is like. There is no other god in the history of various religions who has given us such a testimony. This testimony inspires adoration, admiration, love, and worship from men (male and female). This should inspire man to say, "I do," to be joined to this wonderful God as their husband.

The Covenant: A Mutual Marriage Vow between God and Israel

> Then I passed by you and saw you, and you were indeed at the age for love. So I spread the edge of My garment over you and covered your nakedness. I pledged Myself to you, entered into a covenant with you, and you became Mine. This is the declaration of the Lord GOD.
>
> I will judge you the way adulteresses and those who shed blood are judged. Then I will bring about your bloodshed in wrath and jealousy.
>
> – Ezekiel 16:8, 38, HCSB

> Indeed, your husband is your Maker – His name is Yahweh of Hosts – and the Holy One of Israel is your Redeemer; He is called the God of all the earth. For the LORD has called you, like a wife deserted and wounded in spirit, a wife of one's youth when she is rejected," says your God.
>
> – Isaiah 54:5–6, HCSB

According to the context of Ezekiel 16, the covenant made by God with Israel on Mount Sinai was actually a marriage covenant. God proposed to Israel, and Israel said, "I do": God and Israel were "married." They entered a union together. Later the prophets wrote often concerning God as the husband and Israel as the wife, or God as the bridegroom and Israel as the bride (Isa. 62:5). The covenant, then, was a marriage pledge from God to Israel where He declared who He is, what He is like, how much He loves her, and how He will take care of her. Israel didn't have anything to worry about for her entire life, except to enjoy all His riches. Then in return, God asked her whether she would make the same pledge and to match Him in every way and be His wife. Israel said, "YES, Amen, we will do it."

Understanding this, then the Ten Commandments were actually a marriage vow, the first three commandments, fit right into place as well as the others which were already described above:

1. Do not have other gods besides me – This is the first of a marriage pledge. God will not commit adultery, meaning God will never forsake the one with whom He has joined Himself and go to another. He is now asking His bride not to have another "man." He is the one, the unique one to His wife, and she will have only Him and be with Him alone. He is her only lover and husband.

2. Do not make images of other gods for God is jealous – God is a jealous husband. He doesn't want to compete with anyone else. He wants His wife to love only Him and not remember any of her past lovers or any other "men." It would be a fair request for a faithful husband to ask his wife to remove pictures of other men who might tempt her. God, in a sense, is asking His bride to remove "pictures" – anything which would remind her of another lover who would pull her away from her one husband, God. God promised to love His wife faithfully, and He expects the same from His bride.

3. Do not take God's name in vain – In western culture, the wife takes on the family name of the husband and marries into the husband's family. Similarly, Israel took on God's name, which means Israel is married to God; thus, everything God is and possesses – all His riches – belong to her. The bride also has God's same name. To take God's name in vain meant Israel, though having God's name, was treating His name as nothing. She did not take advantage of

the riches and power of His name, but acted as if she were poor, weak, and miserable. Let's say Bill Gate's wife, Melinda Gates, went around begging for food dressed in rags. She is the wife of one of the richest man in the world and bears his name but wouldn't be acting like it! What vanity, and how that would shame not just her, but her husband, Mr. Gates. Israel as God's bride, bearing His name, should live and behave as one who possesses God. All God is and has is hers.

God made a marriage vow to Israel and asked her to make the same vow back — she agreed. This became the Old Covenant — a marriage covenant between God and humanity, represented by Israel.

Alas, Israel as the wife didn't keep her marriage vow. She started taking on many lovers (gods), so much so God referred to her as a prostitute. In His jealous rage, He allowed these "lovers" to take advantage of her, beat her, strip her, and take everything away from her (Ezek. 16). Every time she repented, God as her wonderful and faithful husband, came and took her back to bring her back to health and to make her His beautiful wife again (Isa. 54). This is the love story between God and man (Israel).

In the Old Testament prophetic books, this theme of Israel as the unfaithful wife — including God allowing judgment to befall her, His faithfulness to not forsake her, and ultimately His grace in taking her back as His only beloved; especially, from the book of Hosea.

God "Breathes Himself Out" through the Word
Thus, in reading "All Scripture" — both "testaments"; His words to us are the very breath of God, His Life-giving breath. God "breathes Himself out" through the Word, enabling man to receive Life.

> . . . every Writing is God-breathed, and profitable for teaching, for conviction, for setting aright, for instruction that is in righteousness.
> — 2 Timothy 3:16, YLT

> It is the Spirit who gives life; the flesh profits nothing. The words that I speak to you are spirit, and they are life.
> — John 6:63

The giving of God's Law is His speaking which is recorded in the Scripture. His speaking is simply His "breathing out." Paul refers to this as the Law being "God-breathed" ("*All Scripture is God-breathed*" – 2 Tim. 3:16). It is impossible to speak without breathing out. When God spoke the Law, it was full of His breath. His breath is life to man. God "breathes out" so man can "breath in" and receive God's breath: His life. Jesus said His Word – His speaking – is Spirit and life. Man receives breath and life from God's speaking (in the Scriptures).

God's intention in speaking forth the Law enables man to receive His breath through His speaking thereby becoming alive with Him. The real profit in Scripture for teaching, conviction, and instruction is the breath of God being ministered into the hearer (reader).

Without receiving God's breath through His Word, Scripture is just black and white letters – like any other book which can teach and instruct. But what is *profitable* occurs when man receives God's breath bringing life into its teaching and instruction in righteousness. Whenever believers come to read the Bible to hear God's speaking, they should not forget to breathe in God's Spirit, through faith and prayer.

In point of fact, "don't hold your breath" – learn to "breathe in His Word" – for the words He speaks to us are Spirit (pneuma or "breath") and Life (John 6:63).

Negative Purposes of the Old Covenant

The Old Covenant also had negative purposes, such as exposing man's sinful nature.

> . . . for by the law is the knowledge of sin.
> – Romans 3:20

> Moreover the law entered that the offense might abound...
> – Romans 5:20

> I would not have known sin except through the law...For apart from the law sin was dead.
> – Romans 7:7b–8

When Adam and Eve ate of the forbidden tree, they didn't just disobey God. They ingested sin into their being. This sin is considered to be "satanic life and nature" which came into man. It can be said it affected Adam's DNA and mutated his genetics, making all subsequent generations sinners by nature. Though men had sin and committed sins, they didn't know the evil things they were doing were sin. They might have thought it was just part of human nature to steal and to murder (just don't get caught doing it). So, it was normal to covet and crave things from persons around them — things which didn't belong to them. They didn't have any knowledge of their sin.

Therefore, God gave the Law so men would come to the knowledge of sin. When the Law came, men realized there was a standard to fulfill. Once they realized this and tried to live by this standard of the Law, they realized what sin was. It was in them. In fact, sin became alive in them to make sure they could not fulfill the requirements of the Law. Many people have a common misperception wherein the Law was given to *control* sin but according to Romans 7:7-8 the Law *caused* sin to abound.

There is nothing wrong with the Law; it is holy and righteous, and it did what God intended it to do. The Law uncovered sin in man, so man could recognize he's a hopeless and helpless sinner who cannot live up to the standard of God's Law.

> For the mind-set of the flesh is hostile to God because it does not submit itself to God's law, **for it is unable to do so**. Those who are in the flesh cannot please God.
>
> – Romans 8:7–8, HCSB

The flesh refers to fallen man and the mind-set of fallen man without the life of God. Man, in his flesh, is hostile to His Creator. The "flesh of sin" in man is an enemy of God, and therefore, not able to submit to God's Law. Even when man is desirous to submit to God's Law, fallen man is unable to do so. It is not possible for fallen man to please God — to fulfill God's Law.

Without the Law, men may think they are quite good. They can live in a way pleasing to a higher power. They can think highly of themselves–just how good and charitable they are to others. The Law's job, however, is to expose what is really in people so men will no longer deceive themselves. Through God's Law, they will hopefully come to their senses and realize their true condition, so they'll turn to Jesus Christ for *salvation*.

A Guardian to Keep Men Safe

> Now before faith came, we were held captive under the Law, imprisoned until the coming faith would be revealed. So then, the Law was our guardian until Christ came, in order that we might be justified by faith. But now that faith has come, we are no longer under a guardian . . .
>
> – Galatians 3:23–25, ESV

One can imagine the danger of living in a lawless society — a society with no law, no law enforcement, and where anything goes. It would be a fearful place. Men would end up openly killing each other. Therefore, the Law was given to guard man, to keep man safe. Many countries today are like one big prison where there are surveillance cameras everywhere to make sure people do not break the law; it is intended to keep their citizens safe.

God's desire is not for man to stay under the Law, in its prison. God's purpose is to *use* the Law as a guardian, a pedagogue (a teacher), to safeguard and guide man to faith in Jesus Christ. Before coming to faith, man is like a little child who needs to be under a guardian who will make sure the child does not do anything foolish and harmful. The pedagogue's goal is to lead man to Jesus Christ. The guardian's job is done once man comes to faith in Jesus Christ. Men may try their best to be justified according to Law; however, if they are honest with themselves, they'll admit they are a failure at keeping God's Law. When they arrive at this point of hopelessness before God according to the Law, then they will come to receive the faith of Jesus Christ in order to be justified before God. At that point, the law has done its job as the "school master" who has brought them to saving faith in the Savior!

Freed from the Law and Joined to Jesus Christ

> Or do you not know, brethren (for I speak to those who know the Law), that the law has dominion over a man as long as he lives? For the woman who has a husband is bound by the law to her husband as long as he lives. But if the husband dies, she is released from the law of her husband. So then if, while her husband lives, she marries another man, she will be called an adulteress; but if her husband dies, she is free from that law, so that she is no adulteress, though she has married another

man. Therefore, my brethren, you also have become dead to
the law through the body of Christ, that you may be married to
another — to Him who was raised from the dead, that we should
bear fruit to God.

— Romans 7:1–4

In eternity, God's desire is to be joined to humanity, to be one with
man — to *marry* man. He will be the husband, the male; humanity (male
and female) will be the wife, the female. In the Bible, the exemplary role of
the husband is to be the provider, protector, the giver of riches, and source
of love to the wife. The wife's exemplary role is to be the receiver, enjoyer, a
lover, and the fruit-bearer to the husband. When God declared His nature
and character through the Law, He testified He was qualified to be the
husband. He is the "male" in the universe. The Law is a detailed description
of what a true husband is like. The Law then is not the requirement for the
wife (the female) but for the husband (the male).

Humanity was created by God to be the universal female as the
counterpart to be joined to God as the universal male. This was the
significance of God being the Tree of Life — humanity might ingest Him, be
joined to Him, be one with Him. He would become the source of life within
humanity. Instead, Satan tricked man into declaring his independence from
God, to be god in and by himself. Just as Satan wanted to replace God, he
deceived man to take the same position as he to replace God. And just as
Satan wanted to be the "man" in the universe, humanity took Satan's side
becoming the "man" in the universe taking the place of God. Therefore,
man (male and female) left the position of the female by eating of the tree
of the knowledge of good and evil and became the male.

Fallen humanity (which the Bible calls the "flesh" and the "old man")
took the position of the male; thus, humanity originally created by God to
be the female became trapped inside the fallen man — married and joined
to him. Since fallen humanity took the position of the male, then the law of
the male (God) is applied to humanity. Every "man" in the universe must
live up to the law of the male in the universe. Both Satan and fallen man
must live up to the Law of God.

Basically, God says, "This is what the male — the husband of the
universe — is like; this is who He is and His character." Then this fallen
man — the imposter who has joined himself to Satan — says to God, "I am

now the male of the universe. I don't need you." Then God says, "Okay, if you are the male, the husband, then you need to live and act like one. Let me give you my testimony. This is the Law for you to keep proving you can play the role of the male of the universe." Therefore, the Law is for the husband to keep, to show he is the authentic male.

Satan was the first one to be exposed as unqualified to be the male because he broke God's Law: Satan coveted God's position, which was the source of his rebellion. Then he gave a false witness and lied to Eve (who was deceived) in order to give her a wrong impression of God. Adam knew full-well if he too partook of the forbidden fruit he would be "disobedient" to God – no deception there – just disobedience! Then, acting out as sin in man, we find that this deception and disobedience led to the first murder when Cain killed his brother Abel (John 8:44 – *"the devil . . . was a murderer from the beginning"*). Fallen man (the First Adam), with sin in his flesh, took on the same nature as the devil: therefore, as the "male," fallen man came under the "law of the husband." Of course, this fallen man (the flesh) – not being able keep the law of the husband (God) – is also exposed as not being qualified to be the husband . . . the male of the universe. If fallen man is alive, then the original created man (the female) is also bound to her first husband since she is joined to him, the fallen man. Since her first husband is under the Law and under the curse for breaking the Law, she is also under Law and shares that same curse.

According to Romans 7:1–4, the only way for her to be freed is for her first husband to die. If he dies, then she can marry another husband. The good news is this: Christ died on the cross, the flesh (the fallen man – the old man) was crucified with Him (Rom. 6:6; Gal. 2:20). The old man (the husband) died with Christ. This death released the wife, the original created man, to be joined to a new husband – *the resurrected Jesus Christ*. Now, man as the female has a new husband, and this new husband has proven Himself by fulfilling all of God's Law. Therefore, He is qualified to be the real husband to man; to take care of all of man's needs. Now, man, joined to Christ, can take pleasure in being the "wife," – the *enjoyer*, the receiver, and the lover to Christ, bearing fruit to God.

By joining with the resurrected Christ, united with Him and with His life and nature, she bears the fruit of the Spirit: love, joy, peace, long suffering, kindness, goodness, faithfulness, gentleness, and self-control (Gal. 5:22-23). This is the spontaneous character and expression of the "wife" who is joined with and receives the rich supply from her new, resurrected "husband," Jesus Christ.

It is critical to understand the Old Covenant does not refer to the Old Testament (Genesis to Malachi); it is a *condition* for a relationship with God. The Old Covenant exposes the sin of fallen man. Therefore, although Christians no longer live within the Old Testament period, they persist to live within the framework found in the Old Covenant. Alas! A Christian living under the Old Covenant will read the New Testament and find even more laws under which to be bound — receiving more condemnation! But believers living within the New Covenant, however, can read the Old Testament and find only Jesus Christ — the husband — for their enjoyment.

9

THE NEW COVENANT
(SECTION B)

Four Blessings of the New Covenant

In Section A of this chapter, we discussed the Old Covenant relating to its nature; the reasons why it was given; and the results of the Old Covenant. In Section B, the focus is on the New Covenant. Everyone who understands the good news of the New Covenant should rejoice. People living during the New Covenant period would be considered extremely foolish not to accept the terms of the New Covenant given to us directly by God with thanksgiving. The New Covenant is unconditionally fulfilled *without man's self-efforts*. There are four blessings within the New Covenant. It is described below in two portions: one from the Old Testament and a repeat in the New Testament.

> Behold, the days are coming, says the LORD, when I will make a New Covenant with the house of Israel and with the house of Judah — not according to the covenant that I made with their fathers in the day that I took them by the hand to lead them out of the land of Egypt, My covenant which they broke, though I was a husband to them, says the LORD. But this is the covenant that I will make with the house of Israel after those days, says the LORD: I will put My law in their minds, and write it on their hearts; and I will be their God, and they shall be My people. No more shall every man teach his neighbor, and every man his brother, saying, 'Know the LORD,' for they all shall know Me, from the least of them to the greatest of them, says the LORD. For I will forgive their iniquity, and their sin I will remember no more.
>
> – Jeremiah 31:31–34

For this is the covenant that I will make with the house of Israel after those days, declares the Lord: I will put my laws into their minds, and write them on their hearts, and I will be their God, and they shall be my people. And they shall not teach, each one his neighbor and each one his brother, saying, 'Know the Lord,' for they shall all know me, from the least of them to the greatest. For I will be merciful toward their iniquities, and I will remember their sins no more."

– Hebrews 8:10–12, ESV

It is remarkable in that the New Covenant is spelled out clearly in just two verses in Jeremiah when the Old Covenant law took scores of chapters to describe. This shows the simplicity of the New Covenant. It is direct – to the point. Jehovah God will unilaterally accomplish everything in the New Covenant. In the Old Covenant, Jehovah God kept His side of the bilateral agreement, but Israel, representing mankind, didn't (and couldn't). They repeatedly failed, but this was part of God's design. One of the reasons for God to give the Law, as we have seen in the previous chapter, was to expose man's sinful nature; therefore, they were destined to fail. Meanwhile, God's plan has always been the New Covenant.

God simply declared what He would do in no uncertain terms in three sentences. There is no condition for man to fulfill before God. The prominent parts of the New Covenant indicate God being life to man; man receiving God as life, being joined to God in perfect union; and spontaneously living according to God's nature. God would accomplish what He covenanted to do for man, because the New Covenant was actually in God's heart and His eternal purpose before creating man in the very beginning.

This was God's desire from the very beginning by providing the Tree of Life to man. If man would have eaten the Tree of Life instead of partaking of sin, then man would have received God's life and nature and would have become one with God. Man would express God and have dominion over God's enemy, Satan. Man would not need the last part of the New Covenant relating to forgiveness of sins – because there would have been no fall. If man had not partaken of the tree of the knowledge of good and evil, then man would not have had sin – thus, needing forgiveness. Therefore, the positive aspect of the Old Covenant, as described earlier, affirms God's eternal purpose from the beginning–expressing Himself and being joined to man. God gave the negative aspect of the Old Covenant as a temporary solution to guard man and to expose sin, so that man would welcome the New Covenant, thereby fulfilling what God yearned for from the very beginning. Thus, the Old Covenant would have been unnecessary if man had eaten from the Tree of Life from the start. Now that the New Covenant is available, the Old Covenant is obsolete and ready to completely vanish away (Heb. 8:13). The New Covenant was God's purpose from the very beginning, even before time.

1. The Imparting of the Law of Life into believers

> I will put my Spirit within you, and cause you to walk in my statutes, and you shall keep my ordinances, and do them.
> — Ezekiel 36:27, HNV

> Therefore you shall be perfect, just as your Father in heaven is perfect.
> — Matthew 5:48, HNV

The first thing God provided in His New Covenant was to put His Law in His people's minds and hearts (Jer. 31:33; see also Heb. 8:10). The Law in the Old Covenant was on a tablet outside of man, but the Law in the New Covenant became an integral part of man and his character.

The heart signifies the nature, character, and personality of man's very being. The word "write" indicates inscribing something. The Law inscribed in man's heart means the Law of God is now part of man's nature, just as it is part of God's nature and character. Previously, man had a fallen nature, so he needed to work at following God's Law which was foreign to him. He had to work at it with much effort, because the Law was alien to him. This is like a monkey trying to act like a man! As hard as a monkey tries, it will eventually fail, because it is still a monkey. In the New Covenant, man does not have to try to follow God's Law because the nature of God's written law is now written upon man's nature, his heart.

How does this happen? The New Covenant is the Spirit of God Who comes into and becomes an integral part of man. The Spirit of God is no longer outside (or simply "upon") man, but within man — joined in perfect union with man. This portion found in Jeremiah 31 is a prophecy for believers living within the bounds of the New Covenant. This fact of the

Spirit of God coming into man is the vital difference between the old and the new. This mysterious union between divinity and humanity as seen in the God-Man, Jesus Christ (as "fully God" and "fully man") is difficult to explain. How can today's humanity in general partake of that divine nature (1 Peter. 1:5)? Grappling with this mystery, many Bible expositors use various descriptive terms such as: blended, grafted, joined, mingled, becoming one and more. No matter the mystery of God and man becoming one and the descriptive words used, it is necessary to understand God and man are still distinct and distinguishable - just as Jesus said of a husband and wife's union: "The two shall become one flesh" (Genesis 2:24; Matthew 19:5;; Mark 10:8; Ephesians 5:31); yet, clearly, one is the husband and the other is still the wife - though two, they are one. Even so, the joining together between humanity and divinity does not produce a third species. When Christians say - "A New Creation" (2Cor. 5:17) some have suggested that an entirely new species other than humanity was created. No, the new creation is simply the joining of divinity with humanity which was accomplished in Jesus Christ.

Notice, it is the Spirit Who causes man to walk according to His Law. It is no longer man's effort working to keep God's Law; rather, the Spirit of God with His life and nature is what causes man to live by God's Law. With the Spirit within man, God gave a promise: "*You shall*" keep my Law (Ezek. 36:27). The word "*shall*" means keeping God's Law is inevitable. Due to the Spirit of God in man, man shall keep and do God's laws. Sooner or later, man shall, without a doubt, without a choice, predictably, express the very life and nature of God.

This is akin to the Lord Jesus saying, "*You shall be perfect as your heavenly Father is perfect.*" After telling the disciples about the *expanded* Law, which is humanly impossible to keep and laughable to suggest one can attempt to fulfill it, He gave a promise they shall be perfect or complete as their heavenly Father. Why? Because they are born of God, and God is their Father. Like father, like son. God's characteristics will be in His sons. This is like an earthly father telling his newly born son, "You shall grow up and be like me — able to run, play ball, talk, and work with me." Even though the baby is completely helpless at that point, the father knows because the baby is born of him and possesses his life, one day the baby will grow up to be a man like him. This is the essence of the New Covenant, God's Spirit coming into man.

Therefore, no condemnation now exists for those in Christ Jesus, because the Spirit's Law of life in Christ Jesus has set you free from the law of sin and of death. What the law could not do since it was limited by the flesh, God did. He condemned sin in the flesh by sending His own Son in flesh like ours under sin's domain, and as a sin offering, in order that the Law's requirement would be accomplished in us who do not walk according to the flesh but according to the Spirit.

– Romans 8:1–4, HCSB

The entrance of the Spirit into man brings the Law of divine life into man. This is the Spirit's Law of Life. Every life has a law. This law is not outside of life; rather, the life is the law. An apple's "life" will bear apples. It will never bear oranges or bananas. That is the law of the apple's life. It is completely dependable and predictable. The life-law of a dog will cause this dog to run, bark, wag its tail, and grow hair like a dog. When human beings produce an offspring, it is predictable that – based on the law of life – the child will grow with human characteristics. No prayer is needed – "Lord, please make sure that my baby is human!" That would be a ridiculous prayer.

The Spirit of God with His life also is a law. This law is not the same as the Ten Commandments outside of man requiring man to act and behave like God. Rather, when the Spirit enters man and joins man with God's life and nature, this law of divine, eternal life enters as well. This is the Law which frees believers from the law of sin and death and fulfills God's requirement in every believer. It is no longer man's effort to fulfill the requirements of God's Law, but the Spirit's Law is their law of life. What freedom from condemnation when a person realizes it is God's Law of life which shall inevitably fulfill the highest requirements of God's character in each and every believer!

What the external Law could not do since man's flesh is sinful, God terminated that flesh (viz., the "flesh of sin") on the cross. He then was able to enter man with His Spirit, and by His Law of life caused His character to be fully expressed in man; thus, God and man together fulfill God's external Law.

Therefore, the New Covenant is not conditional. How wonderful is this New Covenant! God *will* do it and He *is* doing it, unilaterally! Man's part is simply to enjoy God as life and to allow God's life to grow and mature.

(Please read the four chapters on life in the books, *One and One Life &
Glory,* to understand man's part in cooperating to let God's life grow in
the believer).

A believer should no longer place attention and emphasis on keeping
God's external Law but focus on the Spirit — the relationship of God within
them as this eternal, divine life.

> ...who also made us sufficient as ministers of the New Covenant,
> not of the letter but of the Spirit; for the letter kills, but the Spirit
> gives life.
>
> – 2 Corinthians 3:6

Here, the ministry of the Spirit is uniquely associated with the New
Covenant and clearly disassociated with the letter of the Law in the Old
Covenant. The New Covenant is all about the minister imparting and
dispensing the Spirit Who gives this eternal, divine life, whereas the Old
Covenant, with its letter of the law, kills. What a contrast!

Believers today have been made sufficient (or competent) ministers of
the New Covenant; they are able to minister the Spirit. If they minister the
Spirit to people, then they bring people into the New Covenant. If they
minister the letter of the law, however, they bring death (condemnation,
paralysis, division, and other spiritual weaknesses). It is one or the other.
Therefore, believers need to be clear concerning the New Covenant with
the Spirit of life and leave behind the Old Covenant with its letter of the law.

2. He Is Our God and We Are His people

> But you are a chosen race, a royal priesthood, a holy nation,
> a people for His possession, so that you may proclaim the
> praises of the One who called you out of darkness into His
> marvelous light.
>
> – 1 Peter 2:9, HCSB

To be God's people is much more than just a group of human beings
acquired by Him. The Greek word for "people" in Hebrews 8:10 and 1 Peter
23:9 is *laos*, which means, "A people, tribe, nation, all those who are of the
same stock and language" (Thayer's Greek Lexicon). The word "stock"
means "the descendants of one individual" which is a group having unity of

descent (Merriam-Webster). So, when God says, "They shall be My people," it is very significant indeed.

In the New Covenant, believers are not just a mass of human beings belonging to God as the Creator; their ancestry is *God*. They descended from God. They are the same "kind" as God. They are no different intrinsically in their life and nature. They are His people, His relatives, and they communicate with each other using the same language.

When God said, "they shall be my people," this did not have the same meaning as the owner of some puppies saying, "These are my puppies." Rather, it would be like Jacob in the Old Testament looking at Israel today and saying, "These are my people," since they are his offspring. See the difference? A human and a puppy are two different kinds of species with different languages; however, Israel's ancestry is literally from Jacob.

How can believers be God's people and from His lineage? The reason is God's Spirit is in them. Since believers are born of God and are now inextricably joined to Him with His life and nature, they are God's people.

Yet, God is still their God. God is still the distinct One to be uniquely worshipped and adored for eternity. The uplifting of human beings becoming God's people in the way of birth does not diminish in any way God's status, glory and uniqueness; rather His people can express Him and proclaim His praise at the highest level above all creation. This proclamation is not just in words but also as His people. The very life and nature of God is multiplied, and His glory is magnified. Therefore, being God's people is wonderful for His believers and glorious to God.

3. Knowing God

> Nevertheless you have an anointing from the Holy One, and you all know. I have not written to you that you do not know the truth, but that you do know it, and that no lie is of the truth . . . Now as for you, the anointing that you received from him resides in you, and you have no need for anyone to teach you. But as his anointing teaches you about all things, it is true and is not a lie. Just as it has taught you, you reside in him.
>
> – 1 John 2:20–21, 27, NET

The third blessing of the New Covenant reveals no one needs to teach God's people to know God; all shall know Him from the least to the greatest. There are two different Greek words for the word "know" in Hebrews 8:11. The first "know" is from the Greek word, *ginosko*, and the second "know" is from the Greek word, *oida* (or its verb form, *eido*). According to Vine's New Testament Expository Dictionary, *ginosko* frequently suggests inception or "progress in knowledge," while *oida* suggests "fullness" of knowledge. According to J.N. Darby, *ginosko* signifies objective knowledge — what a man has learned or acquired. *Oida* conveys the thought of what is inward — the inward consciousness in the mind or intuitive knowledge not immediately derived from what is external. Based on these definitions, the third blessing says believers in the New Covenant do not need man to teach them an external, objective knowledge of God, because each and every one has an inward, intuitive knowing of God in fullness.

Knowing God in the way of *oida* for believers is the same way Jesus knows (*oida*) the Father. In John 8:55 Jesus said to the Jews concerning God: You do not know (*ginosko*) Him, but I know (*oida*) Him. Unbelieving Jews did not have a concept of knowing God internally, but Jesus, as the Son, knew God in full, inwardly, and intuitively. It is very significant for believers to know (*oida*) God in the New Covenant the same way as Jesus knows (*oida*) God, the Father. How is this possible? It is only because of the first blessing of the New Covenant; namely, the Spirit of God is residing in the believer becoming part of their inward being. The Spirit of God is in them, like the Spirit being in Jesus; therefore, they can intuitively and inwardly know God in full just as Jesus did while on earth.

In 1 John 2:20 there is support for this same thought. God, the Holy One, anoints believers. This anointing is the Spirit (Acts 10:38), and because of this anointing, all believers know (*oida*) the truth. They do not need men to teach them because the anointing Spirit teaches all things related to the truth. This teaching causes them to reside or remain in Jesus Christ. This does not mean believers do not need any external teachers to instruct them from the Bible concerning the truth. It does mean if they pay attention to the anointing within them, the Spirit will witness in them, and they will intuitively know what is and is not the truth as they listen to Bible teachers. It is the Spirit in them Who discerns what is healthy, acceptable truth, and what to reject and avoid.

The goal of the Anointing's teaching is for believers to remain and reside in Jesus Christ. The anointing Spirit is not for teaching believers which car to buy, which class to take, or what career to choose, but to always live in Jesus Christ — to remain in Him. As believers live through the day, the anointing is constantly moving. This moving is a witness to the reality they are in Him. The anointing Spirit's work is consistently bringing believers back to Jesus Christ when they are experientially distracted. This is the third blessing of the New Covenant: believers know (*oida*) God as the truth, making them unmovable as they reside in Jesus Christ.

4. Sins Are Forgiven and No Longer Remembered

> Therefore, let it be known to you, brothers, that through this one forgiveness of sins is proclaimed to you, and by this one everyone who believes is justified from everything from which the Law of Moses could not justify you.
>
> – Acts 13:38–39, NET

The last blessing God extended with the New Covenant is, "*I will forgive their iniquity, and their sin I will remember no more.*" This certainly is wonderful news for all humankind, for all are sinners. This forgiveness is accomplished only through Jesus Christ.

Faith in Jesus Christ is the sole necessity for justification . . . to be made righteous in God's sight. God has an amazing memory. On one hand, God can never forget man's sins no matter how hard men try to please God by the works of the Law. On the other hand, once a person believes *into* Jesus Christ, God forgets all of man's sin. To God, it is as if man never sinned. When Satan tries to accuse a believer before God, God will say to Satan, in effect: "What are you talking about? I don't have any record of this person's sins. This one is sinless and righteous in My judgment."

To most believers, this is the first and most important blessing: being forgiven by God. But to God, it is the least important! This is the last item of the New Covenant. God's eternal purpose was not to forgive man's sins. God's eternal purpose was to be joined with man in eternal union.

Sin came into the picture in Genesis 3 and put a stop to God's plan; therefore, God had to clean up sin in man before continuing with His eternal plan. After man was cleansed from sin through the cross of Jesus Christ, God continued His plan of coming into man and becoming one with man. The first three blessings of the New Covenant were part of God's eternal plan; the last item relating to sin was a temporary setback God had to solve, which He did.

Therefore, Christians should not fill their thoughts with the issue of sin and forgiveness of sin. Once forgiven, they need to give their attention to enjoying God in Jesus Christ with the working of the Spirit's Law of life. Believers are of the same tribe and language as God and know God inwardly and intuitively in full.

The Effective Date and the Executor of the New Testament

The New Covenant (New Testament) took effect with the death of Jesus Christ.

> Likewise He also took the cup after supper, saying, "This cup is the New Covenant in My blood, which is shed for you."
> – Luke 22:20

> For where there [is] a testament, there must also of necessity be the death of the testator. For a testament is in force after men are dead, since it has no power at all while the testator lives.
> – Hebrews 9:16–17

The Greek word for "covenant" and "testament" is the same word: *diathēkē*. *Diathēkē* is "a promise or an agreement made with an oath." The testament is a person's will, that is, what that person will distribute to others in the event of his death. A testament is fully enforced or effective at the time of death. All the items in a testament before the death of the testator are promises, but once the testator dies, they are no longer promises, but a bequest. The items rightfully belong to the recipient (or the inheritor) declared in the will or testament. For example, a father may write in his will or testament he will give his house to his son. Before the father dies, it is only a promise. Legally, the father can change his mind and change his will to give the house to someone else. But if the will says the house is to be given to the son, and the father dies, the will can no longer be changed. In fact, as soon as he dies, ownership of the house transfers to the son; it is his inheritance. It is a done deal, and nothing can change it.

The New Covenant became effective at the death of Christ. God, who made the covenant, shed His blood with the death of Jesus Christ (Acts 20:28). Jesus declared the cup, representing the shedding of His blood, is the cup of the New Covenant. Jesus' death made the New Covenant effective, or "in force." Before his death, only God's promise wherein one day a New Covenant for His people would prevail. That promise was fulfilled and executed when Jesus died on the cross. No longer a promise from God, the New Covenant was an enforceable and effective will or testament.

The writer of Hebrews says a testament has no power when the testator still lives. Since the testator died — Jesus Christ — the New Testament is fully in force with all authority. What is written is no longer a list of promises, but a bequest for all believers — their inheritance.

This is very significant. Whatever God promised is now a bequest. It is rightfully the believers. Most believers still read the Bible as God's promises. They may pray, "Lord, remember your promise in your Word," or "I claim what you have promised to me." However, Paul in 2 Corinthians 1:20 said *all* the promises of God in Christ are YES and AMEN. They are no longer promises, but bequests for believers to receive and enjoy freely for themselves. The New Covenant with its four blessings includes all of God's promises. All other promises made by God may be considered sub-points of the four, just as all the statutes and ordinances in the Old Testament are sub-points of the Ten Commandments. Understanding the New Testament is enforceable through Christ's death. What has been spoken as a promise now rightfully belongs to believers. This should instill in believers the boldness to freely take hold of their inheritance. It is rightfully theirs.

Jesus Is the Executor (Guarantor) of the New Covenant

Today in resurrection, Jesus is the executor (or guarantor) of the New Covenant.

> But now He has obtained a more excellent ministry, inasmuch as He is also Mediator of a better covenant, which was established on better promises.
>
> – Hebrews 8:6

> How much more shall the blood of Christ, who through the eternal Spirit offered Himself without spot to God, cleanse your

conscience from dead works to serve the living God? And for this reason He is the **Mediator of the New Covenant**, by means of death, for the redemption of the transgressions under the first covenant, that those who are called may receive the promise of the eternal inheritance.

– Hebrews 9:14–15

Compared to the Levitical priesthood in the Old Testament and the animal sacrifices which could never take away the sins of the people, Jesus Christ has obtained through His death and resurrection a *better* ministry. The Old Testament priests were operating under the Old Covenant, but Jesus Christ is guaranteeing God's people will receive all New Covenant items.

In these verses the Greek word for "mediator" according to Vine's Expository Dictionary means, "one who acts as a guarantee." Jesus, being the Mediator of the New Covenant means He guarantees the terms of the New Covenant (testament) will be fulfilled to the beneficiaries. In the modern era the person who guarantees the beneficiary receives all the items of the inheritance or bequests is called an executor.

The better ministry of the Lord Jesus Christ is as the guarantor or the executor of the New Covenant. Since His resurrection and ascension, Jesus' ministry is to make sure believers receive all that is rightfully theirs according to the New Covenant, which is fully in force due to the death of the Testator.

The four blessings of the New Covenant are no longer promises, but bequests which have been accomplished and are just waiting for the beneficiaries (believers) to partake of them and inherit them as their own. There is nothing more for beneficiaries to do other than to claim what is rightfully theirs in order to enjoy their inheritance.

On one hand the Lord Jesus is praying in the heavens for believers to realize what is theirs; on the other hand, He is working out every item of the New Covenant from within believers. Therefore, in every way and from every angle, Jesus is working to make certain every item of the New Covenant is made real and enjoyed by believers

Receive All that God Has Accomplished by Faith

This only I want to learn from you: Did you receive the Spirit by the works of the law, or by the hearing of faith?

Therefore He who supplies the Spirit to you and works miracles among you, [does He do it] by the works of the law, or by the hearing of faith?

But that no one is justified by the law in the sight of God [is] evident, for "the just shall live by faith."

. . . that the blessing of Abraham might come upon the Gentiles in Christ Jesus, that we might receive the promise of the Spirit through faith.

– Galatians 3:2, 5, 11, 14

Since the New Covenant is in effect, everything God promised is now a bequest. There is a guarantor (executor) of the "will" to make sure beneficiaries receive what is rightfully theirs. What next? The only thing left to do is simply have faith to receive what already belongs to all mankind just for the taking. There is no payment or condition; believers only need to take and enjoy. This is faith. Faith is realizing what is already there: receiving, accepting, taking, and enjoying it.

This would be like a father who died and left $10 billion in the bank as an inheritance for his lost son. The lost son was living on the street like a beggar. The executor of the father's estate goes out to look for the son, to give the son the good news he is the beneficiary of the $10 billion bequest. He also gives the son a bank debit card and a check book. However, the son does not believe what has been told to him and continues to live on the streets, though the money is rightfully his and sitting in the bank in his name. Notwithstanding, because of the son's unbelief, it does not benefit him at all. Maybe one day, he will be so hungry and desperate he will muster up enough faith to use his bank debit card for ten dollars. Lo and behold, it worked and he got the money. The next time, he might venture out to use his debit card for $100. Eventually through experience, his faith increases where he writes a million-dollar check!

This is what Christ has done for all of humankind. Believers are the only ones who benefit, because they have faith to claim what is theirs: forgiveness with resurrection power. They have ascended to have all-things under their feet. It is as if believers have blank checks. They should just write what they want the "I AM" to be to them. This faith can receive all bequests of the New Covenant. This is not just for initial salvation but also for every step of the journey with Christ, for every environment and difficulty believers encounter — with the expectation of fulfilling God's calling. It is all there for the taking, by faith. Believers started by faith and will continue to live by faith. Praise the Lord for the New Covenant!

Salvation: Irrevocable, Eternal, and Secure

> . . . who has saved us and called us with a holy calling, not according to our works, but according to His own purpose and grace which was given to us in Christ Jesus before time began.
> — 2 Timothy 1:9

> And I give them eternal life, and they shall never perish; neither shall anyone snatch them out of My hand.
> — John 10:28

> For the gifts and the calling of God are irrevocable.
> — Romans 11:29

Since salvation provided through the New Covenant is a unilateral gift from God; therefore, all that is needed to receive salvation is faith (also a gift from God). Many believers have the assurance their salvation is secure: Once a person has believed and receives Jesus Christ as their Savior, no matter if they go through periods of moral failure — seemingly rejecting God — yet, their salvation is eternal. The above verses are commonly used to support this point of view. First, it is God who does the calling; this calling is for His purpose. Since it was not dependent on man's doing to begin with, then no matter if a believer temporarily falls away, God is faithful to His own purpose and grace to finish what He has begun.

We find a poem, a "faithful saying" given by Paul in 2 Timothy 2:11-13:

> *"This is a faithful saying:*
> *For if we died with Him,*
> *We shall also live with Him.*
> *If we endure,*
> *We shall also reign with Him.*
> *If we deny Him,*
> *He also will deny us.*
> *If we are faithless,*
> *He remains faithful;*
> *He cannot deny Himself."*

Here, from our perspective, our salvation is assured; for since we died with Him, we shall also live with Him. Now, those who endure with Him — press on to know Him in fullness as stewards of His grace — then we shall reign in life through Christ alone. However, if we deny Him, He will deny us the reign of the "servant kings" – notwithstanding, if we come to the point of being faithless, he remains faithful still because He cannot deny Himself! What assurance is this!

At the time of faith, Jesus Christ came into the believer to join with him and give him eternal life. This eternal life is not in the future. It arrives at the very moment of faith in Jesus. Because this life is within believers, they shall never perish. There is no condition given to sustain eternal life. Once a person has it, that life is now part of him or her — no matter what they do, or how much they try to run away from the Lord — eternal life is now fused within them and cannot be un-fused . . . *He abides faithful still*! It is like eating food. Once food is eaten and digestion starts, the elements of the food become part of the body. It is impossible to separate the food digested from the body. Jesus Christ is our *real* food. Once eaten through faith, He is one spirit with the believer — the two can never be divided. There is nowhere to run — it is impossible to undo.

Faith is a gift. Eternal life is a gift. Every item of the New Covenant is a gift. Once God has called a person to participate in these gifts, His gifts and calling are irrevocable. He gave and He called, and neither is reversible, even by God. What a wonderful assurance! Salvation does not depend on man to be activated. Salvation does not depend on man to be kept. God truly did it all, and there is nothing for man to boast about in relation to salvation (as if man deserved even one iota of it). All the glory and praise goes to God, the Lord Jesus Christ.

People will then say, "What is the point of man having a will to choose? Don't people have to *do* something to receive salvation?" The answer is YES. Men need to choose to hear the good news. They need to decide if they wish to hear the news of what Jesus has done for them. They are already judged and condemned, on death row, awaiting their sentence to be carried out: death! They desperately need a pardon — they need to hear the good news of Jesus Christ Who took the penalty for their sin. When they hear this — then they receive the gift of faith.

If they are not willing to read or listen to this wonderful news of salvation, then they do not have a chance to be rescued (saved). In our next section we will show how one's *will* to choose is mandatory for every believer.

Coming Judgment: Motivation to Enjoy and Dispense

Although a believer's salvation is secured, Scripture also reveals believers will still be judged at the Lord's second coming (viz., at the "Judgment Seat of Christ" — 2 Corinthians 5:10: *"We must all appear before the judgment seat of Christ to receive the things done in the body, whether good or bad."*). Sometimes these portions of Scripture are interpreted to mean believers can lose their salvation if they are unfaithful.

Because these verses seem to conflict with other Scriptures; therefore, certain camps among believers argue and divide over the matter. One side believes strongly once someone is saved by grace — then they are always saved (let's call this the "grace" side). The other side says: "What about those who have fallen away from the Lord and are living in sin? How can they be saved?" (Let's call this the "work" side).

Those on the "grace" side will counter Christians living in sin were never saved in the first place. Those on the "work" side teach believers can lose their salvation if they are not faithful. The "grace" side will accuse the "work" side for making salvation a matter of works and not of grace — believers must work for their salvation, nullifying the grace of God.

The "work" side may accuse the "grace" side of having a "cheap grace," so, they only want salvation without the obedience to follow the Lord's commands.

This section will attempt to harmonize both sets of verses, so both are accepted without contradiction, thereby, providing comfort or security for believers — yet still motivating them to grow and be faithful during the course of their Christian life.

Believers Shall Still Be Judged at Jesus' Coming

> Why do you pass judgment on your brother? Or you, why do you despise your brother? For we will all stand before the judgment seat of God.
>
> — Romans 14:10, ESV

For we must all appear before the judgment seat of Christ, so that each one may receive what is due for what he has done in the body, whether good or evil.

— 2 Corinthians 5:10, ESV

Paul clearly teaches in Romans and 2 Corinthians all believers will have to stand before Christ for judgment. Believers will be judged by what they have done when they were alive on earth in their physical bodies; have they done good or evil? They will be judged based on whether they have practiced oneness with all believers by a non-judgmental receiving of all those who have received salvation through faith in Jesus Christ. Wait, didn't this chapter concerning the New Covenant make a strong case for the unconditional and unilateral work of God — namely, believers cannot work for their salvation and have eternal security? Now, Paul says there is judgment based on how believers have lived and acted . . . isn't this *conditional*? This seems to be a complete contradiction to the New Covenant.

There seems to be more bad news for the "grace" side:

. . . work out your own salvation with fear and trembling.

— Philippians 2:12

This is one of the more perplexing verses in the Bible, which seems to contradict the idea of God doing the work for man's salvation by grace. Here Paul clearly says believers need to "work out" their own salvation. "*Fear and trembling*" sure sounds like there is an unknown element at the time of judgment, and whether one passes the judgment or not is not assured. Those on the "grace" side will cite the next verse wherein it is God who is working in the believer (Phil. 2:13); therefore, there is no need to worry since God will affect His salvation in them. This is a good argument from a one-sided point of view, but from an unbiased reader, that simply does not explain away verse 12, which says believers need to work out salvation in fear and trembling. This is just one verse out of a body of Scripture verses wherein the "work" side can cite from their point of view; salvation can be lost if the believer does not continue faithfully as a Christian.

The Standard of Judgment for New Covenant Believers

In the Old Covenant the standard for judgment is whether the Law is kept. True, in the New Covenant everything is done by God and the initiation and continuation for man to be saved is only grace through faith. Then on what basis or standard will God judge believers? To fully dive into this topic would take multiple chapters; instead, let's consider the key points with direction for further studies, if so desired.

> . . . for you are still of the flesh. For while there is jealousy and strife among you, are you not of the flesh and behaving only in a human way? For when one says, "I follow Paul," and another, "I follow Apollos," are you not being merely human? What then is Apollos? What is Paul? Servants through whom you believed, as the Lord assigned to each. I planted, Apollos watered, but God gave the growth. . . . For we are God's fellow workers. You are God's [cultivated] field, God's building.
>
> For no one can lay a foundation other than that which is laid, which is Jesus Christ. Now if anyone builds on the foundation with gold, silver, precious stones, wood, hay, straw — each one's work will become manifest, for the Day will disclose it, because it will be revealed by fire, and **the fire will test what sort of work each one has done.** If the work that anyone has built on the foundation survives, he will receive a **reward.** If anyone's work is burned up, he will suffer **loss,** though he himself will be saved, but only as through fire.
>
> ~ 1 Corinthians 3:3-6, 9, 11-15, ESV

This is a key portion of Scripture to show first there is a standard of judgment based on a believer's deeds. Second, it also is made clear believers are still saved even if they do suffer at the time of judgment; therefore, these verses show the harmonizing of both the "grace" and "works" sides — they do not contradict each other.

Paul clearly pointed out the problem with the Corinthians: They were fleshly by causing strife and divisions among the saints. They declared their preference or allegiance for the minister from whom they received help. They identified themselves by their favorite minister. This seemingly innocent group identification, which is common today among Christians, was condemned by Paul as fleshly. By extension, proclaiming, "I am of minster so-and-so," is like saying, "I belong to such and such a church (which is led and presided by a particular minister so-and-so)."

Paul continued to say they were merely servants or ministers which were not worthy for the saints to boast in them (1 Cor. 3:21). All genuine ministers, whether through their preaching or teaching, can lay only one unique foundation: Jesus Christ. Although, each minister may have their styles, methods or directions of service, they should only lay one foundation. This book on truth is describing that same foundation — Jesus Christ with His unsearchable riches.

It is in the context of Christians being divided among themselves due to differing preferences in ministers, that Paul used the analogy of various materials believers are using for the building. Using wood, hay, and straw to build is referring to such divisive group identity based on a minister's teaching or personality. Since the foundation is Jesus Christ, then the material used for the building must also be precious — material which can go through the test of fire. No matter how good a minister of the Lord is or how much help he/she has provided, believers cannot uplift such a person to cause division in the Body. If you do, then you are building with wood, hay, and straw (i.e., "stubble"). Just consider this: Even before the time of judgment, thousands upon thousands of Christians have suffered loss due to disappointments or failures of their esteemed minister. This is a precursor of the material exposed as destructible under testing.

Paul is warning believers who were causing divisions over their boasting of their favorite minister that such division-causing-identity cannot stand the test of fire. Sooner or later their divisiveness will be burnt up. They will be left with nothing and suffer loss. All believers are needed and expected to build up God's temple. However, they need to do so by using the same indestructible material as the foundation: gold, silver and precious stones.

All believers comprise the Temple of God. The Temple of God is one. Causing divisions among believers is a destruction of the Temple of God (1 Cor. 3:16-17). This is a serious matter which should cause believers to repent from splintering the Temple of God to building up the one Temple of God.

In showing the need for growth and building up of God's Temple, Paul used an analogy of a farm. A plant is a beautiful picture of growth and building. It is an appropriate analogy to help explain growth and building. A seed is planted into the earth and is regularly watered. The life in the seed makes use of the soil and the water to produce a plant. The content of a plant is 100 percent made up of water plus the minerals of the soil. The plant grows by photosynthesis: the sun causes the water in the plant to exchange for poisonous carbon dioxide (CO_2). In the process, oxygen is released and carbohydrates (sugar, or energy) and cellulose are generated for the growth and building up of the plant. The life (DNA) of the seed will spontaneously determine what kind of plant (an apple, orange, or rose, for example) will manifest itself when it is grown.

The Bible says the seed for planting is Jesus Christ as the Word of God (1 Pet. 1:23); the watering is the Spirit (John 7:39); and the sun for growth is the Father (Rev. 21:23). When a believer is full of the Spirit (water), then everything poisonous of Satan (CO_2) is utilized as an ingredient to generate energy (sugar). This causes growth (cellulose) — even a release of the Spirit (oxygen) to enliven others. The plant itself is the joining and mixing together in the most profound way of bonding between earth (humanity) and water (the Spirit). The "DNA" of the seed, Jesus Christ, determines the maturity the plant will have in conforming to His very image. This is how a "plant" (believer) grows to become God's building, His harvest, fulfilling His eternal purpose.

Every believer (one who is regenerated with the seed) is the field God is cultivating. So, in that sense, every believer should be growing and building on the foundation of Jesus Christ. They all need to produce something organic for God's building during the time they are here on earth. The day of judgment will decide the final testing by fire to see what each believer has produced for the building up of His Body. If the material is gold, silver, and precious stones, then fire will only improve on its glory. A believer will receive a positive reward. But if the material used by the believer is wood, hay, or straw (stubble), then certainly it will be burned up — the believer shall suffer some form of loss. A believer shall still be saved, but "*as by fire.*" Their salvation is assured — *He cannot deny Himself* — but the journey at that time is through fire rather than through faith.

Gold, silver, and precious stones representing materials which can go through the fire of God's judgment are only what is directly related to the Triune God. Wood, hay, and straw (which cannot go through God's judgment) are related to fallen humanity, the flesh, without the elements of the Triune God. Believers should care for the growing "seed of life" within them, which will only produce the indestructible material for God's building. If a believer neglects to grow and dispense life for building, then he or she is left with his original elements of wood, hay, or straw. Such a believer will suffer loss. Any suffering of loss on the day of judgment is not good news. After this suffering of loss, the person is still saved, but through the fire of the Judgment Seat of Christ — known as the Bema. Although the result is still salvation, the journey this person will go through at that time will not be pleasant, since it is through fire.

This is a stern warning to believers. Although they have received the divine seed at regeneration, they are to continue to grow and produce Christ for the building up of the one body with all believers. This also shows that the standard of judgment for a believer is whether they are producing precious materials for the building up of the ekklesia, or are they continuing to be fleshly by causing divisions in their uplifting of differing ministers.

No matter how much a minister has been successful in ministry, no one can borrow from his/her success for the building. A minister's faithfulness and contribution cannot be transferred to those who prefer them. Just because you boast in their ministry doesn't mean you yourself grew and contributed to the building. Each believer has to produce for themselves; each has to build with proper material themselves. We all need to grow and contribute gold, silver, and precious stone for the building.

This is similar to watching a basketball game. All the fans can brag about the greatness of their favorite players, but it has no bearing on whether the fans can play well themselves. God is not looking for fans of His ministers. He wants all his people to participate and contribute in the building up of His Temple by growing and sharing Christ themselves.

> For land that has drunk the rain that often falls on it, and produces a crop useful to those for whose sake it is cultivated, receives a blessing from God. But if it bears thorns and thistles, it is worthless and near to being cursed, and its end is to be burned.
> – Hebrews 6:7–8, ESV

In the context of these verses, the "land" is clearly referring to genuine believers who have *"tasted the heavenly gifts"* and *"shared in the Holy Spirit"* (Heb. 6:4). The land (believers) who have received God's blessing of grace should be producing food for building up, but instead the writer of Hebrews says it produces thorns and thistles. At the Judgment Seat of Christ, the Bema, these believers are close to being cursed. Though not actually cursed (since they are saved), they will still suffer a sort of "fire" or "burning." The standard shown for judgment here is related to producing something that can feed others for building up.

> And the Lord said, "Who then is the faithful and wise steward, whom his master will set over his household, to give them their portion of food at the proper time? Blessed is that servant whom his master when he comes will find so doing. Truly, I say to you, he will set him over all his possessions. But if that servant says to himself, 'My master is delayed in coming,' and begins to beat the menservants and the maidservants, and to eat and drink and get drunk, the master of that servant will come on a day when he does not expect him and at an hour he does not know, and will punish him, and put him with the unfaithful. And that servant who knew his master's will, but did not make ready or act according to his will, shall receive a severe beating.
>
> – Luke 12:42–47, RSV

In this parable, Luke describes a faithful and wise steward. This steward's master honored him for dispensing and serving food to the master's household in due season. Referring back to Chapter 7 on *Oikonomia*, this was a faithful steward in God's economy: he provided food regularly to grow God's household. The unfaithful servant should not be considered an unbeliever, since he considers the Lord *"my master"* who will come back. He even knew his master's will. Certainly, an unbeliever would not consider the Lord as his master and would not know His will. Instead of feeding the household, however, the unfaithful steward mistreated his fellow servants; therefore, his portion at the Lord's coming back is punishment, even a severe beating.

In the three scriptural portions above, the standard of judgment for a believer seems clear: it is based on the divine seed one has received growing up into maturity — feeding through service or ministry to God's people. This standard is very different from law keeping according to the Old Covenant; rather, it relates to life receiving and life dispensing via the New Covenant. The Lord has done everything. His anger and judgment are then toward those who do not continue to receive by faith all He has accomplished and to serve God in love as food to the needy in the world.

The goal of this chapter was to awaken in the heart of the believer the seriousness of being a faithful steward of the Lord's vineyard. Although the New Covenant is unilateral and unconditionally fulfilled by God, this does not mean believers can "kick back" while receiving some sort of "free pass" no matter what they do after they are regenerated by divine life. It is precisely because God has done everything that His anger and judgment extends toward those who do not take advantage of it and enjoy all He has already accomplished.

The parable in Matthew 22 describes a king who prepared a great feast. Everything was prepared. People were invited to the feast at no charge. His anger was toward those who didn't come to take freely all what He had prepared for them to enjoy. Certainly, this parable can be interpreted toward unbelievers, but it sets the same principle even toward believers. The Lord is still calling His believers to dine with Him as seen in Revelation 3:20. God is after saints who will continue to receive by faith all He has accomplished and is now rightfully their inheritance. It is this continual receiving of His riches which causes a believer to build up the one Body of Christ, growing into maturity. Believers will be judged by how much they have matured through receiving and enjoying His riches.

Simultaneously, the receiving of His riches is integrated with and dependent on believers willing to dispense His riches as stewards to others. God is a sharing and giving God; therefore, those who are truly growing in Him must also share and give to others. This dispensing of His riches is what will cause His ekklesia to be built up (His One Body practically expressed) — fulfilling His eternal purpose. Therefore, a believer's judgment is also based on their faithfulness to be a dispenser of the unsearchable riches of Jesus Christ. In the New Covenant God has done everything; believers now have the privilege and responsibility to enjoy and dispense/share what they have received, to take in and give out. This is completely different from the standard of judgment in the Old Covenant.

When the Lord Jesus returns to judge by bringing in the manifestation of His kingdom upon the earth, His kingdom will last a thousand years before the ending of time and the beginning of eternity (Rev. 20). At the Lord's return, the resurrection of all believers will occur (viz., the "resurrection of the just"), and, together with those that are still alive, they will be judged before Him. Some Bible teachers have suggested it is during the millennial (1000 years) kingdom faithful believers will "rule and reign" with Christ, while unfaithful believers (viz., those *"saved as by fire"*) will use this time to grow to maturity, as described by phrases in the verses just quoted: "saved through fire," "near a curse," and "receive punishment." This topic certainly can use more development, but according to the definition of truth, what reward or "saved as by fire" to believers looks like during the millennium is not an item of truth. Since it is not an eternal item, it is not an item of truth to discuss further in this book.[23]

For now, calling attention to these verses raises the possibility believers (though saved) should not be passive and lethargic concerning the coming Judgment Seat of Christ; rather believers need to wake up. . . arise to be well-pleasing to the Lord by being full participants in the New Covenant; growing to spiritual maturity, while contributing to fulfill the Lord's desire for the oneness of all His believers as prayed for in John 17.

10

THE COMPLETE GOSPEL
OF JESUS CHRIST

The gospel is a major topic of truth; and since this book is on ONE TRUTH — what better way to conclude this text than sharing the "Truth of the Gospel!" Every Christian has heard the gospel and just about all of them support the preaching and spreading of the gospel throughout the earth. Therefore, it is indispensable to have a focused discussion about the gospel in a book on truth. Our discussion of the gospel will be more profound than the general understanding of the gospel understood by most Christians. This topic of the "gospel" will be approached in its completion, its fullness. Chapters 10 and 11 will not present a partial gospel, but the complete, full, or the *completion gospel*.

> But I know that when I come to you, I shall come in the **fullness** [completion] of the blessing of the gospel of Christ.
> — Romans 15:29

"Completion" is derived from the Greek word "*plērōma.*" It is translated in most versions as "*fulness.*" The actual meaning includes completeness or completion, that which fills up. This terminology was used at the end of Romans which Paul wrote as the "gospel of God" and preached to the saints in Rome (Rom. 1:1, 15). After explaining the gospel for 15 chapters, he used this term *the completion . . . of the gospel* (Rom. 15:29). The complete gospel needs the entire book of Romans to explain its meaning. Nevertheless, these final two chapters will try to explain the completion gospel in a condensed manner.

In the New Testament, there is the gospel of God (Rom. 1:1; 1 Pet. 4:17), the gospel of Jesus Christ (Mark 1:1; 2 Thess. 1:8); the gospel of the grace of God or the "gospel of grace" (Acts 20:24); the gospel of peace (Rom. 10:15; Eph. 6:15), and the gospel of the kingdom (Matt. 4:23; 24:14). All these descriptions combined constitute the *completion gospel*. This is an aspect of truth believers must understand, appreciate, and ultimately preach!

The Gospel is for God's Eternal Purpose

The gospel is not just for individual sinners to be saved and go to "heaven" one day; rather, the gospel is preached to ultimately fulfill God's eternal purpose. The gospel has a central role in the realization or completion of God's eternal purpose. God's eternal purpose is such an all-encompassing and essential matter of truth; yet, so inadequately taught and discussed in main-stream Christianity. Therefore, an entire book was dedicated to this topic by the same author (Henry Hon) entitled: *ONE EKKLESIA: The Vision and Practice of God's Eternal Purpose*. It is worth reading and studying through this book to consider this matter. Repeating some of this material at this juncture is appropriate.

After reading the first eight chapters of Romans, Christians should be very familiar with most of the elements of the Christian faith. It is Jesus Christ as the Savior of the world. It is Jesus Christ sent by God who loved the world so much He sent His only begotten Son to die and resurrect for all believers — for their ultimate justification, unto glorification. This is certainly good news: all sinners can now become sons and daughters of the Living God. However, what about God's eternal purpose?

God's eternal purpose is not just to have many individuals who become His children and then-to heaven. God's purpose is completely wrapped up in the building up of His *ekklesia* (which is the Greek word mistranslated to "*church*" in most English versions). Jesus Christ came not just to save individual sinners, but to have these regenerated (born again) believers built up into a spiritual house, the Body of Christ, the Messiah, into His *ekklesia*.

Let's briefly review the subject of God's eternal purpose. His eternal purpose is centered on Christ and His *ekklesia*.

> "And I also say to you that you are Peter, and on this rock, I will build My church (**ekklesia**), and the gates of Hades shall not prevail against it."
>
> — Matthew 16:18

And He put all [things] under His feet, and gave Him [to be] head over all [things] to the church (**ekklesia**), which is His body, the fullness of Him who fills all in all.

– Ephesians 1:22-23

...to the intent that now the manifold wisdom of God might be made known by the church (**ekklesia**) to the principalities and powers in the heavenly [places], according to the eternal purpose which He accomplished in Christ Jesus our Lord....

– Ephesians 3:10-11

Salvation came to Peter when He recognized Jesus the Christ, the Son of the living God. It was a revelation directly from God. Every person needs a direct revelation concerning Jesus Christ in order to have faith to follow Jesus. At that very moment of revelation concerning Jesus Christ, Peter was changed. His name was changed from Simon to Peter (a stone). That is how a person is revolutionized. Every believer can give a personal testimony of their personal revolution/revelation at the time of faith in Jesus Christ. Every believer has had a transformation which cannot be explained. At one time, they were typical sinners living in this satanically-controlled world; then, the next minute there was this repentance from sins with a desire to follow Jesus Christ. Suddenly they would have a desire to give themselves to God's purpose. This transformation can only happen through a direct revelation from God concerning His Son Jesus, the Christ, the Messiah

However, seeing Who Jesus Christ is, is but half the revelation. As the Christ, the anointed one sent for a purpose; after this recognition, Jesus unveils the second half of the revelation: He will build His *ekklesia*. That is the purpose of being the Christ: the building of His *ekklesia*. It is at this point that Jesus expressly told them of His impending death and resurrection. His death and resurrection are not just to save sinners from "hell" so they can go to heaven, but ultimately, they are saved for the building up of His *ekklesia*.

His *ekklesia* has many descriptions — here are some of the major ones: The Body of Christ; the Temple of God; the Household of God; the Bride of Christ; the Kingdom of God; the New Man; and the New Jerusalem. These descriptions show various aspects of God's people built up into one. God the Father needs many sons and a dwelling place; therefore, the *ekklesia* is His family, His household, and temple. The *ekklesia* as the bride describes God's people as the counterpart of God the Son, uniting together as one couple in eternal love. The Body of Christ is the physical manifestation of God the Spirit. She is His Body wherein the indwelling Spirit is expressed.

The One New Man is the warrior fulfilling God's original purpose whereupon through man, Satan is defeated. Satan is defeated by the new humanity created in Jesus Christ — a New Creation. The Kingdom of God is where Christ the King with His followers as a "kingdom of priests" shall reign over the entirety of God's creation. The built-up *ekklesia* is the eternal New Jerusalem where humanity is joined in everlasting relationship as His One Bride in union with the Triune God. God is in man and man is in God in eternal harmony and unity. She is the perfect match between humanity and divinity for eternity.

All the various descriptions of the Lord's *ekklesia* require oneness among God's people. Would God the Father be happy to see His children fighting and divided from each other? There can only be one temple as God's dwelling place. Can a body be divided? Are there two brides of Christ? Paul emphatically states ONE New Man — so making peace (Eph. 2:15). Certainly, with one King, there can only be one kingdom of God. Eventually, it is one New Jerusalem for eternity. None of these descriptions would make sense if there is division among God's people — indeed, that includes one New Covenant. Therefore, the building up of the Lord's *ekklesia* is the bringing together into one all of God's previously divided people. This is truly good news for all humanity.

The Two Aspects of the Gospel: Grace and Peace

The word "gospel" means good news. The gospel is fundamental to the Christian faith. The gospel is the gospel of Jesus Christ, who He is and what He has accomplished. This is what every believer should preach. All believers have been charged to preach the gospel of Jesus Christ (Mark 16:15). Since He is the Son of God, the gospel is also known as the gospel of God. The gospel speaks of Jesus Christ being God who became flesh. He is both God and man. Jesus Christ then went to die on the cross as the sinless perfect God-man. He resurrected on the third day and ascended to heaven. He was crowned with glory and honor as the Lord of lords and King of kings.

Through His work, fallen humanity has been redeemed, justified, sanctified and glorified to become sons of God. Furthermore, He poured-out His Spirit in order for His regenerated people to join with Him in building up His *ekklesia*, His One Body which is the fulfillment of God's eternal purpose:

> In Him you also [trusted], after you heard the word of truth, the gospel of your salvation; in whom also, having believed, you were sealed with the Holy Spirit of promise, ...
>
> – Ephesians 1:13

> To me, though I am the very least of all the saints, this grace was given, to preach to the Gentiles the unsearchable riches of Christ ...
>
> – Ephesians 3:8, ESV

The gospel of Jesus Christ is the truth. Every item of the truth is good news. Typically, Christians only consider the gospel to be the following: Jesus Christ dying for man's sins whereby whoever believes in Him will not go to perdition (hell; i.e., perish); rather, that person will go to glory (heaven). This gospel is not the entirety of the gospel of Jesus Christ. So, Paul says he preaches, *gospelizes*, the unsearchable riches of Christ.

This means Paul is preaching all of Christ's unsearchable riches, which together are the gospel, the good news, which needs to be preached. In fact, every facet of the truth is the gospel. The truth in a nutshell is the Triune God embodied in Jesus Christ fulfilling God's eternal purpose through His death, resurrection, ascension, and the out-pouring of the Spirit. His Spirit is now working in all His followers to manifest, in time, the accomplishment of God's eternal purpose. This entire truth can be considered as good news which needs to be preached and announced.

The Gospel of Grace

> For I delivered to you first of all that which I also received: that Christ died for our sins according to the Scriptures, and that He was buried, and that He rose again the third day according to the Scriptures ...
>
> – 1 Corinthians 15:3-4

> For by grace you have been saved through faith, and that not of yourselves; [it is] the gift of God, not of works, lest anyone should boast.
>
> – Ephesians 2:8-9

> I may finish my race with joy, and the ministry which I received from the Lord Jesus, to testify to the gospel of the grace of God.
>
> – Acts 20:24

The gospel of grace (aka, *the gospel of the grace of God*) is typically what is preached around the world. Missionaries sent out over the world during the last couple of centuries — into the very heart of Africa and Asia — were preaching this gospel.

This is the message recognized by all believers — even unbelievers as the gospel. In short, this gospel announces Jesus Christ came as the Son of God to die for the sins of humanity and resurrected on the third day, so whoever believes in Jesus Christ shall not perish but have eternal life. All of this is accomplished by God's grace. This salvation cannot be achieved through any works of righteousness nor by self-efforts; rather, a person can only be saved through grace. God showed favor to us, though man does not deserve any of it (cf. Eph. 2:8-9).

This has been preached throughout the world. It is through this gospel that billions of people on earth consider themselves to be Christians. All the followers of Jesus can and should praise God for the gospel of grace spreading throughout the earth.

No doubt this gospel still must be continually preached since there are still billions of unreached people. Additionally, as the population continues to increase, there will always be new souls who will need to hear the gospel of the grace of God.

Although this gospel has been prevailing throughout the earth; yet, God's eternal purpose concerning the building up of His *ekklesia* has not been accomplished.

There are billions of Christians, yet they are all so divided. Christians have been solely focused on salvation and/or the means whereby salvation can be experienced.

The various stages of salvation by Christians — including justification, sanctification, and ultimate glorification — have, in the main, ignored the building up of the Lord's One Body, His *ekklesia*. In fact, the more Christians focus on salvation and what it looks like, the more divisions are generated.

Just consider how many divisions and sects have been established over the topic of sanctification or holiness. There are hundreds, maybe even thousands, of divisions created over methods whereby holiness can be achieved or how a Christian should live and act if that person is to be holy.

In fact, it seems those who focus on holiness as a necessary manifestation of salvation cause more divisions than those who they might consider as "worldly Christians."

Worldly Christians are satisfied with a transfer from hell to heaven. They are not the ones typically causing divisions among believers over spiritual or doctrinal disputes. Of course, the less spiritual Christians can and do cause divisions over other matters such as politics, race, culture, or income inequality, like the rest of mankind.

The gospel of grace is for the salvation of individuals. Often, it is said that just because a person is born into a Christian family, that person still needs to have personal faith in Christ. They need to come to a personal salvation experience.

Parents cannot believe for their children; neither can a child believe for her parents — notwithstanding baptizing infants or presenting them in dedication to the Lord still practiced among believers. Salvation is a personal-based experience — it demands a personal revelation and a personal trust in Jesus Christ resulting in a personal encounter with the Lord Jesus!

The Gospel of Peace

> Now this he did not say on his own [authority]; but being high priest that year he prophesied that Jesus would die for the nation, and not for that nation only, but also that He would gather together in one the children of God who were scattered abroad.
> – John 11:51-52

It can be said the gospel of grace is good news to unbelievers, but the gospel of peace is good news for divided believers. Just as forgiveness of sins came into effect through the blood of the Lord's cross, even so, peace between two of the most divided and hostile peoples was accomplished through the same cross.

In 1 Corinthians 15:3 we find one of the most often quoted verses in the Bible which shows us Jesus Christ died for man's sins and was resurrected on the third day. It is truly a wonderful and comforting passage. At the same time, John 11:52 is rarely quoted regarding the full reason why Jesus Christ died. It is abundantly clear from John 11:51-52 that Jesus Christ died for the Jewish nation (Judah — as understood in its context), *"and not for that nation only, but also that He would gather together in one the children of God who were scattered abroad."* God's desire was to bring His scattered children into ONE. The Jews of Judea, at that time were mainly composed of the tribes of Judah, Benjamin, and the Levites — those who came back from the Babylonian Captivity beginning cir. 586 BC, returning to Judea approximately 538-537 BC at the edict of the Persian King Cyrus the Great. In fact, the word "Jew" is a derivative of the word "Judah" and was not in use until around 600 BC.

Then who are *"the children of God who were scattered abroad"* in John 11:52? For this understanding, it is important to go back to the history of Israel (when the 12 Tribes of Israel were united) — back to the time when the 12 tribes of Israel divided into "two houses." The 10 tribes of the north (known later as Israel, Jezreel, Ephraim, Samaria); and the 2 tribes in the south known as Judah. We get confused sometimes because Judah can be called Israel, and, of course, Ephraim is likewise called Israel (as well as Jezreel and Samaria).

The Southern Kingdom was composed of Judah and Benjamin (with the Levites) with Rehoboam as their king at the time when the United Kingdom of David was divided — known as the "breach of Jeroboam" (2 Chronicles 10-11). This was when the Northern Kingdom was comprised of 10 tribes with Jeroboam as their king. These two kingdoms after their split never came back together again until the gospel was preached to the Gentiles (we will see more of this later) — for the Northern 10 tribes (Ephraim) were "swallowed up of the nations" (Hosea 8:7-8) . . . how could they ever again be identified?

Around the year 745 BC the Northern Kingdom was invaded by Assyria, which began carrying away the 10 tribes of Israel until their capital, Samaria, was conquered in 722 BC and eventually all the "Israelites" were brought into Assyrian captivity by 712 BC (over the course of some 33 years) during the siege of Jerusalem by King Sennacherib as found in 2 Chronicles 32; thence, began in earnest the migration of a foreign people into the former area of Israel occupied by the 10 tribes known as Ephraim. It was a common strategy of the Assyrian empire to migrate and swap populations among the nations they conquered. Certainly, some of the 10 tribes might have migrated to the Southern Kingdom, but the majority were carried off and scattered among all the nations within the Assyrian empire. Therefore, the Bible says Israel was swallowed up by the nations (Hos. 8:7-8).

Now that the 10 tribes, or at least the vast majority (some demographers conclude upwards between 12 and 15 million persons) became assimilated into the nations, they truly became a scattered people! Through intermarriage among the population of all the nations, their bloodline has been thoroughly dispersed. God's children have definitely and irreversibly been scattered abroad; swallowed up (the same word used to "*swallow up*" Jonah by the great fish—Jonah 1:17). We can safely say the ten tribes scattered abroad are now part of the Gentile or "heathen" nations ("heathen" in the sense of not being "holy" as per Israel which was separated out from all the other nations).

The *children of God* in John then referred to both those of the Jewish nation (Judah or Judea) and those of the Gentile nations (wherein Ephraim had been "swallowed up" or assimilated). It was through His death that He would bring them back into one. His death is for the oneness of His people.

> For He Himself is our peace, who has made both one, and has broken down the middle wall of separation, having abolished in His flesh the enmity, [that is], the law of commandments [contained] in ordinances, so as to create in Himself one new man [from] the two, [thus] making peace, and that He might reconcile them both to God in one body through the cross, thereby putting to death the enmity. And He came and preached peace to you who were afar off and to those who were near.
> — Ephesians 2:14-17

With John 11 in view, Ephesians 2 makes this bringing together of Jews and Gentiles as His children very clear. Judaism refers to the religious practices kept by Judah, the Jews. Judaism is a religion maintaining all the Mosaic laws and ordinances — even the "traditions" of the "fathers." Due to these regulations, Jews and Gentiles were the most divided people in the history of the world. They were so divided they could not socially eat together — there was such "enmity" or "hatred" between the two.

This division was God-ordained according to the various ordinances in His commandments. These ordinances stipulate only clean food could be eaten (as described in the *Torah*), the days to keep holy, and how one ought to dress. These ordinances became a cause of enmity or hostility between Jews and Gentiles. Due to this division, it would be impossible for God to realize His eternal purpose of having One Body in Christ, or one new man comprised of both Jew and Gentile; thus, defeating His enemy, Satan! But God, through the death of His Son, His Cross, *"put to death the enmity"* – that awful hatred!

God's desire is to have all His people, from every tribe, tongue, people and nation, become one in Him. This is the building, His Holy Temple – His *ekklesia*. In order to accomplish God's eternal purpose: the creation of His One New Man by bringing His divided people together, Jesus Christ came to die on the cross and abolished the enmity.

Through His death He terminated this generational hatred caused by these laws; thus, the hostility between these most divided peoples resulted in peace between them both through the blood of His cross – creating the One New Man. How could there be One Body if two divided people could not eat together? How could they literally break bread together in remembrance of the Lord? It was impossible before the cross. Now, not only is it possible to be truly one, it is required for those who were previously divided, now they can come together to eat and drink in celebration of the Lord's death and resurrection.

This is peace through the blood of His cross (Eph. 2:14-18). The peace between two divided peoples is what Jesus died to accomplish. Just as believers need to have faith in Jesus Christ's death – death caused God to forgive their sins – they now need to believe all divisive barriers between and among God's people have been terminated; thus, making peace This peace needs to be preached. This is good news. It is amazingly good news, for all God's people are made one through the blood of His cross. Therefore, Ephesians 2:17 says Jesus preached peace. Peace needs to be *gospelized*. This is not the peace between an individual believer and God as in *"we have peace with God"* (Rom. 5:1). This is peace between the most divided people on the planet – in order to create from that horrendous division: One New Man.

Peace is not just the absence of war and conflict. According to *Strong's* definitions, it is positive and active. It includes: prosperity, rest, and becoming one or unity. The equivalent Hebrew word is *"Shalom"* which includes: Happiness, health, safety and wholeness. *Peace* is a wonderful word describing a state or environment every person should desire.

> . . . endeavoring to keep the unity of the Spirit in the bond of peace. [There is] one body and one Spirit, just as you were called in one hope of your calling . . .
>
> – Ephesians 4:3-4

> . . . and having shod your feet with the preparation of the gospel of peace;
>
> – Ephesians 6:15

> And the God of peace will crush Satan under your feet shortly. The grace of our Lord Jesus Christ [be] with you. Amen.
>
> – Romans 16:20

Continuing with Jesus' death on the cross bringing peace in Ephesians 2, we now find in Ephesians 4 that the topic of unity and peace is strengthened when Paul says, "*endeavoring to keep the unity of the Spirit in the bond of peace*" (Eph. 4:3) since "*There is one body and one Spirit, just as you were called in one hope of your calling; one Lord, one faith, one baptism; one God and Father of all, who is above all, and through all, and in you all*" (Eph. 4:4-6).

It is due to this bond of peace wherein divided believers can endeavor, even persevere, to keep the unity of the Spirit. Peace was realized through the cross of Christ; moreover, unity is of the Spirit. All those born of the Spirit have the inborn nature to be one with all other believers. It is the nature of the Spirit within each believer which enables Christians to be one, as one as the Father and the Son are one (John 17: 21). True unity among believers cannot be negotiated or compromised, it is uniquely of the Spirit. Believers are charged to keep or guard this unity in the uniting bond of peace.

The peace our Lord wrought through the cross is a bond which unites and joins all diverse believers together. The Greek word for "bond" here is a compound word made up of "union" and "chain." This peace brings previously divided peoples into a union like a chain which cannot be broken. A person cannot claim to have peace if such peace is not causing a uniting in Spirit, as well as fellowship with those with whom there would normally be division. This peace is active. It is not a passive peace where you stay at home by yourself to experience peace. This is not referring to an individual having "peace with God." That personal peace can be experienced all by oneself. However, the peace found in Ephesians 4 causes the follower of Jesus to be united with other believers no matter the depth of separation or the gulf created by hostility. This is the peace Christ died to generate among these most divided peoples.

This peace motivates believers to seek fellowship with those who are different from themselves. It is this uniting bond of peace which causes all Christians, regardless of diversity, to become one. The word endeavoring is also translated "to be eager" (Strong's G#4704 – "to use speed"). This word commends itself to doing something with diligence and haste. It's a matter of anxious reconciliation and endeavor. Frankly, far too often Christians who find themselves divided from their brethren use "waiting on the Lord" or "let's pray about it" – all the while placing aside all anxious reconciliation and earnest endeavor to "keep the peace."

For this unity among Christians, there needs to be an "endeavoring." Based on the unity of the Spirit already present in every believer and the bond of peace created by the cross between previously divided peoples – every believer must endeavor. Don't be passive, don't be discouraged, don't give up on the oneness of God's people. The Holy Spirit is with you – Jesus Christ has accomplished peace. Thus, let's make the effort, let's be motivated, let's be encouraged to endeavor to keep the oneness of the Spirit. Endeavoring to be in peace and unity with all believers is to walk worthily of God's calling (Eph 4:1). God has done everything in calling us and saving us. Now, will we do something that would garner His admiration? It is worthy to live and walk to accomplish the oneness of God's people.

Notwithstanding, while the gospel of grace for personal salvation has spread throughout the earth generating millions upon millions of Christians; yet, who is preaching the gospel of peace? Though there are myriads of Christians, they have been made ineffectual as an influential force upon society around them. Jesus said that "*a kingdom divided against itself cannot stand*" (Matt. 12:25). Christians have been divided by the tens of thousands of different churches and denominations – that number is still increasing. No wonder the Lord's prayer in John 17 is for His people to be one so the world will believe in Jesus Christ. It is through the building of the Lord's one *ekklesia* Satan's kingdom can be crushed and defeated (Matt. 16:18).

Certainly, very few Bible teachers are preaching the gospel of peace. What is alarming is the fact most Christians have not the slightest awareness what exactly is this gospel of peace? Due to this ignorance, most Christians are satisfied with their personal salvation and have accepted the divided state among God's people as a *fait accompli*. Most do not believe it is wrong and against God's plan to be divided. Alas! Some affirm divisions within His One Body are part of God's plan! **Just as most unbelievers do not know they need salvation from sin until they hear the gospel of grace; even so, most Christians do not know they need salvation from division and sectarianism until they hear the gospel of peace!**

In fighting God's enemy, believers, as God's warriors, need the entire armor of God. This armor is needed to fight for God's move, to complete God's eternal purpose. Ephesians 6:10-18 tells us God's armor covers God's warrior from head to toe. One of the items needed to complete the armor of God is the binding of the soles of the feet with *the preparation of the gospel of peace*. Feet are for running, for moving and for stomping. It is wonderful for a warrior to have an armor ready to fight, but what if this warrior does not have feet or what if the soles of his feet are not protected from sharp objects? When a warrior's feet are protected, he is ready to move, to travel, to run and even to step on serpents. What gives him such ability? It is the gospel of peace. The movement of this warrior is through preaching the gospel of peace. In fact, it can be said without the preaching of the gospel of peace, God's warrior has no move on the earth. God needs His warrior for the battle against His enemy, and the warrior needs the gospel of peace for his feet in order to move and stomp on the enemy.

How critical and essential is the gospel of peace in God's move! Even if believers have the rest of their armor; yet, if they are not preaching the gospel of peace, then God's move has no feet, no move. Christians are at a standstill. The gospel of peace is essential for the move of God. In fact, the preaching of the gospel of peace *is* the move of God to accomplish His eternal purpose.

When Christians are divided, God is hindered from moving. When the gospel is preached to bring divided believers together, God is moving, and He is building His *ekklesia* for His eternal purpose.

Eventually, according to Romans 16:20, it is under the feet of the saints who are actively reaching out to other believers in fellowship (greeting), that Satan is crushed under the God of peace. It is the God of peace working in believers, uniting them together in the bond of peace, whereupon Satan is finally crushed. Defeating of God's enemy Satan through the building up of His *ekklesia* displays God's multi-faceted wisdom whereupon His eternal purpose is fulfilled (Eph. 3:10-11).

According to God's plan, He will not lift His little finger to directly defeat Satan — this Rebel who has little fear of God (Job 1-2; Matt. 4:1-11; Mark 1:12-13; Luke 4:1-13; 1 Peter 5:8; Revelation 12:10). Yet he knows full well, it is humanity that ultimately defeats him. Satan's goal is to divide man with the aim that mankind through wars, human diseases, murder, etc., would destroy themselves.

We see this immediately after the fall of man in Genesis 4. Cain, a son of Adam and Eve, divided from Abel through jealousy, ultimately murdered his brother. This has been the history of mankind ever since this first murder: Divisions are taking place among nations, races, social classes, even down to the family unit. Through these divisions, wars have been waged, with death and murder as their rotted fruit.

To counter Satan's tactic of division, God, through the work of Jesus Christ brought in peace and unity. It is in the uniting of divided people by bringing them together in peace wherein God's wisdom is manifested; Satan is ultimately defeated; and God's eternal purpose is fulfilled. Crushing Satan and putting him to an open shame is one of the main purposes of the building up of the Lord's *ekklesia*, the new humanity in Christ Jesus.

This is the reason preaching the gospel of peace for the uniting of God's people is critical and essential. Knowing this, Satan has blinded believers to the need for the gospel of peace. Satan is more than satisfied to keep the gospel of peace hidden, or to deceive Christians to consider the matter of peace to be reserved for the Millennium . . . a veritable impossibility, given nearly 2,000 years of division.

No, Satan is not defeated and crushed through the myriads of believers who have come to salvation through the gospel of grace. However, he is doing his very best to blind Christians from the gospel of peace, so they stay divided and separated. In such a state, Satan is still alive and well having rule over this present world.

It's time to end Satan's reign. It's time to bring God's people together in one. It's time for the preaching of the gospel of peace!

The Gospel of the Kingdom

"And this gospel of the kingdom will be preached in all the world
as a witness to all the nations, and then the end will come."
                                                    – Matthew 24:14

There is a thought among Christians wherein the kingdom of God
is inclusive of everything God created including what is contained in
the physical universe. Certainly, that can be the broadest definition of the
kingdom of God. Nevertheless, the term "kingdom of God" or its synonym
"kingdom of heaven" was not used in the Old Testament; rather, it was
at the introduction of Jesus Christ that it first was used. Additionally, the
gospel of the kingdom was critical since the Lord promised when the gospel
of the kingdom would be preached in all the world, then the end of the age
would come. Let's consider this vital topic.

Due to this verse in Matthew 24:14, Christians have done their best to
preach the "gospel of the kingdom" in order to hasten the Lord's second
coming. When western missionaries started to preach the gospel in Africa
and Asia, the gospel of the kingdom in the main was the gospel of Jesus
Christ and specifically the gospel of grace. Without a doubt this is part of
the kingdom message. Since this gospel has virtually reached every country
throughout the earth and the end is still nowhere in sight, many preachers
began to consider "the gospel of the kingdom" must be more than just
bringing sinners to salvation. . . maybe this "kingdom message" can be
manifested in other ways, other realms?

Since the advent of Pentecostalism in the beginning of the Twentieth
Century, the practice of casting out demons or "deliverance" has become a
common prayer practice among this form of Christianity. The verse cited for
this practice in relation to the kingdom of God is found in Matthew 12:28:
"*But if I cast out demons by the Spirit of God, surely the kingdom of God has come
upon you.*" Due to this teaching, much of the focus relating to the kingdom
of God is on casting out demons. Of course, the matter of casting out
demons has been in practice both by the Catholic and Orthodox Churches
for centuries. Although an important exercise, the practice of casting out
demons or evil spirits was unmentioned in the epistles; notwithstanding,
God's kingdom continued to be a major topic. Therefore, it is safe to say the

emphasis of the gospel of the kingdom for the end times is not a matter of casting out of demons — it is something far more significant!

In the last few decades, Christian preachers and teachers have started giving messages on aspects of Christian understanding and experiences with a focus on the kingdom of God. Generally, the emphasis was — and still is — to come under the authority of King Jesus, the Lordship of Christ (viz., "Lordship salvation"); and exercising dominion over society. If Christians are under the King's ruling, then they have the authority to affect society around them. The foundation of this understanding stems from the Lord's *ekklesia* He is building, and this *ekklesia* has the authority to bind and loose on the earth (Matt. 16:19).

Additionally, whatever the Lord's *ekklesia* binds or looses on earth corresponds with what God is doing in the heavens. This authority reflects the original practice of the Greek *ekklesia* which the Lord Jesus appropriated: *I will build my ekklesia.* The Greek *ekklesia* was the beginning of democracy in Greece cir. 600 BC, which was a form of government where all citizens of a city were called out for assembly — each one was given a voice to express their own opinions on a subject affecting the city. After discussions and debates, the matter was brought to a vote. The majority vote would win; a decree was made; and actions taken. The *ekklesia* legislated what took place in that society. In this sense, the Lord's *ekklesia* is very much related to the authority of God's kingdom.

Therefore, based on this understanding, the preaching of the gospel of the kingdom is first and foremost obedience to the authority of King Jesus in our daily living. Furthermore, exercise of this authority in the *ekklesia* is manifested as kings on earth to legislate the affairs of society. Under this understanding, Christians should set up God's kingdom throughout the earth as God's government in various "marketplaces" such as education, entertainment, business, human governments, neighborhoods, science, etc. Those under this concept of the kingdom believe this is the gospel of the kingdom which needs to be preached to all the nations . . . then the end will come.

This line of teaching is not wrong in and of itself. In fact, this kind of teaching has been popular on and off for almost 500 years starting from John Calvin, one of the main reformers. Actually, an entire doctrine of such a concept was developed by St. Augustine in his *City of God* wherein the "Church" was able to justify Roman rule over the masses.

Many of the Puritans who first migrated to the United States from Europe had similar convictions in setting up God's kingdom in human society. The Moral Majority movement in the USA formed in 1979 was spreading a similar message. Indeed, the NAR movement (i.e., New Apostolic Reformation) embodies most of these concepts.

The problem is this: Whenever or whatever these kinds of movements have achieved in their influence over society, they fall abysmally short of their goals with little lasting influence. Over time, Satan is still the ruler over the kingdoms of this world. This kind of preaching of the gospel of the kingdom has had negligible effect on society throughout the centuries of its inept run. Additionally, the Lord's *ekklesia*, the Body of Christ, continues her fragmenting and divisive trend — evermore disintegrating and dividing. There must be an alternative or additional understanding concerning the gospel of the kingdom which Christians must recognize; otherwise, doing the same thing over and over will repeat history and not result in the desired outcome . . . the ending of the age unto the Second Coming of the Messiah!

So, what is the preaching of the gospel of the kingdom which would bring us all closer to the end of the age? Let's start this consideration with the following:

> . . . and saying, "The time is fulfilled, and the kingdom of God is at hand. Repent, and believe in the gospel."
> – Mark 1:15

> Being asked by the Pharisees when the kingdom of God would come, he answered them, "The kingdom of God is not coming in ways that can be observed, nor will they say, 'Look, here it is!' or 'There!' for behold, the kingdom of God is in the midst of you."
> – Luke 17:20-21 ESV

> And He said to them, "Assuredly, I say to you that there are some standing here who will not taste death till they see the kingdom of God present with power." Now after six days Jesus took Peter, James, and John, and led them up on a high mountain apart by themselves; and He was transfigured before them.
> – Mark 9:1-2

From the New Testament's writing, there is no doubt the coming of the kingdom of God is the coming of Jesus Christ. Jesus Christ Himself is the kingdom of God. Matthew and Mark first announced this kingdom of God (heaven) is at hand before introducing Jesus Christ. Jesus Himself declared Himself, as the kingdom of God — He was in the midst of His disciples. Then He said some of them would see the kingdom coming in glory. A week later He was transfigured before them in His glory. These verses clearly show Jesus Christ Himself is the kingdom of God. The gospel of the kingdom of God is certainly the gospel of Jesus Christ.

> And they sang a new song, saying, "Worthy are you to take the scroll and to open its seals, for you were slain, and by your blood you ransomed people for God from every tribe and language and people and nation, and you have made them a kingdom and priests to our God, and they shall reign on the earth."
> — Revelation 5:9-10 ESV

However, God's purpose was not simply to have one person as His kingdom; rather, His kingdom would expand to include people from every tribe, tongue, people and nation. Therefore, many more people need to be transferred into His kingdom (Col. 1:13) from the kingdom of darkness. This transfer happens through the new birth. A person needs to be born or reborn into the kingdom of God; therefore, John 3:5 says no one can enter the kingdom of God unless a person is born anew (born again); born from above or regenerated. Being born of God is the only way to enter the kingdom of God or have the kingdom expand. It is through the gospel of grace wherein myriads upon myriads of individuals have been brought into the kingdom of God. One cannot be born through works of the flesh (John 1:12-13). It is all by grace.

As has been seen, the kingdom of God is one. It must be composed of people who are united. A kingdom cannot stand if it is divided against itself (Matt. 12:25). That is also true for the kingdom of God. **Therefore, the gospel of the kingdom must include the uniting together of previously divided peoples from every tribe, tongue, people and nation.**

The Rebuilding of the United Kingdom of David

Remember it was discussed earlier in this chapter how the kingdom of David was split back in the days of Rehoboam and Jeroboam? Ever since that split, (the division between the southern two tribes and the northern ten tribes) the kingdom of David in the land of Israel has been under domination by other kings and nations. Although Judah and Benjamin (with the Levites) went back to rebuild the temple and Jerusalem around 538 BC; after 70 years of Babylonian captivity, they continued to be under the power of other kings for almost 2,500 years. This confirms that when a kingdom is divided it cannot stand — it will become desolate, laid waste.

The rebuilding of the United Kingdom of David happened in Acts 15 according to James' interpretation of the prophecy found in Amos 9:11-12.

> And certain [men] came down from Judea and taught the brethren, "Unless you are circumcised according to the custom of Moses, you cannot be saved." . . . But some of the sect of the Pharisees who believed rose up, saying, "It is necessary to circumcise them, and to command [them] to keep the law of Moses" . . . "Now therefore, why do you test God by putting a yoke on the neck of the disciples which neither our fathers nor we were able to bear? . . . 'After this I will return And will rebuild the tabernacle of David [i.e., the "United Kingdom of David"], which has fallen down; I will rebuild its ruins, And I will set it up; So that the rest of mankind ["Edom" according to the Greek Septuagint] may seek the LORD, even all the Gentiles [i.e., "nations" or "ethnos"] who are called by My name, says the LORD who does all these things."
>
> — Acts 15:1, 5, 10, 16-17

Many Jewish believers at the time of Acts considered the kingdom of God to be theirs. They, having the heritage of the kingdom of David, of whom is the forefather of Jesus Christ, deemed they were — and still are — the formation of the kingdom of God. More so, to many Jewish believers, the kingdom of God must be a Jewish kingdom. Therefore, they considered their laws and traditions to be indispensable as part of God's kingdom.

Although Gentiles also believed and received the Holy Spirit in the same fashion as Jewish believers, they still considered Gentile believers needed to abide by the same laws and traditions as Jews. Thus, many Jewish believers tried their best to convince Gentile believers to come under the law such as circumcision, diet and keeping a strict Sabbath. Jewish traditions and law became a gulf of separation and division in the Body of Christ between Jewish and Gentile believers; and, as a result, the enmity and hatred between Judah and the Nations persisted.

In Acts 15, Paul and Barnabas with some Gentile believers went to Jerusalem to settle this factious matter. After presenting what the Lord had done in granting salvation to the Gentiles, Peter spoke up and said something very significant, referencing history. He said Jewish believers should not put a "*yoke*" upon Gentiles which the Jews themselves could not bear (Acts 15:10). In using this word "*yoke*" it invoked the same word used in the split between Rehoboam and Jeroboam (2 Chron. 10:11).

The division of the kingdom happened because Rehoboam wanted to increase taxation upon the Northern ten tribes while exploiting their labor, which was described as a "*heavy yoke*" (1 King 12). The word "yoke" was used eight times referring to this taxation and labor exploitation. It was due to this yoke the Northern ten tribes decided to divide from the kingdom of David. Peter by referring to this yoke brought into memory the reason the kingdom was divided. Basically, Peter was saying the customs and traditions (ordinances) of the Jews was a heavy yoke. A yoke which in past times divided the United Kingdom of David; therefore, let's not allow such a "yoke" as circumcision ("*Unless you are circumcised according to the custom of Moses, you cannot be saved*" – Acts 15:1) to divide the Body of Christ.

James continued this thought with his astonishing conclusion by citing a prophecy from Amos 9:11-12. He declared Gentiles, joining with Jews in the faith of Christ, are the very rebuilding ("raising up the ruins") of the Tabernacle of David or the United Kingdom of David. Remember, the Northern ten tribes were swallowed up by the nations (Hosea 8:7-8); therefore, they became "*scattered among the nations.*" Now, James under the inspiration of the Spirit declared these Gentiles joining with Jews through faith in Christ is the rebuilding of King David's United Kingdom. His understanding was this: The Gentiles represented the ten tribes assimilated by the nations; now, by those being called out from among the nations wherein they were scattered, joining with the Jews (the two tribes), together [i.e., the Ten Northern Tribes and the Two Southern Tribes] they would once again become the 12 united tribes of Israel. What a revelation!

King David was the prefigure of Jesus Christ. The kingdom of David prefigures the kingdom of Jesus Christ, the kingdom of God. According to James' interpretation of prophecy, the Jews and Gentile believers becoming one in the Lord's *ekklesia* is the rebuilding of the United Kingdom of David. Indeed, expanding and building up the kingdom of God is from one person to a corporate person. This corporate person is the One New Man composed of both Jews and Gentiles including all those of every tribe, tongue, people, and nation (i.e., "*the rest of mankind*" or "*Edom*").

Therefore, preaching the gospel of the kingdom has to include uniting previously divided peoples into one. Moreover, James went a step further in his prophetic pronouncement regarding the incursion of the called out from among the nations coming into the Lord's *ekklesia*: "*So that **the rest of mankind** may seek the LORD, even all the Nations* [viz., Gentiles] *who are called by My name, says the LORD who does all these things*" (Acts 15:17; Amos 9:12). Not only would Ephraim once again be united in the Kingdom of God with Judah, but Edom or MANKIND would be as well. "*Jacob have I loved, but Esau* [the Edomites] *have I hated*" would now be brought into the Tabernacle of David!

We find in 1 Chronicles 13:13-14 the Ark of the Covenant was temporarily placed in the house of Obed-Edom the Gittite where upon Obed-Edom (meaning "the servant of Edom") was greatly blessed for three months. Later we find in 1 Chronicles 15:18, 21, 24-25; 16:38 Obed-Edom did not forsake the Ark of the Covenant when it was moved into the Tabernacle of David in the City of David (Jerusalem) — he and his 69 Edomite brethren became the gatekeepers of the Tabernacle of David . . . "*because His mercy endures forever*" (1 Chron. 16:41).

Imagine, those of Edom/Esau became the gatekeepers in the United Kingdom of David — the Tabernacle of David! What mercy is this!!

Today, Christians are speaking of the results of the kingdom of God, such as authority over society, without understanding and emphasizing this kingdom of God must be one; which includes uniting of those normally divided from and hostile to each other. This is indeed good news: people who are naturally divided enemies are now united in the righteousness, peace, and joy of the Holy Spirit (Rom. 14:17). **This is the gospel of the kingdom.**

Truly, the gospel of peace is a critical and essential part of the gospel of the kingdom — just as the gospel of the grace of God comprises its complimentary portion. It is the gospel of peace declaring all walls of division formally between these most hostile peoples are now terminated through the death of Jesus Christ. This is the rest of the gospel message missing today. This is the portion of the gospel needed by all people and especially among Christians. Therefore, it is against the truth of the gospel to accept the normality of Christians being divided. To suggest unity among believers will not become a reality until the second advent of Christ militates against the message of the gospel of peace. It is time to preach the entirety of the gospel of the kingdom. It is the very fulfillment of the One Body of Messiah – wrought by the preaching of the gospel of peace – that will, in fact, result in the Second Coming of Messiah and the end of the age: *THIS GOSPEL OF THE KINGDOM SHALL BE PREACHED IN ALL THE WORLD, THEN SHALL THE END COME!*

In conclusion, the gospel of the kingdom is the combination of all the gospels. It is the gospel of God who loved the world and sent His Son. It is the gospel of Jesus Christ: Who He is and what He has done through His death, resurrection, ascension, and the out-pouring of the Spirit. It is the gospel of grace since it is not of works whereof sinners can be forgiven and regenerated to become sons of the Living God. It is also the gospel of peace which brings divided people together into oneness in the rebuilding of the United Kingdom of David, the kingdom of God. Every aspect of the gospel needs to be preached. However, it is the gospel of peace which has been the most obscured, obfuscated, and terribly neglected. It is the gospel of peace which will bring in the unity for the kingdom of God and the prophesied end of the age, the Second Coming of Messiah!

Divisions Contradict the Truth of the Gospel

> Now when Peter had come to Antioch, I withstood him to his face, because he was to be blamed; for before certain men came from James, he would eat with the Gentiles; but when they came, he withdrew and separated himself, fearing those who were of the circumcision And the rest of the Jews also played the hypocrite with him, so that even Barnabas was carried away with their hypocrisy.
>
> – Galatians 2:11-13

In Antioch, Peter with other Jewish believers were eating and in fellowship together with Gentile believers. They were practicing the oneness of the Body of Christ, the Lord's *ekklesia*. They were in the reality of the gospel of the kingdom. Then some Jewish Christians came from Jerusalem, from James (although it seems insufficient to suggest James sent them). At that point, Peter took the lead to withdraw and divide from these Gentile believers — all other Jewish believers followed. All of them separated and divided themselves from the Gentiles. This action directly contradicted and opposed the gospel. It was destroying the work of the gospel. It had become a "perverted" – a "distorted" – a "different" – "another" or "other gospel" (Gal. 1:6-9). It became a gospel where Paul said of those who preach such: *Let him be accursed* — ANATHEMA! (Gal. 1:9).

Therefore, Paul had to publicly rebuke Peter declaring he was not walking according to the "*truth of the gospel*" and was but a "men pleaser" (Gal. 1:10; 2:5, 14). This powerful and intentional phrase "***truth of the gospel***" was used in describing Peter's transgression (Gal. 2:5, 14). *Truth of the gospel* means the reality behind the gospel. It can be inferred to mean the purpose of the gospel; what the gospel was to accomplish. Jewish believers separating and dividing themselves from Gentile believers was against the very reality or purpose of the gospel — the goal of the gospel was not only to save sinners but to restore the United Kingdom of David so the rest of mankind (the nations) could enjoy the Tabernacle of David in its fullness! This gospel is not just to bring sinners to glory, but ultimately it is to bring previously divided people into unity and become one as the kingdom of God for the Almighty, through this Oneness, to take dominion, thereby crushing Satan beneath our feet!

Christians cannot simply accept the status quo of having divisions and factions in the body of Christ, awaiting the Second Coming of Christ "to bring it all together." Believers cannot continue to perpetrate divisions and separation from other believers considering it as normative without negative consequences. Rather, there needs to be a radical change in understanding to appreciate joining divided believers together in unity. Repent, for the kingdom of God!

Today, there may be millions of preachers preaching the gospel of grace, but how ironic it is, while they are preaching the gospel of grace, they themselves are divided from other believers; thus, destroying the very reality of the gospel. In fact, their gospel preaching may be intended to grow and expand their own defined group, denomination, ministry, which, as a practice, may not have meals and fellowship with other believers aside from their own defined group.

Just about every minister is preaching the gospel of grace and every believer seems to be charged to do likewise. How many are preaching the gospel of peace whereby divided believers are brought together in oneness? How many are even aware the gospel of peace needs to be preached? What's worse, how many even have the understanding and appreciation of the gospel of peace?

Without the gospel of peace, the gospel of the kingdom is not yet preached in fullness. We need the gospel of the kingdom to be preached in all the nations, then the end shall come. The gospel of peace is the completion of the gospel of Jesus Christ. It is the one thing lacking in preaching today: This is the gospel of the kingdom. Now is the time for all ministers, preachers, all Christian workers, and believers to arise and preach the gospel of peace, the complete gospel of the kingdom. This is the completion of the gospel of Jesus Christ — *"the fullness* [completion] *of the blessing of the gospel of Jesus Christ"* (Rom. 15:29).

11

THE COMPLETION GOSPEL IN ROMANS

The four gospels, in general, can be considered as the gospel of Jesus Christ before His death and resurrection. Romans can be considered as the gospel of Jesus Christ after His resurrection. Many theologians esteem Romans to be Paul's complete theology of the Christian life (aka, "the Romans Road").

First, let's consider the background when Paul wrote the epistle to Rome. At that time, he had not yet been to Rome, nor was there a record of any other apostle having gone to Rome. Nevertheless, from his writing, "*To all who are in Rome, beloved of God, called to be saints*" (Rom. 1:7) it is apparent there was a sizable community of Christians in Rome. How did so many believers come to live in Rome?

History confirms that under the administration of the Roman Empire there was unrestricted and relatively safe travel throughout its territory. Rapidly expanding commerce brought diverse peoples to and from the Capital which was Rome. Citizens and freemen of the Empire took advantage of this and were able to travel — locating freely within Roman territory. Many slaves were brought there to serve the citizens of Rome (normally known as "barbarians" but anyone aside from Roman citizens could be a slave). There was also a large population of Jews in Rome. This is clearly affirmed by the backgrounds of the twenty-seven people named in Romans 16, plus the five groups of people Paul mentioned (some say 36 various names).

Although Paul personally brought some in Rome to faith in Christ, and at least a couple became his fellow workers such as Prisca (Priscilla) and Aquila, it is also reasonable to assume many were brought to faith by other apostles and preachers who were active during Paul's time. Certainly, some could have come to Christ in Judea. Perhaps, when they went to Jerusalem for the feasts, they heard the gospel through the ministry of the Twelve

Apostles, or through Philip in Samaria, or from one of the many scattered believers who went throughout the territories preaching the gospel (Acts 11:19).

In Rome, they had become collections of believers meeting in different homes who had come to faith in Christ through various preachers; they were as diverse as the population of Rome. There were well-to-do believers with large households, as well as slaves, Jews, Greeks, barbarians, Roman citizens, and freemen from throughout the Empire. In such a situation, it certainly would have been easy for the Christian community to segregate and separate themselves from each other. Naturally, those with similar cultural backgrounds, socioeconomic status, ethnic identities, apostolic preferences, and especially those with a kosher diet would prefer to group themselves together.

As expected from these deep-seated divisions and hostility between Jews and Gentiles, Paul's main challenge was bringing these two groups of believers together in Rome. Remember how Peter with other Jewish believers separated themselves from eating and fellowshipping with Gentile believers in Antioch? (Gentiles; Grk. "*ethnos*" or those called out from the nations – Gal. 2:2-16) If Peter could become factious, even after the revelation of the rebuilding of the United Kingdom of David in Acts 15:16-17, it would be easy and natural for Jewish and Gentile believers in Rome to separate themselves from each other. If Paul could solve this problem in Rome in order to build up the One Body of Christ, then, in comparison, all other divisions between Barbarians and Romans, or slave and freeman, would be simple. The building up of the Lord's One Body depended upon the "wall of separation" (Eph. 2:14) being broken down. Let's review the book of Romans with the unity of God's people in view, and division being the problem for Paul to resolve.

Paul addressed this letter to the "*saints in Rome*" (Rom. 1:7). He didn't write this letter to any specific group, not even the group of saints meeting as the Lord's *ekklesia* in Priscilla and Aquila's house (nor is any leadership designated in his epistle to the Romans). He wanted all the saints in the various groups to hear the same message directly from him; so, after reading they could come together in one fellowship. Although he was addressing "saints" – those who already had faith in Jesus Christ – yet he said he was preaching the gospel to them (Rom. 1:15). According to our current understanding the gospel message is for unbelievers. Why would Paul need to preach the gospel to those who had already believed in Jesus Christ? It's because they were divided; therefore, they needed to hear and understand the entire gospel of God (Rom. 1:1) concerning His Son, Jesus Christ, Who died and resurrected (Rom. 1:3-4) for His eternal purpose to be fulfilled.

Since the challenge was to bring divided and separated believers into One Body, Paul started by showing no matter the gulf of differences between Jews and Gentiles, they still had a common heritage. The first commonality is condemnation by God — the *"wrath of God has passed to all humankind for all have sinned and come short of God's glory"* (Rom. 3:23). In Romans chapters 1 through 3 Paul made evident, whether Jews or Gentiles, whether "chosen" with God's law or without law, both were sinners falling short of God's glory — under the sentence of "judgment." There is no advantage of Jews over Gentiles or vise-versa regarding condemnation.

As people equally condemned — under God's wrath, both needed common redemption through the death of Jesus Christ (Rom. 3:24). Without exception, the only common way to justification available before God is through faith (Rom. 4-5), the faith of Jesus Christ (Rom. 3:26). In Romans 4, while the Jews considered Abraham to be their forefather, it made clear Abraham is the father of faith for both Jews and Gentiles (for *"righteousness was imputed to him"* before Abraham was circumcised — Rom. 4:22). Romans 6:3-4 unveils both Jews and Gentiles have been "put to death" through Christ's crucifixion and burial. Now, both are sanctified (made holy) the same way. . . by their common identity in Christ.

Romans 7 reveals, whether a Jew under the law or a Gentile without law, both have a common struggle with indwelling sin, and both need the indwelling Spirit as found in Romans 8. It is this Spirit who brings both once-divided people into the glory of the sons of God.

From a salvation perspective, Romans 8:29-30 ends with glorification — this should be the finality of the gospel. Glorification is the end goal of every believer's salvation journey. Through these eight chapters, one's salvation is made complete: starting with justification through faith; then sanctification through identification in Christ's death and resurrection; then transformation through the indwelling and leading of the Spirit; and finally, glorification or the transfiguration of the body unto becoming mature sons of God (Rom. 8:29) — ultimately, bringing in the new heaven and new earth. These first eight chapters of Romans are the work of the gospel of the grace of God: all are saved by grace (Rom. 3:24); and after entering grace, all need to stand and remain in grace through the entire salvation journey (Rom. 5:2). Yet, this is only half the book of Romans. Why is there a need for another eight chapters (Romans 9-16)?

Although individual salvation is established and completed, God's purpose is still not fulfilled. The Lord still needs His One Body to crush Satan's head (Rom. 16:20). The Jews and Gentiles are still divided and no doubt gathering separately in Rome; therefore, Satan was not crushed at the end of Chapter 8; therefore, another eight chapters are needed before we see Satan crushed at the end of chapter 16.

Believers Were Divided: Who Is Special and Chosen?

The bulk of Bible commentary on the book of Romans has been focused on Romans 1-8. These first 8 chapters clearly have a systematic progression. Whereas, Romans 9-16 are usually taken in a piecemeal fashion with various disjointed doctrines selected within these chapters. Romans 9 is a pillar of support for those holding the doctrine of predestination. Those leading individuals to salvation will find verses in Romans 10 indispensable for gospel preaching. Romans 11 is essential for studying the end times in relation to Israel in Bible prophecy. The doctrine of the Body of Christ with the priesthood of all believers can be found in Romans 12. Those objecting to Reform theology's bid of influencing and shaping government will no doubt make use of Romans 13. Ministers with a socially liberal perspective will derive their doctrine from Romans 14 and 15. Romans 16 has no theology at all other than to exploit a few verses to ostracize troublemakers in a church, while showing Paul's familiarity with various saints in Rome.

What if Paul also wrote Romans 9-16 with a systematic development? What would be the logical progression? From the gospel's perspective, Romans 1-8 is the work of the **gospel of the grace of God** (Rom. 1:16; cf Acts 20:24), turning condemned sinners into glorified sons of God. In Romans 9-16 readers will be shown the work of the **gospel of peace** (Rom. 10:15; cf. Eph. 6:15), turning believers in divided groups into one unified Body giving glory to God and crushing the head of His enemy – Satan (Rom. 16:20).

> As it is written, "Jacob I have loved, but Esau I have hated." . . . even us whom He called, not of the Jews only, but also of the Gentiles [ethnos or nations]? As He says also in Hosea: "I will

call them My people, who were not My people, And her beloved, who was not beloved." "And it shall come to pass in the place where it was said to them, 'You [are] not My people,' There they shall be called sons of the living God."

– Romans 9:13, 24-26

While the background of one's individual salvation journey starts with sin and condemnation (Romans 1-3), Romans 9 starts with two divided groups: Israel (representing the Jews) and *Esau* (the rest of "mankind"), the Gentiles. The word "*mankind*" in Acts 15:17 is translated in the *Septuagint* [ancient Greek version of the "Hebrew Scriptures"] as *Edom* (aka "Esau"). Anyone who reads Romans 9:13, will consider God is unfair: He hated Esau and loved Jacob. Those who identify with Jacob, the chosen people, can no doubt feel honored and even proud. Jacob can feel pity for Esau. But since it was God's will, the Jews, considering themselves to be the pure descendants of Jacob, the true Israel (i.e., the totality of Israel) can be justified in their contempt for Esau — "*the rest of mankind*," in which the Jews have classified all non-Jews to be Gentiles. Those who identify themselves with Esau (the rest of mankind or the Gentiles) will feel dejected, humiliated, and rejected.

Moreover, those "*scattered among the Gentiles*" — those who were considered "*not beloved*" but now those scattered Ephraimites (viz., Israelites) who were "*not My people*" are now considered "*her beloved*" and "*sons of the living God*" — well, obviously, Romans 9 has in view the "*gathering together in ONE the children of God who were scattered abroad*" (John 11:52). Imagine what Jewish believers were thinking as they were reading these "*prophetic Scriptures*" (Rom. 16:26) being expounded by Paul!

Yes, just a few verses later, God calls those Gentiles — those Israelites scattered among the nations — who were no longer His people "His people," and those that are not beloved, "beloved" (cf. Hosea 1:6-11; 2:1; Rom. 9:25-26). Isn't that wonderful? God has just completely reversed Himself from hating Esau to loving Esau; from rejecting Ephraim to calling her "beloved" — now all mankind (Gentiles) — whom the Jews (Israel — the House of Judah) had considered to be inferior; even as unclean dogs, now they are the ELECT OF GOD? WOW!

Paul quoted from Hosea 2:23 "*I will call them My people, who were not My people*" in reference to Esau. However, in context Hosea was speaking of the so-called "Lost Ten Tribes of Israel" known as Ephraim, Jezreel, Samaria . . .

those *"scattered among the nations"* (cf. Hosea 8:7-10). These are the same people who were called Gentiles in Acts 15 where James referenced them to be Ephraim, the lost ten tribes coming back to rebuild the kingdom or the Tabernacle of David. **By applying Hosea's prophecy, Paul lumped two groups of people together into one common group called Gentiles: Ephraim (as the lost ten tribes) and Esau (the rest of mankind).**

Remember the context found in Paul's remarks primarily deals with the division between Jewish Christians and Gentile (*"ethos"*) Christians. Even as Christians, those with Jewish heritage were considering themselves as beloved Israel (even "exclusively Israel"), while considering believers from among the nations (aka, Gentiles) as inferior. That was the reason Jewish believers were motivated to compel Gentile believers to be like them — keeping the laws contained in ordinances according to Moses and their traditions. Now, Paul in Romans 9 showed through the prophetic Scriptures (Rom. 16:26) the Gentiles are also beloved and deemed His people. Therefore, Jewish believers should accept them, love them as God loves them. Jewish believers should no longer consider themselves superior to Gentile believers since God has only one people, and those being called out from among the nations are now part of the same people as Israel — ALL ISRAEL (Rom. 11:26).

Let's skip Romans 10 for now and jump to Romans 11 for further consideration.

> And if some of the branches were broken off, and you, being a wild olive tree, were grafted in among them, and with them became a partaker of the root and fatness of the olive tree . . . You will say then, "Branches were broken off that I might be grafted in." Well [said]. Because of unbelief they were broken off, and you stand by faith. Do not be haughty, but fear. For if God did not spare the natural branches, He may not spare you either.
>
> – Romans 11:17, 19-21

The situation is now reversed: Gentile believers feel special and superior by pointing out that Israel (Judah, the Jews) was cut off. God pruned and cut-off Israel for their unbelief and they, the Gentiles, as the wild olive branch are now grafted into Christ (the root of the green olive tree-Jeremiah 11:16), enjoying all His riches. God has cut off Judah-Israel. He has terminated everything Jewish! It is the age of the Gentiles. The Gentiles are now the "chosen ones" — "*Israel* [Judah] *has not obtained what it seeks; but the elect* [those called out from among the nations] *have obtained it*" (Rom. 11:7). In their own eyes Gentile believers think they can now denigrate all the practices of Jewish believers. Why are they still practicing the Sabbath or keeping the Levitical diet? Don't they know God has terminated all these ordinances and laws?

Knowing Israel is no longer part of the olive tree (broken off), Gentile believers now consider themselves to be superior over Jewish believers. Those Gentile believers separating and dividing from Jewish believers can find support with this thought: If God cut them off, we can also cut off the Jews. If anyone practices anything Jewish, let's support God's decision by withdrawing from them; these Jewish believers need to know God has already cut off Israel.

Paul reprimanded the Gentiles: Don't be proud, don't boast. If they do, God can also cut off these Gentiles. If these Gentile believers divide and cut off Jewish believers, God will cut them off from the enjoyment of the riches of Christ. They will no longer be under God's cultivation to receive nourishment and the pleasure of His grace.

Paul was taking his metaphor of the olive tree directly from Jeremiah 11:16-17: "*The LORD called your name, Green Olive Tree, Lovely and of Good Fruit. With the noise of a great tumult He has kindled fire on it, and its branches are broken. For the LORD of hosts, who planted you, has pronounced doom against you for the evil of the house of Israel and of the house of Judah . . . .*" What is critical to note here is the ONENESS of that singular Green Olive Tree — yes, branches (Israel/Gentiles and Judah/Jews) but ONE ROOT that bore them both (Rom. 11:16-17). BOTH branches are considered "holy" (Rom. 11:16) — "set apart" by God Himself.

Paul's conclusion was, neither group is better. Whether one identifies with the Jewish group or with the Gentile group — neither group is special or superior over the other. Neither group is exclusively the selected or chosen ones. God has committed all in disobedience (Rom. 11:32). In fact, it was and still is this superior group identity which is dividing and causing a separation among believers — and it's not just ethnic divisions; it is a multitude of practices and doctrines, as well as individual "styles" which are causing division in the Body of Christ.

There is only one Body of Christ. There should not be sub-groups in His One Body. If there is a division between these two groups of Jews and Gentile believers, then both are disobedient because both are dividing the Body of Christ, His *ekklesia* (Matt. 16:18). Whichever divided group you consider yourself to be in, whichever group you have identified yourself with, whether Jewish or Gentile (or even sub-groups within these two major groups), and you consider your group superior and separate from the others; yet, God has counted all such divided Christians under disobedience!

When a person recognizes he or she is being disobedient, then God can show mercy. God's mercy is upon those who acknowledge their disobedience in dividing from other believers. Just as for individual salvation wherein there needs to be an acceptance of being a sinner who needs redemption before salvation can proceed according to Romans 3; even so, now if one is in a divided state where fellowship is withheld from those dissimilar, that person needs to recognize it is disobedience, even rebellion. It is at this point God's mercy is available. God's mercy is shown upon such a repentant person who is ready to be built up into the One Body of Christ. Just as sinners need to repent in order to receive salvation, even so, a believer who is divided from their brethren needs to repent in order to become one with other diverse believers so they can enjoy all the riches of Christ within the Body of Christ.

In Romans 10 we find the preaching of the *gospel of peace* is what brings believers together:

> But the righteousness of faith speaks in this way, "Do not say in your heart, 'Who will ascend into heaven?' " (that is, to bring Christ down [from above]) or, " 'Who will descend into the abyss?' " (that is, to bring Christ up from the dead). But what does it say? "The word is near you, in your mouth and in your heart" (that is, the word of faith which we preach): that if you confess with your mouth the Lord Jesus and believe in your heart that God has raised Him from the dead, you will be saved . . . For there is no distinction between Jew and Greek, for the same Lord over all is rich to all who call upon Him . . . And how shall they preach unless they are sent? As it is written: "How beautiful are the feet of those who **preach the gospel of peace**, who bring glad tidings of good things!"
>
> –Romans 10:6-9, 12, 15

What was needed to bring those divided groups together into one was the gospel of peace. Sinners need the gospel, but so do divided believers. Believers who are divided need to hear the gospel — the gospel of peace. *How beautiful are the feet of those who preach the gospel of peace!* It is this gospel of peace which brings believers together who once identified themselves in various divided groups.

This is not **another gospel** as Paul calls it in Galatians 1:6-7 (*"which is not another"*); no, it is the very *"truth of the gospel"* (Gal. 2:14). The gospel of peace is in fact the gospel of Jesus Christ. He is the One who came down from above as God. He died and went into the abyss as the God-man. He was raised from the dead as the life-giving Spirit to be in the heart and in the mouth of every believer. It is with the heart they believe in His resurrection and with the mouth they confess Jesus is Lord. The same confession which gave sinners initial salvation is the same confession which will save believers from division. Jesus Christ is rich to all those who call on His name — regardless of whether one considers himself a Jewish believer or a Gentile believer. Those recognizing they are in a divided state will call out to be saved in order to enjoy the Lord's riches. This is the gospel of peace which needs to be preached to all believers in division.

What caused divisions between Jewish and Gentile (Greek) believers? According to this chapter, it was the law of Moses. Jewish believers considered the law was nonetheless needed to establish their own righteousness unto salvation (Acts 15:11: *"But we believe that through the grace of the Lord Jesus Christ we shall be SAVED in the same manner as they."*).

Faith to them was not enough to be saved, the law was still needed. They were like those in Galatia who started in faith by the Spirit but went back to perfect themselves by seeking justification through the law using self-effort (Gal. 3:3-5). Paul admonished them and told them they were bewitched. They should not go back to law but continue by faith in the Spirit. Certainly, the matter of whether the law was needed for righteousness "unto salvation" would cause a dispute between Jewish believers and Gentile believers.

It is tragic whenever something is added to the one faith of Jesus Christ among believers (Eph. 4:5), **because any addition to the faith of Jesus Christ in order to achieve another level of salvation or further sanctification will always cause division among the saints of the Lord.** Speaking of Gentiles, Peter says: *"And made no distinction between us and them, PURIFYING their hearts by faith"* (Acts 15:9).

Therefore, Paul brought them back to the basics, the gospel of Jesus Christ, the simplicity of salvation. It is just Jesus. No matter how long a person has been a Christian or how scripturally learned, it is still just Jesus: Who He is and what He has done. Can it be simpler than believing in your heart God raised Jesus from the dead, and calling out upon His name to be saved? NO! "*For there is no distinction between Jew and Greek, for the same Lord over all is rich to all who call upon Him . . . for whoever calls on the name of the LORD shall be saved*" (Rom. 10:12-13).

The gospel of peace, which alone can bring divided believers together, is not something else other than Jesus Christ. It is not complex doctrines, higher learning or special practices. There is peace between all believers when they come back to this simplicity — the singleness of Jesus Christ.

Consider what divides Christians today; it is not Jesus Christ. It is Jesus plus something else. A certain kind of doctrine such as whether one can lose salvation, a practice such as whether one speaks in tongues or not, or a form of living such as whether it is holy enough. Those who have divided themselves from other believers due to Jesus plus something else need to hear the gospel again — the "fullness" or "completion" gospel again! Bringing believers back to the simplicity of faith in Christ alone is the very gospel of peace. Those who preach the gospel of peace are considered peacemakers. They are blessed and their feet are beautiful (Rom. 10:15). Those feet are for God's move on the earth to build up His one *ekklesia* by reconciling once divided believers together into one fellowship — the fellowship of Jesus Christ (1 Cor. 1:9).

Unfortunately, the Journey of Salvation from Romans 1-8 Has Caused Many Divisions

If we consider the time of Reformation beginning with Martin Luther as the initiation of the journey through salvation, then Romans 3 with justification by faith started one of the biggest divisions within the Body of Christ — the division between Protestants and Catholics. Both preach Jesus Christ; yet, both have many other doctrines and practices in addition to Jesus Christ separating them. In both groups, there are myriads of genuine believers who affirm the faith of Jesus Christ — are regenerated by the Holy Spirit. Additionally, those in each camp may consider God has chosen them and rejected the other. Therefore, due to group identity, a believer who goes to a Protestant church may not fellowship and break bread with one who identifies himself as a Catholic, and vice-versa. So how can individuals in either one of these groups get saved from division into the enjoyment of the oneness of the Body of Christ?

The *gospel of peace* is sorely needed. The gospel of Jesus Christ is again needed to be preached to those divided in Protestant and Catholic churches. Those who hear this gospel will receive faith to realize barriers have been broken down between believers. No matter which group with whom they may associate, they can fellowship freely with others not in their group. By hearing the gospel again, those divided are brought back to Jesus Christ and His riches — together with those who have the same faith, enjoying the same riches.

Though the gospel can be preached to many at one time, receiving of the gospel is up to each individual. Although the gospel of grace can be preached to hundreds or thousands at a music concert or an event; yet, the revelation and acceptance is personal. This is also true of the gospel of peace. This gospel can be preached in a denominational church to many Christians all at once, but the revelation and acceptance is also personal. The church as an organization, like an event, cannot receive the gospel, it is up to each individual.

The point is this gospel of peace is not for bringing together the Protestant and Catholic churches. The gospel cannot be received by an organization, it can only be received by individuals. To those who receive the gospel of peace — they will realize all walls dividing believers can be broken down, extending fellowship to all kinds of believers without partiality.

As Christians progress through the epistle to the Romans, in addition to justification by faith, there are more and more healthy doctrines supporting believers in following Jesus. The subject of sanctification or holiness is unveiled in Chapters 6 and 7, and the matter of the Spirit in chapter 8. Just as Martin Luther discovered justification by faith in Romans chapters 3, 4 and 5, even so, many ministers have uncovered additional helpful doctrines over the last few centuries. Each discovery has helped a portion of the followers of Jesus.

Those who have received these doctrinal benefits have been revived and energized. Naturally, since they were helped by these illuminations of the Spirit through ministers who discovered these teachings, they found it helpful to join themselves with these various ministers or churches (or "ministries") which brought them into a new understanding and experience. Since they are grouped with those who had arrived at a similar state of spirituality, they considered themselves truly blessed — due to these new and helpful understandings and experiences. Their thanks to God for their awakening and revival brought them to those who espoused these more progressive discoveries from the Scripture. In fact, God really has shown them favor! Indeed, most have found themselves truly blessed and chosen to have benefitted from such restoration ministries. This seemingly innocent and natural progression has unfortunately resulted in believers separating and segregating all the more from other believers who have not yet arrived at their understanding or who have taken a different approach in following Jesus with a different understanding.

As an example, Joe was a typical church-going Christian who became born again when he was younger. He was going to church regularly, but he also liked to party with friends. His church attendance started to drop. One day someone asked him to listen to a preacher. The preacher spoke concerning being filled with the Holy Spirit and how to experience the baptism of the Holy Spirit. Joe was intrigued. He went a few more times, then started to pray for this experience. A minister prayed for him and he got filled with joy and started manifesting a gift of the Spirit. He was so strengthened; he gave up partying with his friends. He joined this new church which helped him — he felt special. He felt he finally found a church God favored. When he looked back at the people in His old church, he thought, "They are really missing the mark, deficient". Those in his old church thought Joe was deceived. They no longer fellowship with each other.

Another example: Jill came to Jesus in a "Spirit filled" church; however, after a few years, she started backsliding. She didn't know whether she was still saved because people in her church told her she needed to live a holy life if she were truly saved. She was constantly under condemnation. She doubted whether the Lord was with her. One day she heard a minister preaching "all of grace and not of works." Additionally, nothing can separate her from the love of God. Once she is saved, she cannot lose her salvation. She was so relieved! Her love for God was renewed. She felt so special because now she knew God loved her so much, no matter her condition. She joined the church because it helped her understand she could never lose her salvation. She thought the people in her old church were wrong for thinking God could actually change His mind if a believer backslid, as if salvation were based on one's works and not on God's unchanging love and grace.

These examples are but a few of the myriad of illustrations wherein believers depart from one church to another and in so doing, unwittingly cause division. Now, consider there are thousands of Bible teachers who have a desire to help Christians with various combinations of doctrines and practices in the Bible. Undoubtedly, many will be helped by such ministers. If an individual gets help through minister "so-and-so" with what is perceived to be his dynamic practice or teaching, then that individuals will consider that group which helped him to be specially selected by God. Therefore, naturally, believers identify themselves according to the group or the minister which benefited them. They will often stay in association or fellowship only with those in their newly-found group from whence they originally got such great help.

Now, here we are, centuries after the Reformation. Thousands upon thousands of Bible ministers, millions upon millions of Christians later. Alas! Believers are divided by group identity and everyone who has received help thinks their church or group is special and "chosen." This may all have happened gradually without any sinister intent. Therefore, Romans doesn't end in chapter 8 – it purposefully continues with chapters 9-16 in the preaching of the gospel of peace in order to bring believers together into one fellowship. After the first eight chapters, believers can still be divided into various groups — each group has seemingly valid reasons to believe they are chosen of God, superior. Yet, each, as far as God is concerned, is disobedient because His people are still divided. It is time to recognize God's mercy is needed on His rebellious, divided people.

The gospel of peace, on the one hand illuminates the believer's disobedience in being divisive and factious; and on the other hand, gives salvation and supply with the riches of Christ (Rom. 10:12). This illuminating revelation and supply causes a believer to repent anew which in turn brings God's new mercies (Rom. 11:32). At this point, those who have obtained mercy (Rom. 11:30-32) continues into Romans 12 where these "mercies" issue forth in the One Body of Christ:

> I beseech you therefore, brethren, by the **mercies of God**, that you present your bodies a living sacrifice, holy, acceptable to God, [which is] your reasonable service. And do not be conformed to this world, but be transformed by the renewing of your mind, that you may prove what [is] that good and acceptable and perfect

will of God. For I say, through the grace given to me, to everyone
who is among you, not to think [of himself] more highly than
he ought to think, but to think soberly, as God has dealt to each
one a measure of faith. For as we have many members in one
body, but all the members do not have the same function, so we,
[being] many, are one body in Christ, and individually members
of one another.

– Romans 12:1-5

Romans 12 begins with the *"mercies of God"* which is a clear reference
back to the end of Romans 11. It is when you, a follower of Jesus, hear the
gospel of peace and repent of your disobedience, even rebellion, for being
divisive, that you are now ready to see and experience real Body Life. You
are ready to present yourself to the Body of Christ. If you only associate and
fellowship with those in a designated group and not with others, you are
not yet ready for true Body Life. You cannot present yourself to the Body
of Christ. The Body of Christ is constituted with both Jews and Gentiles;
therefore, the Body of Christ does not belong to any one group no matter
how scripturally correct or spiritually advanced they are. The Body Life
found in Romans 12 cannot happen within any one divided group of people.
It's not that you have to leave a group from where you got help; however,
what is necessary is to be delivered from being limited to that singular
group. It is only then you are ready to present yourself to the entire Body of
Christ; ready and willing to fellowship with all believers no matter which
group with whom they may or may not identify.

This attitudinal transformation, wherein the believer's identification
finds fellowship with the entire Body of Christ, through the renewing of the
mind, enables one to think differently. This renewed thinking is not to think
of oneself more highly than one ought to think. Remember in Romans 9-11
Paul was exposing the disobedience of those in divided groups because they
thought they were superior or "chosen" compared to others? Then, through
the gospel of peace, they received mercies to have their minds renewed. The
renewed mind appreciates all other members in the Body no matter be they
Jews or Greeks, rich or poor, bond or free, etc.

It is this renewal of the mind which can value all believers as individuals
beyond group identity. A renewed mind cannot see believers with a label;
rather, it sees every believer as a member of the Body of Christ — every

member is necessary. There are many different and diverse individual members, but only One Body. Generally, every church or group gathers together Christians who are similar; just like a Jewish group will gather Jewish Christians and a Chinese church will gather Chinese people, a Pentecostal church will gather those who practices the gifts of the Spirit, etc. However, by Romans 12 believers have been released into the freedom of the Body of Christ. In the Body there is diversity in function (Rom. 12:4, 6); yet, absolutely one in fellowship.

The context of the word "world" which believers should "not be conformed to" (or not to allow the "world to squeeze you into its own mold") is not focused on sin and the glamour of the secular world; rather, it is the religious world with divided groups and churches. Most Christian teachers apply this verse back to sanctification which Paul has already thoroughly addressed in Romans 6-8. In these later chapters, Paul is addressing divisions within the Body and having a superiority complex among Christians. Don't be conformed to that world! The transformation here is being delivered from this divisive world among Christian believers into the freedom of the inclusiveness of the Body of Christ.

The Secular World Is Not the Problem in Causing Division

> Let every soul be subject to the governing authorities. For there is no authority except from God, and the authorities that exist are appointed by God . . . Owe no one anything except to love one another, for he who loves another has fulfilled the law . . . Love does no harm to a neighbor; therefore love [is] the fulfillment of the law.
>
> – Romans 13:1, 8, 10

When Paul wrote to the Romans, Nero was the Emperor. Undoubtedly, Nero's regime was the worst government in history facing the early Church. Nevertheless, the Scriptures urged the saints to be subject to the governing body. Paul didn't ask or suggest believers become political and overthrow or change the government (the author is not suggesting Christians should neglect their civic duty to vote if they are citizens of a democratic society).

Basically, he said to trust God for those in authority. The problem with division is not due to government. Human government is not the source of division in the Body of Christ. In fact, when a government persecutes believers, believers who are suffering are enjoined to drop their factiousness and become one. Due to unity, they become revived, strong, and fruitful.

Basically, Paul's point in Romans 13 is "let's not get distracted with human government, good or bad." If believers have a heart for the oneness of the Body, then love is needed. Love is the fulfillment of the law. Remember back in chapters 9 and 10 Paul addressed a controversy concerning keeping the Mosaic law? Well, here is the fulfillment of all the laws: love one another (Rom. 13:8)! Love those who are dissimilar, those with different doctrinal views, and those with diverse experiences and perspectives — *"he who loves another has fulfilled the law"* (Rom. 13:8).

Not Judging but Receiving One Another

> Let not him who eats despise him who does not eat, and let not him who does not eat judge him who eats; for God has received him . . . One person esteems [one] day above another; another esteems every day [alike]. Let each be fully convinced in his own mind.
>
> — Romans 14:3, 5

> . . . that you may with one mind [and] one mouth glorify the God and Father of our Lord Jesus Christ. Therefore receive one another, just as Christ also received us, to the glory of God.
>
> — Romans 15:6-7

By Romans 14, being in One Body and loving one another is no longer a theory — it has become pragmatic. Jewish and Gentile saints are now assembling together for meals and fellowship. Instead of meeting in separate, divided groups, they are coming together as the Lord's *ekklesia* According to 1 Corinthians 11, when the Lord's *ekklesia* assembles together, it's necessary there should be diversity among believers represented from various factions. Yes, factions — but not "factious." They could come together for meals, break bread to remember the Lord, and fellowship around Jesus Christ.

In Romans 14, there were some who ate meat (presumably unclean meat) and some who ate only vegetables. Some treated one day special (likely, the Sabbath), and others treated every day the same (Rom. 14:5). Previously, in Romans 9-13, these saints might find it much easier to gather separately: Those who would not eat meat would have their own meals and fellowship separately from those who enjoyed eating all kinds of meat. Those who would consider one day special would meet on that day different from those meeting at any day of the week. Therefore, many of these saints might have gathered exclusively with those who were similar and divided from those who were different when it came to gathering, worshipping, and fellowshipping together on certain days. Let's face it—it's just more "comfortable" to gather within your "comfort zone."

Now, in practicing the One Body, they assembled together at the same place and time. In such a situation, love is needed not to judge one another, but rather to receive one another. It can be quite awkward in the beginning with the propensity to judge those dissimilar from you. Thus, from Romans 14 to the beginning of Romans 15, the focus is on receiving one another in fellowship; although, perspectives and understanding might be conflicting and contrary. It is in such a diverse environment where love and unity can be manifested.

Though diverse, they became one mind and one mouth to glorify God. It does not mean they all agreed to eat meat or keep the same day. *Unity is not uniformity or conformity*—it simply meant their minds were now focused on Jesus Christ and not on their differences. The gospel of peace made them one to glorify God. It is noteworthy: God did not receive glory in Romans 1-8. It is not until believers are one that God is glorified. Christians speak much of glorifying God. They may specifically focus on holiness to give glory to God, yet up through the believer's own glorification in Romans 8, there was no mention of God being glorified or receiving glory. However, now in Romans 15 God is glorified in His built up *ekklesia*! Therefore, the following verse charged believers again to receive one another as Christ received each of them. Jesus Christ through His blood on the cross received each of them in their diverse state. Through the same blood of the cross, He brought peace between those who were in conflict . . . bringing both of them into One New Man—into a Perfect Man (cf. Eph. 2:15; 4:13). It is here where God gets the glory from the manifested One Body of Christ.

The Kingdom of God Manifested

> . . . for the kingdom of God is not eating and drinking, but righteousness and peace and joy in the Holy Spirit. For he who serves Christ in these things [is] acceptable to God and approved

by men. Therefore let us pursue **the things [which make] for peace and the things by which one may edify another.**

– Romans 14:17-19

Paul was a preacher of the kingdom of God 'till the very end of Acts (Acts 20:24-25; 28:31). Clearly, he was absolute for the kingdom of God. Here, in his complete theological work on the Christian life, the kingdom of God is revealed. The kingdom of God is where previously divided believers are united in the Lord's *ekklesia*. This is indeed significant! In Romans the kingdom of God is not domiciled in casting out demons or in the context of influencing the secular marketplaces of society; rather, it is amid diverse believers receiving, loving, and fellowshipping with one another in one accord.

The kingdom of God is not related to outward practice – whether one eats, drinks, keeps days, dresses a certain way, or keeps certain laws. It is "*righteousness and peace and joy in the Holy Spirit.*" Righteousness refers to justification by the blood of the Lamb; peace is between once divided peoples; and joy is the experience or manifestation by all those in such a harmonious environment. This is the kingdom of God. Every time believers assemble in oneness with those who might naturally be contrary to them – this is the kingdom of God being manifested. Therefore, pursue peace and build up one another!

But why do you judge your brother? Or why do you show contempt for your brother? For we shall all stand before the judgment seat of Christ.

– Romans 14:1

It is also significant in this chapter where relationships between believers may conflict with each other – herein is the judgment seat of Christ revealed.

The fact there is judging and contempt between believers assembled means there were divergent views and practices. An environment with such divergent views and practices is one that is ripe for judging and contempt – whoever gives in to their natural reaction and remains in that state, would be liable to be harshly judged by Christ at His coming. This is serious!

According to the context of this verse, to be approved under Christ's judgment, believers must receive, fellowship, love and build up one another. This is not referring to a group of Christians who are like-minded and like each other; rather, it is referring to those dissimilar and diverse from each other.

The Completion Gospel

> But I know that when I come to you, I shall come in the **fullness**
> [or "completion"] **of the blessing of the gospel of Christ** . . .
> Now I beg you, brethren, through the Lord Jesus Christ, and
> through the love of the Spirit, that you strive together with me
> in prayers to God for me . . . Now the God of peace [be] with
> you all. Amen.
>
> – Romans 15:29-30, 33

Nearing the end of his epistle, Paul used this phrase: *the fullness or completion of the blessing of the gospel of Jesus Christ*. Remember, the entire book of Romans is Paul preaching the gospel of Jesus Christ to the saints there. He preached being saved by the gospel of the grace of God in Romans 1-8; and now, the gospel of peace wherein believers are brought into unity — into the kingdom of God (Romans 9-16). It is at this point the gospel of Jesus Christ has come to its fullness . . . the completion of the gospel of Jesus Christ. Romans 1-8 is the first part of the gospel of Jesus Christ — Romans 9-16 is the completion of the blessing of the gospel of Jesus Christ!

Without the preaching of the gospel of peace, the gospel of Jesus Christ is not complete. It is far past time for ministers and preachers to arise to preach the *completion gospel*: both grace and peace. This is the gospel of the kingdom of God! To highlight and punctuate the gospel of peace as the operating subject of these chapters, Paul ends this section of his writing with: *The God of peace be with all the saints, amen* (Rom. 15:33).

But wait, Satan still needs to be crushed!

Proactively Greet to Initiate this One Fellowship

> Likewise [greet] the church [ekklesia] that is in their house.
> Greet my beloved Epaenetus, who is the firstfruits of Achaia
> to Christ . . . Greet Asyncritus, Phlegon, Hermas, Patrobas,
> Hermes, and the brethren who are with them. Greet Philologus
> and Julia, Nereus and his sister, and Olympas, and all the saints
> who are with them.
>
> – Romans 16:5, 14-15

Those assembling together in the manner of Romans 14 and 15 would be considered as the Lord's *ekklesia* according to 1 Corinthians 11-14 (See: Henry Hon's book: *One Ekklesia*). The Lord's *ekklesia* is where diverse believers assemble for meals and enjoy the oneness of fellowship as the Body of Christ, the Messiah, in giving glory to God. In Rome, the *ekklesia* was happening at Priscilla and Aquila's house (i.e., *"the ekklesia that is in their house"* – Rom. 16:3-5). Apparently, there were other individuals who would not be included in this *ekklesia*; also, many other believers were gathering in other separated groups based on the description in Romans 16.

Therefore, Paul commanded the saints in Rome to proactively and intentionally go out of their way to greet one another. They needed to leave the comfort of their natural surroundings with those who were like themselves. They needed to get out and greet those with whom they were unfamiliar.

Just about all teachers of the Bible have considered Romans 16 to be Paul's own salutation/benediction or greeting of various saints in Rome. It is understood to be: Greet so-and-so for me (as in "say hello, or hi, from me, Paul"). As such, the application of this portion is relegated in trying to remember all the saints if you are going to write a letter and don't leave anyone out! However, upon further consideration with the enlightening of the Spirit, it was not Paul sending personal greetings; it was Paul commanding the saints in Rome to go and greet all these various people listed in that chapter. They were to go and greet numerous believers who found themselves segregated from one another in Rome. In fact, he emphatically told them to do this greeting seventeen times – it was not "optional" – it was "mandatory" – an injunction!

The word "greet" is not just saying "hi" when walking past someone. The word for "greet" in the Greek means: *to embrace, to be joined, a union, to visit or joyfully welcome a person* (Strong's and Thayer's) It was customary for greetings to take place by entering a house with the occupant welcoming that person to stay for a while (Matt. 10:12; Acts 21:7). Greetings included intimate dialogues with another person (Luke 1:40-55; Acts 21:19). Additionally, the Greek verb form for "greet" as found in Romans 16 is *aorist middle deponent imperative*; which means Paul was commanding whoever was reading his letter to take continual action to go and greet those listed. This greeting is the initiation of fellowship. They needed to continue doing this greeting whether they had done so in the past or not. Likewise, it isn't a matter of just "meeting" someone as in:

"Hi, how are you doing?" No, no, no — it's a matter of not only seeing but "greeting" — getting to know them!

It is consistent through all the epistles wherein the verb form for "greet" is different whether the greeting is done by someone remotely in another locality or done face to face in the same locality. For example, in Romans 16:16: "*Greet one another with a holy kiss. The assemblies* [ekklesia] *of Christ greet you.*" In this verse, there are two "greets." The first one obviously is in-person, a face-to-face greeting. The second "greet" is from all the assemblies. Obviously, the saints in those assemblies were not in Rome. Therefore, the verb form is different. Specifically, it was not imperative, a command; rather, it was indicative, a simple statement of fact. Over 37 times greetings were used in all the epistles. In every single instance, when it was face to face, it was imperative, a command; however, when it was remote, it was indicative. Without a doubt, all the greetings in Romans 16:3-15 were Paul commanding recipients of his letter, which were all the saints in Rome, to go greet all the saints in those verses. It was not Paul doing the greeting from afar. He was literally commanding, charging, the saints to intentionally, proactively, and continually to go and greet all the various saints in Rome.

They needed to do it in-person, face-to-face, and intimately with a kiss. Why is that important? It is important because every believer's situation and relationship with one another in Rome was the closest example of what it is today. Presently, there are a variety of factions and groupings of various believers. These various groupings are generally a result of comfort and familiarity due to similarity in ethnicity, doctrine, worship tradition, and so on. Additionally, none of the first-century apostles founded any of the groups we have today. Today, the one fellowship of Jesus Christ is fractured, and the practice of true oneness is severely limited.

Therefore, today is precisely when the gospel of peace in Romans is needed, and specifically the last chapter with the command to go greet, is as critical as it was 2,000 years ago in Rome. Believers today are to obey the Scriptures just as those in the First Century. God's people should take similar action to go and greet brothers and sisters individually, as well as those associated with other groups. They should continue to do this regardless of whether they have done so in the past.

Members of a home group from the same "church" might enjoy a homogeneous fellowship because they're going to the same church — but that's not, per se, an *ekklesia*. An *ekklesia* occurs when brethren from diverse groups of believers come together to "meet and greet" one another and find themselves meeting with very diverse believers who have assorted doctrines and practices but find their oneness of fellowship in Christ alone!

Therefore, greeting was not Paul's casual addendum to his otherwise intensely theological discourse. No, it was Paul's way of engineering a mixing of normally segregated people and expanding the one fellowship among all the saints in Rome. If they did not proactively go and greet other believers who were normally not associated with their grouping, then segregation and division would persist, eventually becoming systematized and institutionalized after a period of time.

By enjoining those who would obey Paul's injunction to go and greet all these various followers of Jesus in Rome, whether they be Jews or Gentiles, slave or free, it would initiate fellowship among all the Lord's followers in Rome. Such vibrant fellowship is the reality of the one *ekklesia*. This is what is upon the Lord's heart.

Without this ongoing greeting in Romans 16, Paul's theology concerning salvation, justification, sanctification, glorification resulting in the One Body of Christ, would be utterly deficient. Without purposeful outreach to have vibrant fellowship with all those of the same faith, but not in the same grouping, the saints would succumb to gravitational separation, finding themselves with their "own kind" — whether ethnically, doctrinally, politically, socio-economically, or personality-wise. The result: division and sectarianism.

Therefore, every believer can start preaching the gospel of peace by simply going and greeting those believers unfamiliar or even contrary. Fellowshipping with them concerning the person and work of Jesus Christ. This act of extending oneself to greet others in Christ is by itself preaching the gospel of peace. Many Christians consider that preaching needs a sizable audience. No. Just as preaching the gospel of grace is effective on a personal basis, preaching the gospel of peace is as simple and personable as visiting and greeting another believer in the environment of any given neighborhood, workplace, or school.

Crushing Satan Is a Fitting Finale

The **God of peace** will soon crush Satan under your feet. The grace of our Lord Jesus Christ be with you.

– Romans 16:20, ESV

This declaration of crushing Satan didn't show up in Romans 8 or up through Romans 15, but at the end of Romans 16 — in fact, we don't hear anything mentioned about Satan, the Devil, the Serpent or the Dragon (Rev. 12:9) until the very last chapter of Romans. Satan being crushed revealed at the end is an answer to the Lord's promise in Matthew 16:18 — "The gates of Hades" would not prevail against His *ekklesia* — His *ekklesia* would crush the gates of Hades, the stronghold and power of Satan. This shows us all 16 chapters of Romans are needed by the saints in Rome to crush Satan under their feet. How? Through the completion gospel wrought by the GOSPEL OF PEACE – THE GOD OF PEACE!

Many Bible teachers have called Romans the unfolding of God's plan of salvation. If Romans was a movie then many readers of Romans would consider chapter 16 with many names as "rolling the credits of the movie" since Romans 15 already ended with what appears as a benediction and a hearty "amen" in Romans 15:33 (i.e., *Now the God of peace be with you all. Amen.*). Just as many people start walking out of a movie when the credits start rolling, many Bible readers would do the same and not pay attention to Romans 16. However, if this last chapter is skipped, the final demise of the villain being crushed by the heroine would be missed. This shows us Romans 16 is the climax of the Romans movie.

This should not be easily dismissed. In Paul's presentation of his complete theological framework, we must recognize the entire letter to the saints in Rome was divinely inspired from Chapters 1 through 16. Each chapter was designed to be exactly where it needed to be with its content precisely expressed. To proclaim Satan being crushed at the end of Romans 16 shows us Satan cannot be crushed by the God of peace under the saints' feet until the practice of greeting is accomplished. Only then is the Lord's assembly (i.e., *ekklesia*) built up.   Yes, it seems incongruous to state it is THE GOD OF PEACE Who crushes Satan under the feet of the *ekklesia* — however, this is the very result of the Gospel of Peace!

Just think — the same beautiful "feet" who preach the gospel of peace (Rom. 10:15), those same "feet" carrying the saints to go greet, are the feet crushing Satan. Indeed, we cannot dismiss the *protoevangelium* found in Genesis 3:15 where the LORD God said to the serpent: "*And I will put enmity between you* [i.e., Satan] *and the woman, and between your seed and her Seed* [i.e., the followers of Messiah]; *He* [the One New Man of Messiah] *shall bruise your* [i.e., Satan's] *head, and you* [i.e., Satan, the Serpent] *shall bruise His* [Messiah's] *heel* [alluding to Messiah's crucifixion]."

Remember the difficulties for Jews and Gentiles even to eat together? What a beautiful sight of fellowship and oneness when the city of Rome witnessed Jews going into Gentile homes to greet them, having a meal together, and vice-versa. The rich or freeman would greet believing slaves by welcoming them into their homes for a meal. Throughout the city, unlikely people would be greeting and fellowshipping together with each other at markets, "coffee shops" and in their homes, from house to house.

As the number of believers in Rome who read Paul's letter increased, the greetings, and thus the fellowship among the saints, exponentially grew. What a testimony to the oneness of believers as they went from house to house greeting each other! Paul ended this section of his epistle to the saints in Rome by instructing his readers to greet one another with a holy kiss. This kind of greeting expressed pure love and intimate fellowship among believers. None would be isolated in their own group, seeing the same believers year after year, but instead would be part of a growing network of homes in one fellowship with much traffic and support between them, because they were indeed one *ekklesia*.

Today, most believers are segregated and isolated in their church or in their home. If believers would accept Paul's directive to seek out other believers and "meet and greet" them, the Lord would have a way to build up the ekklesia, His body. There are so many churches, ministries and Christian groups today with believers isolated from each other. It is essential in God's purpose for believers to heed Paul's command to go and greet fellow believers not in their own grouping.

In God's eyes all His children are in one family — in the One Body of Christ — the Household of Faith (cf. Gal. 6:10). As such, believers should not acknowledge any division, no matter what church or denomination may be segregating Christians. Greetings to believers who meet in the Catholic Church should have the same fervency and love in their greetings given to believers who may identify with a Baptist Church, a Pentecostal Church, a non-denominational church, or even a believer not attending any church at all (so-called "*dones*"). For the purpose of mutual greetings among believers, no recognition should be given to which church a person belongs (since churches are artificially organized by men). For someone to say: "This is my church" – well, it may be the building or group you're currently attending, but Jesus said: "*I will build MY EKKLESIA and the Gates of Hades shall not prevail against it*" (Matt. 16:18) – it's His, NOT yours!

No matter which church one belongs to or if a believer is completely outside the institutional church, everyone needs to proactively greet and receive other believers. What if believers with an emphasis on Pentecostal experiences greets those who disparage the gifts, like speaking in tongues? What would happen if those with a preference for reformed theology greeted those who preach salvation is a choice? Believers would automatically become one in the reality of the Body of Christ, and non-essential doctrines which do not "save" in the first place, as well as pet practices, would fade in priority – these peripherals would cease being an issue between believers. Subsequently, intimate fellowship in Jesus Christ alone will cause the ekklesia to bloom from house to house. This will take place outside of and despite almost 2,000 years of separation within institutional Christianity.

How can believers testify to the God of Peace if they are divided? However, the God of Peace is in action and magnified among all the greetings of disparate believers. Therefore, Satan being crushed is an appropriate ending for this epistle, but not before. In Matthew 16:18, Jesus was giving the promise, or a prophecy; here however, Paul and early believers were living out the reality of the practical building up of the ekklesia, the Kingdom of God, which crushes Satan. When believers are in oneness, in this one fellowship, built on the one foundation – Jesus Christ, with all her members functioning and active – then Satan is crushed! It is the oneness of believers that defeats the enemy and satisfies the Lord's desire in His prayer found in John 17: The prayer for His people to be one as the Father and the Son are one.

The Conclusion of Paul's Gospel

> Now to Him who is able to establish you according to my gospel and the preaching of Jesus Christ, according to the **revelation of the mystery** kept secret since the world began
>
> – Romans 16:25

> This is a great mystery, but I speak concerning Christ and the church [ekklesia].
>
> – Ephesians 5:32

Paul declared at the very end of this epistle: It is his gospel, the preaching of Jesus Christ. He ended it the same way he started: . . . separated to the gospel of God, to preach the gospel to the Romans (Rom. 1:1, 15). This proves Romans is the entire gospel of God which needs to be preached. Don't be preachers of a half gospel — preach the **completion gospel** (Rom. 15:29). It is through this preaching that the mystery kept secret since the world began is revealed.

The gospel is not just to save sinners, so that they may go to heaven, but to complete the mystery of God. The great mystery hidden is Christ and His *ekklesia*, the fullness of the One who fills all in all (Eph. 1:22-23). This *ekklesia* must manifest the coming together into one all those previously divided and separated people of God. This is God's eternal purpose!

This can only take place when believers receive the "fullness" or "completion" of Jesus Christ (John 1:16) through the hearing of the completion gospel as preached by Paul in the entire book of Romans — especially, the final half of Romans (Romans 9-16).

What is this mystery the gospel would unveil? In Colossians 2:2 we find the "mystery of God" is Christ: ". . . *that they may know the mystery of God, even Christ*" (ASV). Then, we find in Ephesians 3:4-6 Paul speaks of the "*mystery of Christ*" which is His Body: "*you can perceive my understanding in the mystery of Christ . . . that the Gentiles are fellow-heirs, fellow-members of the body, and fellow-partakers of the promise. . .* (ASV). Taken together, Paul declares in Ephesians 5:32 the great mystery is Christ and His *ekklesia*!

Ephesians 1:23 says: the *ekklesia*, the Lord's body, is the "fullness" or "completion" of the One who fills all in all. It is mysterious and awesome that God's plan is His *ekklesia*, His people in oneness, who become God's completion or fullness. This word "completion" (*plērōma*) is the same Greek word as the "completion" of the gospel of Jesus Christ (Rom 15:29). It is the completion gospel: both the gospel of grace and the gospel of peace which will usher in the built-up *ekklesia* being the "completion" of God. Truly this has been a hidden mystery, but now revealed through Paul's "*completion of the blessing of the gospel of Jesus Christ.*" Let's start preaching this COMPLETION GOSPEL so the world shall believe the Father sent the Son . . .

"*That they all may be one, as You, Father, are in Me, and I in You; that they also may be one in Us, THAT THE WORLD MAY BELIEVE THAT YOU SENT ME*" (John 17:21). Yes, Satan is crushed beneath our feet AND the world shall believe as the prevailing Gospel of Peace unites His people in the Oneness wrought in Messiah — that wondrous mystery before the world began, but now revealed through His UNITED saints, His One Body — Christ in you Jews and in those being called out from among the Nations, the Hope of Glory!

About The Author
HENRY HON

HENRY HON is a "serial entrepreneur" and engineer who was graduated from the University of California, Berkley. He is a frequent conference speaker and writer on themes related to Jesus' statement: "I will build my Ekklesia" (Matt. 16:18). And Jesus' prayer: That His people may be ONE as the Father and the Son are ONE so that the world may believe in Him (John 17:21).

Hon's growing audience includes both domestic (North America) and an outreach to Africa (Nigeria) and Asia. Raising up local "ekklesia-style" gatherings; encouraging evangelical ministries to "team-up for the faith of the gospel" and uniting the Body of Christ wherever the opportunity avails itself. Henry is the founder of One Body Life ministries — supporting ministries for the sake of His One Body. He and Sylvia have been married for over forty years with four children and a growing number of grandchildren. Currently, he resides in the Bay Area of Northern California—He can be reached through www.onebody.life

OTHER BOOKS
BY HENRY HON

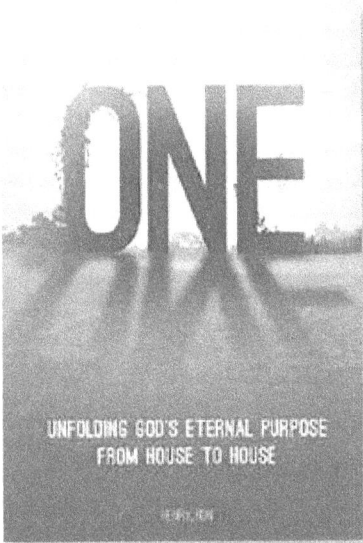

Unfolding God's Eternal Purpose from House to House . . . John 17 reveals Jesus' prayer - His heart's desire would be He wants all people, irrespective of differences in background, ethnicity, politics, and/or socio-economic status, to be ONE. Just as Jesus and the Father are perfectly ONE, Jesus desires His people to be included in this complete oneness. Jesus gave three gifts in His prayer for accomplishing this ONEness: Eternal life, Truth (God's Word), and His glory. This is the author's first book expounding on these three gifts which makes believers ONE — A ONEness to cause the world to believe in Jesus Christ.

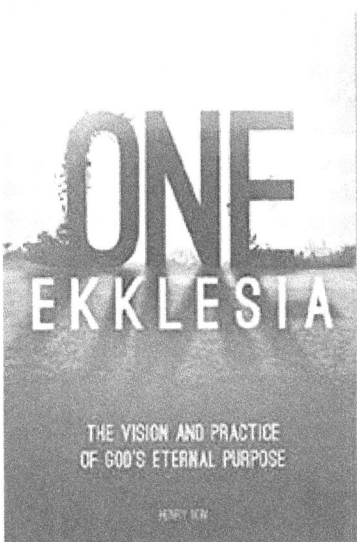

The Vision and Practice of God's Eternal Purpose (Now in AUDIO on Amazon as well) . . . ONE EKKLESIA is not about how to improve your church, leave your church, or to start a better church. Rather, its vision and practice are to fulfill the Lord's prayer for His people (whether attending church or not) to be ONE so the world will believe. It is a practical oneness of diverse believers impacting the world. This will ignite the holy fire of God spreading uncontrollably . . . the next and final revival.

Both @ www.onebody.life and on Amazon.com

BIBLIOGRAPHY

Austin-Sparks, T. The Centrality and Supremacy of the Lord Jesus Christ. Online Library of T. Austin-Sparks.

Coneybeare and Howson. Life and Epistles of St Paul. Grand Rapid, MI: WM. B. Eerdmans Publishing Co.

Lee, Witness. The Economy of God. Anaheim, CA; Anaheim, CA: Living Stream Ministry

Lee, Witness. The Organic Aspect of God's Salvation. Anaheim, CA; Anaheim, CA: Living Stream Ministry

Mackintosh, C.H. Genesis to Deuteronomy. Neptune, NJ: Loizeaux Brothers

Mackintosh, C.H. The Mackintosh Treasury. Neptune, NJ: Loizeaux Brothers

Murray, Andrew. The Two Covenants. New Jersey: Spire Books

Murray, Andrew. Abide in Christ. New Kensington, PA: Whitaker House

Murray, Andrew. The Spirit of Christ. Minneapolis, MN: Bethany House Publisher

Nee, Watchman. Normal Christian Life. PA: CLC

Scroggie, W. Graham. The Unfolding Drama of Redemption. Grand Rapid, MI: Zondervan Publishing House

Vine, W. E. Vine's Expository Dictionary of New Testament Words. Public domain: www.blueletter.org

BIBLE VERSIONS USED

Unless otherwise noted, all scriptural verses are taken from New King James Version (NKJV). Copyright © 1982 by Thomas Nelson. Used by permission. All rights reserved.

[DBY] Some of the scriptural verses taken from Darby Version have been revised to conform to modern English. Public domain version.

[ESV] English Standard Version copyright © 2001, 2007 by Crossway Bibles, a publishing ministry of Good News Publishers. Used by permission. All rights reserved.

[RSV] from the Revised Standard Version of the Bible, copyright © 1946, 1952, and 1971 the Division of Christian Education of the National Council of the Churches of Christ in the United States of America. Used by permission. All rights reserved.

[NET] THE NET BIBLE®, NEW ENGLISH TRANSLATION COPYRIGHT © 1996 BY BIBLICAL STUDIES PRESS, L.L.C. NET Bible® IS A REGISTERED TRADEMARK THE NET BIBLE® LOGO, SERVICE MARK COPYRIGHT © 1997 BY BIBLICAL STUDIES PRESS, L.L.C. ALL RIGHTS RESERVED

[NIV] THE HOLY BIBLE, NEW INTERNATIONAL VERSION®, NIV® Copyright © 1973, 1978, 1984, 2011 by Biblica, Inc.® Used by permission. All rights reserved worldwide.

[ASV] Thomas Nelson & Sons first published the American Standard Version in 1901. This translation of the Bible is in the public domain.

[WBT] The Webster Bible was translated by Noah Webster in 1833 in order to bring the language of the Bible up to date. This version of the Bible is in the public domain.

[HNV] The Hebrew Names Version is based off the World English Bible, an update of the American Standard Version of 1901. This version of the Bible is in the public domain.

END NOTES

1   ANSWERS list 41,000 current denominations. Their article presents 5 major groups of Christians with scores of subsets within these. See: How Many Christian Denominations Are There? @ https://www.answers.com/Q/How_many_Christian_denominations_are_there - Retrieved on 04.26.19.

2   Gesenius' Hebrew-Chaldee Lexicon for "I am"

3   Gesenius' Hebrew Chaldee Lexicon for "Jehovah"

4   Vine's Expository Dictionary for "Jesus"

5   Strong's Definition for "Almighty"

6   Vine's Expository Dictionary

7   Dr. Doug Hamp's article on **Zohar Three In One – Evidence of the Trinity from a Jewish Writing** traces the development of the "three in one" God in ancient Hebrew writings – this is found @ http://www.douglashamp.com/zohar-three-in-one-evidence-of-the-trinity-from-a-jewish-writing/ and is developed in Dr. Hamp's presentation at the ONE IN MESSIAH CONF. (Sacramento, CA – March, 2018) @ https://www.youtube.com/watch?v=CaXXHEQphCY

8   In Isaiah 63 we have an amazing account of what can only be seen as the expression of the Triune God in the words of the prophet Isaiah: (1) The Son – not only is "*This one who is glorious in His apparel*" bespeaks from Isa. 63:1-9 of the Redeemer, the Savior..."*So He became their Savior...In all their affliction He was afflicted, and the Angel of His Presence saved them*" – "the Angel of His Presence" has been taken to be an expression of the "pre-incarnate Christ" – (2) The Holy Spirit: "But they rebelled and grieved His Holy Spirit...Where is He who put His Holy Spirit within them" (Isa. 63:10-11) – (3) The Father: "Doubtless You are our Father...You, O LORD, are our Father" (Isa. 63:16).

9   http://www.theopedia.com/modalism

10   The Bible Hub @ https://www.biblehub.com/john/1-18.htm provides numerous English translations of John 1:18 expressing the same concept: Jesus, the Son of God, is God.

11   Luke 3:23: "*Now Jesus Himself began His ministry at about thirty years of age*" – Doug Krieger in his text, **Signs in the Heavens and on the Earth, Man's Days are Numbered, and he is Measured** suggests Jesus probably commenced His ministry in the year 29 AD in the month of Tishrei on the Hebrew Calendar or 29 29 AD + 3 months unto 30 AD and that He was "cut off" (died) on Nisan 13/14 (spring) of 33 AD (Julian Calendar) having ministered on earth for 3 ½ years or 42 months (or 29 AD/3 months; 30 AD, 31 AD, 32 AD, and 3 months of 33 AD = 3 ½ years (Jesus would have commenced His ministry at the baptism by John on the Day of Atonement in 29 AD—Luke 3:21-22. However, Krieger continues, that if Jesus were born on Passover, 1 BC then He would have lived 9 months of 1 BC/1 AD [there is no zero year] and another 31 years unto the end of 32 AD making him precisely 31 years and 9 months of age + an additional 3 months of 33 AD making Him a full 32 years of age or precisely 33 years of age having died on His birthday!

12   Doug Krieger: The traditional understanding and definition of the doctrine of the "Trinity" is that there are **three infinite persons**, sharing the same substance, making up one God; or one God divided into three parts. This doctrine of the Trinity as commonly understood destroys the "paternal relationship" of the Father with His Son. This teaching concludes that the Father and His Son are simply "role playing" their respective parts—Jesus is not really God's Son. This falsehood or glaring misunderstanding outright rejects the grand plan of redemption! The inexhaustible love of the Father expressed to us in the Savior— "a savior" who is NOT the Son of God—so, He's just role playing? Therefore, the Father really didn't give up anything when He sent the Son, Jesus, to die for the sins of the world? Again, the classical "Trinitarian doctrine" states the following: "There is one God: Father, Son, and Holy Spirit, **a unity of three co-eternal persons**." Still others affirm but "one Being" Whose Name is "God," and that Jesus and the Holy Spirit

are also "Gods"—yet, they are all part of the Godhead. Some suggest that there are actually two Persons of the Godhead—the Father and the Son, with the Holy Spirit being a kind of power or force, but not the "third part" of the Godhead. While still others conjecture the Godhead is made up of three separate Gods—God the Divinity of the Father; God the Divinity of the Son; and God the Divinity of the Holy Spirit—each of these separate powers are unified in purpose—that purpose being the grand plan of redemption.

No to all the above—there is but ONE PERSON, He is God—Father, Son and Holy Spirit. Although it seems inexpressible and/or contradictory; yet, **there are THREE PERSONS in ONE PERSON (better to say there are *THREE in ONE PERSON*)**—how else could the Father send the Son and the two grant us the Promise of the Spirit (John 14:16-18)? This unique distinction of Father, Son and Holy Spirit within the Godhead "appears" as three but is inseparably one!

The question persists: Why was it that the 300 Bishops and Deacons at the Council of Nicaea in 325 AD declared there are THREE PERSONS within the Godhead? Yes, their Nicaean Creed resulted in **(1) God the Father, Son and Holy Spirit are One; (2) All three persons of the Godhead have existed from eternity past; and (3) Jesus Christ and the Holy Spirit are God—co-equal with God.**

Yet, this "Catholic" teaching of the Godhead is sorely deficient, even accommodating to the Roman/Greek understanding of the "gods" in that the ancient world's understanding of the "gods" as "distinct persons" being made of the "same substance" (i.e., all "divine substance") could readily be viewed by polytheists who could now perceive "three gods" could now be placed at the top of the pantheon of the gods who are one in substance (i.e., divine). Alas! No wonder, then, Emperor Constantine could now find justification in opening his government's support of the "temple of the gods" (with their priesthoods, as well as assorted accoutrements and practices AND eventual hierarchical system) by converting these temples into "churches"—which he rapidly implemented, telling these "temple priests" to "convert" or perish! And more so—all Jewish holidays, feast days (e.g., Passover) should be abandoned—no "Christian" would be allowed to partake of such "idolatrous" practices; furthermore, Christians should have absolutely nothing to do with Jews—they do NOT have the same "God of the Christians!" Oh, how "accommodating" was Emperor Constantine! And, who be the "demigods"? Yes, part "god" and part "man"—therefore, all the more under Constantine's clever absorption of "Christendom" into the pagan world came a distorted doctrine of the God-Man. Yes, Jesus was the true God-Man, but He always was with the Father but "took on the form of a man" for us and our salvation.

Now, the Jews, isolated from all things "Christian" could readily conclude— "These Christians have a different God than we do!" Thus, "the middle wall of separation" was once again erected between the two—the Jew and the Gentile. One of the most visible results of this "separation" was believers flooding into these "pagan temples" thinking they were "the Church" (i.e., "churches")—for now there was no need to meet from "house to house" because persecution would no longer exist . . . the "places" to meet up with God were these once awful pagan temples—the TEMPLE OF THE GODS!

Indeed, the site of the Oracle of Delphi (or "Python" as in SNAKE)—where consultation with the "gods" for making "earthly decisions" (e.g., "Should I or King Leonidas go to war with the Persians?" = asked to the female Oracle)—was, as a site in Greece, abandoned by 381 AD; to wit: "Tell the king that the flute has fallen to the ground. Phoebus does not have a home anymore, neither an oracular laurel, nor a speaking fountain, because the talking water has dried out."

(https://en.wikipedia.org/wiki/Delphi). Its disuse resulted both from the Council of Nicaea and later by Emperor Theodosius' persecuting pagan worshippers.

More egregious, however, was Baal Worship (satanic ritual) with vast swaths of ancient temples which were designed to be places where communication or FELLOWSHIP with the gods (who took on many names) took place—to inquire, through payment, with "false prophets" (Ref. Elijah's slaying of the "false prophets of Baal") during FORNICATION (female or male) what commercial decisions and other social courses of action should take place by those "inquiring" in these temples. The Greek and Roman world was filled with these Canaanitic sexual distortions—it was not only "profitable" but sensually deviant, even demonic! Therefore, being "called into the fellowship of the gods"—well, everyone knew what was really going on . . . thus, for thousands of years until the 300s AD did the Oracle of Delphi persist. Brethren, *"our fellowship is with the Father and with his Son Jesus Christ"* (1 John 1:3). *What FELLOWSHIP has light with darkness* (2 Cor. 6:14)? In a phrase: WE'VE BEEN RIPPED OFF! Examining the very nature of the Triune God demands our extreme scrutiny—the "root of this tree has borne plenty of rotten fruit"—coming to grips with these distortions will not be easy.

13   An "Archangel" – of which were Michael (Dan. 12:1; Rev. 12:7-9; Jude 1:9), Gabriel (Daniel 8:15–26, 9:21–27; Luke 1:11-38), Palmoni (Dan. 8:14—viz., "that certain messenger"), and Raphael (the "unnamed angel" at the Pool of Bethesda in the Gospel of John). See also: 1 Thessalonians 4:13-18; Ephesians 6:10-18; 1 John 4:1; 1 Peter 5:8.

14   Anthropological disputes with the historical record are in legion juxtaposed to the Biblical record; however, to go beyond 10,000 years of human history stretches the credulity of "modern man." The Masoretic text gives the creation story to include from Adam through the 21 patriarchs some 2,100 years of history and some 4,000 total years from Adam's creation to the birth of Christ with the approximate 2,000 years of history from Messiah's birth until the present. Doug Krieger gives the year of Adam's creation to have been in the year 3975 BC with the Gregorian Calendar of 2019 AD (2,019 years) providing ample reasoning that we are nigh conclusive of the 6,000 years "allotted to man" (6 days = 6,000 years with the 7th day or Sabbath being the Millennium 1,000-year conclusion or 7,000 years). The Seder Olam Rabbah (cir. 133 AD—Jewish Calendar) gives us today some 5,779 years since Adam's creation; however, this calendar is nigh some 243 years "off" wherein only 5 of the reigns of the Persian Kings is recorded; whereas there were some 13 Persian Kings (See: J. R. Church's "Daniel Reveals the Bloodline of the Antichrist" January, 2010 [Amazon Books]).

15   Doug Krieger calls this the "Elijah Syndrome" – "I alone am left" (1 Kings 19:10, 14). Elijah was fighting the Lord's battle against Jezebel and King Ahab, the prophets of Baal, and considered himself as the "elect of the elect" – yet, the LORD spoke to Elijah: "Yet I have reserved seven thousand in Israel, all whose knees have not bowed to Baal, and every mouth that has not kissed him" (1 Kings' 19:18). Believers, especially in so-called "Restoration Movements" are severely tempted, time and again, to "come out of Babylon" – viewing other Christians as somehow inferior to their dedication to the Lord—viz., "I alone am left." Until and unless this "superiority complex" is dealt with, these believers who, for example, desperately long for the "oneness of the Body of Christ," will find "that which they feared the most has come upon them"—how strange:

They become the most divisive "brethren" in their absoluteness. Their idea of "oneness" forms around the notion that "Only we are left" – other Christians must meet with us in order to experience the "Unity of the Faith," otherwise, they are not absolute for the Lord!

16   http://www.dictionary.com/browse/metamorphoses

17   Strong's Concordance gives us the Greek word *diathéké* meaning will, covenant, testament found countless time in ancient papyri and abundant in NT Scripture (Matt. 26:18; Mark 14:24; Luke 1:72; Luke 22:20; Acts 3:25; Acts 7:8; Rom. 9:4; 11:27; 1 Cor. 11:25; 2 Cor. 3:6; 3:14; Gal, 3:15,17; 4:24; Eph. 2:12; Heb. 8:6, 8-10; 9:4, 15).

18   The timing or inauguration of the New Covenant is a hotly debated topic in Christian theology. It is the contention of this author and his editor that the New Covenant, juxtaposed to the Old Covenant, was revealed through Jesus during His discourse in the Upper Room (Matt. 26:26-30; Mark 14:22-25; 1 Cor. 11:23-26; Heb. 9:11-11-22—specifically). The New Covenant is extended to all who believe into His Name; however, prophetically, that SAME New Covenant will be corporately implemented/accepted to ALL ISRAEL (Judah, in particular) on a yet future day in accordance with Jeremiah 31:31; Hebrews 8:7-13; and Ezekiel 16:60-62; 34:25; 37:26) (i.e., there is only one New Covenant wrought by the blood of Jesus, and it is an "Everlasting Covenant."

19   Galatians 5:1 is the sole NT verse which speaks of "the yoke of bondage" – *"Stand fast therefore in the liberty by which Christ has made us free, and do not be entangled again with a yoke of bondage"* and is directly related to: *"And I testify again to every man who becomes circumcised that he is a debtor to keep the whole law. . . You have become estranged from Christ, you who attempt to be justified by law; you have fallen from grace"* (Gal. 5:3-4).

20   "There is no biblical reference to 613 commandments, although the later rabbinic leaders claimed that all 613 commandments are alluded to within the Ten Commandments. The first actual reference to 613 commandments is found in a lengthy Talmudic passage. There, Rabbi Simlai (third century A.D.) is quoted as saying, "Six hundred and thirteen precepts were communicated to Moses, three hundred and sixty-five negative precepts, . . .and two hundred and forty-eight positive precepts. . ." Based on this comment, medieval Jewish scholars, sought to come to agreement as to the exact enumeration and delineation of the 613 commandments, since there is a good deal of ambiguity in counting." (Dr. Michael Brown – Retrieved on 04.23.2019 @ https://askdrbrown.org/library/are-there-really-613-commandments-torah)

21   The Ten Commandments can be found in the NT: Matthew 5:17-30; 19:17-19; 22:37-40; Mark 10:19; Luke 18:20; etc. – all Ten Commandments are either explicit or implicit within the New Testament (See: Ten Commandments in the New Testament @ http://www.the-ten-commandments.org/ten_commandments-new_testament.html - Retrieved on 04.23.2019)

22   Although the number of NT commands vary, there seems to be abundant agreement there are at least 1,050 NT commands (See: *1,050 New Testament Commands* @ https://www.cai.org/bible-studies/1050-new-testament-commands - Retrieved on 04.23.2019).

23   This issue, known as "Rewards and Losses" is a highly debated topic within certain Christian ranks. With Joseph C. Dillow's release of the "*Reign of the Servant Kings*" a clear demarcation between overcomer Christians from those whose works constitute "wood, hay and stubble" was delineated. Those who would "rule and reign with Christ a thousand years" cannot be the same as those who could have cared less about their Christian life – there are consequences if one chooses to trifle with eternal issues. "Saved as by fire" is one of them!

www.ingramcontent.com/pod-product-compliance
Lightning Source LLC
Chambersburg PA
CBHW070039110426
42741CB00036B/2850